BLACK MAN IN THE WHITE HOUSE

Black Man

E. FREDERIC MORROW

in the White House

A DIARY OF THE EISENHOWER YEARS
BY THE ADMINISTRATIVE OFFICER
FOR SPECIAL PROJECTS,
THE WHITE HOUSE, 1955-1961

Coward-McCann, Inc.
New York

To CATHERINE

ACKNOWLEDGMENTS

A GREAT many good people helped me during my years in the Eisenhower Administration. Despite the fine opportunity afforded me by the President and Governor Adams to serve on the White House staff, I needed friends—not only to help me perform, but to keep me from being overcome with heartbreak and disappointment over decisions that ran contrary to my hopes and beliefs. A few of these persons must be listed here:

The Alfred Moellers of Tenafly, New Jersey, the long-time friends who suggested I start keeping a diary just after the announcement of my appointment to the White House; General Andrew J. Goodpaster, Staff Secretary to the President; Clarence B. Randall, Special Assistant to the President for Foreign Economic Policy; Captain Edward L. Beach, and Captain Pete Aurand, Naval Aides to the President; Douglas R. Price, Executive Assistant; General Robert L. Schulz, Military Aide; Hon. Fred A. Seaton, Secretary of the Interior; Bernard M. Shanley, Special Counsel; General Howard McCrum Snyder, Personal Physician to the President; Colonel Walter R. Tkach, Assistant to the President's Personal Physician; William J. Hopkins, Executive Clerk; James Rowley, United States Secret Service; Major Ralph C. Stover, Chief, White House Police; Grace E. Earle, Chief of Telephone Service.

I want to voice a special tribute to the fine women who served as secretaries and assistants in my office during these years. They served above and beyond the call, and protected me against many a difficult moment. They were: Laura Sherman; Peggy King; Marjorie Hogan; Mary Matheus; Gladys McKay.

7

August 22, 1960

Dear Fred:

On the night of July twenty-sixth, I heard you
give a splendid testimony for the Administration
at the Republican National Convention in Chicago.
The warmth and generosity of your comments
were most appreciated, and I want to thank you
for them.

During the years of your work here, you have
come to know much of the size and scope of the
United States Government.   You know that its
administration requires the talents of many,
many devoted citizens.   Our Nation can never
be run by one man.

As a trusted member of the team, you have contributed much to our record.   Your service and
spirit have meant a great deal to me.

With warm regard,

Sincerely,

Dwight D. Eisenhower

The Honorable E. Frederic Morrow
The White House
Washington, D. C.

INTRODUCTION

I JOINED General Eisenhower's staff as a consultant in August 1952 for the duration of the campaign. His headquarters were in the Hotel Commodore, directly across the street from my office at CBS where I was a member of the public affairs staff. I was on leave from CBS.

A few days after the election, Sherman Adams called me over to the Commodore and said that both he and Eisenhower had been impressed by my work during the campaign and wanted me with them in Washington in some capacity commensurate with my background and training. I was very surprised and flattered, but said I must have time to think about it.

Not once during the campaign had I ever talked with anyone about a Washington position with the Administration. I was happy in my job at CBS and confident that it could lead to important advancement. There were personal complications too. My mother was a semi-invalid, and I had always lived with her in our family home and would have to make some provision for her welfare.

I had many talks with Sherman Adams, and he sent me to see several prominent persons to talk about the kind of spot I should occupy in the White House. Finally a letter from Mr. Adams definitely confirmed the fact that I would be a member of the White House staff and that I would be notified of this officially. He said that in the meantime he was turning over all the details to his assistant Maxwell Rabb. Mr. Adams advised me to tell CBS that I would be resigning, which I did.

After that I met frequently with Max Rabb, and each time there would be a hassle over the salary I could expect in any White House position. I had made it clear that I would not go to Washington for less than $10,000 a year, and I simply could not lower that figure. Max kept trying to induce me to take $1,000 or $1,500 less, and each time I would try to get a firm commitment he would tell me that there were a few more details to be ironed out. By the time the President had moved into the White House my status still had not been established.

The delegation had closed the campaign headquarters at the Commodore, and I began to find it impossible to get in touch with anyone. I phoned the White House dozens of times, only to be told that Mr. Rabb was out or in conference and would call me back. A very distressing period! Several months had passed since I had resigned from CBS, and I was living on savings which were dwindling fast. So was my morale.

Over three months after the Inauguration I finally got through to Bernard Shanley, special counsel to the President, and asked him to please let me know definitely what the score was on my going to Washington. He called me back the next day to tell me that he was very sorry but it had been decided that there was nothing available for me in the White House.

This failure affected me like some kind of complex disease. I tried to eliminate all the reasons why I had not been given the job. The FBI clearance had been swift and sure. I knew that my preparation was adequate. I felt that I had demonstrated my ability during the campaign and that my political record was such that there could be no doubt as to my being deserving. The only remaining possibilities were the personal ones such as prejudice or jealousy.

During all this time, Val Washington, Director of Minorities for the Republican National Committee, had been trying to move heaven and earth to find out the reason for my not getting the promised assignment. Meanwhile, members of the Administration were embarrassed by the treatment I had received, and other efforts were being made to find a "suitable position" for me. Through Val Washington, Charles Willis, Jr., Assistant to Sherman Adams, and others, I was finally offered the position of Adviser on Business Affairs in the Department of Commerce.

It was a new position and a policymaking one of prestige and authority, but the only reason I accepted it at all was because it would put me on the Washington scene. In effect, I took it for purely selfish reasons. However, in a few months I was so fascinated by the requirements of the job and liked my bosses, Sinclair Weeks, and Charles Honeywell,[1] so much that I soon forgot my bitterness at not being assigned to the White House.

This was a pioneering job, and I had to convince a great many people in the Department of Commerce that it was possible to place a Negro in a responsible Government position and have him measure up. Honeywell and Weeks stood by me at every turn, and I owe them deep gratitude for helping me to prove my worth and permitting me to try out my fledgling wings in Washington.

Two years later, one of the most welcome phone calls I have ever had told me to report to Sherman Adams' office "on the double."

I was interviewed, sized up and briefed on a possible staff job in the White House. Mr. Adams, with the President's assent, had decided that I would join the staff. The groundwork had been laid fully; I merely needed to agree on salary, duties, etc. Jim Hagerty's office would make the announcement over the weekend so that the story would get nationwide coverage. On wings of joy, I went back to the Commerce Department to resign.

Friday afternoon I took the Congressional to New York to spend the weekend with my family and tell them the wonderful news. I was in a taxi, speeding up Madison Avenue, when the cab's radio blared the news of my appointment, ending with: ". . . the first Negro ever to be named to a presidential staff in an executive capacity." When the cabdriver turned around to

[1] Weeks, Secretary of Commerce; Honeywell, Administrator of Business and Defense Services.

say "Did you hear that?" he found a passenger with tears in his eyes.

It is difficult to explain my awed feeling the first day I walked through that austere northwest gate of the White House to report for work. It was one of reverence, gratitude and humility, but—rising up like a cloud to envelop me—there was also the awareness of walking into a gigantic fishbowl where the glare of public attention and observation would never cease. I was no longer a private citizen. I was public property.

For the average American, walking into the White House is like walking into a great cathedral. The atmosphere is almost holy. This is a sacred place in our country's history, and the shades of famous and storied figures are all about. To walk here every day in the service of the President is among the highest of privileges. It was an experience I will never forget.

Actually, my official status was not confirmed until almost five years later when at long last I was commissioned formally. The story behind those five years was not told to me until 1958, when Sherman Adams explained why I had not been given the White House position originally promised me. He said he hoped I understood why no one in the Administration had the courage to tell me and spare me those five years of uncertainty and anxiety.

BLACK MAN IN THE WHITE HOUSE

JULY 12, 1955

THE President and Sherman Adams can give the opportunity to serve in this kind of high position, but they cannot control the minds and thoughts of the White House staff. Most of them have been correct in conduct, but cold. It is evident that many do not relish this intrusion of an outsider. There are also those who believe that I am here merely as "window-dressing," and have no real authority or importance. The career staff is the most distressed and the most insecure. My old friends of the campaign train—the "Eisenhower Originals"—are trying to be helpful and thoughtful. Among those I instinctively trust are: Ann Whitman, Tom Stephens, Mary Caffrey, General Robert Cutler, Gabe Hauge, Jim Hagerty, General Howard Snyder, Gerry Morgan,[1] and of course Sherman Adams.

I have been here ten days now and am still having difficulty recruiting an office staff. This is not to be a Jim-Crow office solely made up of Negroes. It is to be like any other office in the White House, and the only criterion for personnel is ability. Neither visitors nor staff will ever refer to my office as "that colored office" down the hall.

I am seeking secretaries from the secretarial pool in the White

[1] Whitman, Personal Secretary to the President; Stephens, Appointment Secretary to the President; Caffrey, Secretary to James Hagerty; Cutler, Special Assistant for National Security Affairs; Hauge, Economic Adviser to the President; Hagerty, Press Secretary; Snyder, the President's Personal Physician; Morgan, Special Counsel to the President.

House. These are trained girls, schooled in White House methods and protocol, and they are invaluable assistants to a novice executive.

So far, all those offered a job by their supervisor have refused. None wants the onus of working for a colored boss. This has not been said this bluntly, but. . . .

So I have been sitting alone in the office, bewildered as how to get going, how to staff, how to find furnishings, and how to make reports. I will not ask Sherman Adams. This may be part of a test to see whether I can take it.

July 15, 1955

TODAY started out like all the others, but late in the afternoon I was sitting in the inner office, brooding on my fate, when there was a timid knock at the door. I opened it to find a shy, frightened girl standing there. She asked if I were "Mr. Morrow." She kept the door opened behind her, as if for protection, and refused to come in to sit down. She literally blurted out her mission.

Her name was Mary O'Madigan. She was from Massachusetts. She was a member of the White House stenographic pool. Impelled by a sense of Christian duty, she had come to volunteer to serve as my secretary. She was aware of the attitude of the other girls in the pool, but felt she could not be true to her faith, and condemn me simply because of my race. She wanted to try.

I was overcome. The girl was crying.

November 6, 1955

GENERAL Wilton Persons, who was in charge of the White House staff while Governor Adams was in Denver, presided over the staff meeting a few days after the President's heart attack. We were briefed on the latest bulletins from the medical staff on the President's condition. Of particular interest was a letter to General Persons written by the President's personal physician, Major General Howard Snyder, explaining exactly what had happened the night the President was stricken. The letter apparently was designed to point out the sensible conduct maintained by General Snyder in diagnosing the illness and in its emergency treatment.

There has been adverse newspaper comment on the original diagnosis offered by General Snyder: "A mild digestive upset." But if the General gave the impression that the illness was less serious than it actually was, it was probably to prevent panic in the sickroom on the part of the President's wife, as well as to spare the President by not informing him, at that early morning hour, that he had a coronary. However, as soon as it was possible to give a thorough examination with proper professional assistance, the information was given to the press immediately.

It is my personal belief that the entire country is impressed with the honesty of the reporting on this matter, and that nothing is being withheld from the public.

Of course, the staff is very disturbed, and we all wonder what this shocking news will mean. Everything has been going along smoothly, and it has never occurred to any of us that health might be the overriding consideration in the 1956 campaign. The country's love for the President is at an unprecedented high, and it is inconceivable that any candidate could challenge him. Now we are faced with the startling fact that he may not be a candidate and that any other Republican nominee will have rough going!

November 7, 1955

I HAVE had a good lesson today on how the vagaries of international political life and one's complete innocence of purpose can conflict and make trouble.

The National Council of Negro Women was holding its annual convention in Washington the latter part of the week. The Vice-President had been asked to speak, or at least to extend greetings to the council. His office called me about the invitation, and I said it would be wise for him to appear, as this was a prominent group and its leaders had been identified with the New Deal in past years. I felt this was a good opportunity for this group to be exposed to the charm and the sincerity of the Vice-President, and suggested that he speak on International Night, the highlight of the convention.

All parties were completely agreed on this when I inadvertently learned that the principal speaker on the International Night program was to be the roving Ambassador of India, Krishna Menon. This immediately provided complications. Mr. Menon has indicated his interest in Soviet patterns and policies and has not been overly friendly with United States' efforts in kindred fields. I felt that the Vice-President's being on the same platform might prove embarrassing, particularly if Mr. Menon used this occasion to tee off on United States policies abroad or at home. It also occurred to me that newspaper commentators, writers, etc., unfriendly to the Administration, might make political capital out of the Vice-President's appearance on the same program, and he could become an innocent victim of editorial rhubarb.

I phoned Mr. Nixon's office and suggested that we call the whole thing off unless he could find time to look in on one of the daytime meetings just to say hello.

November 9, 1955

AN interesting staff meeting this morning, where we discussed details for the President's home-coming from Denver on Friday. We want to keep the reception on a completely informal basis so that protocol will not be involved. The President's plane will land at MATS Terminal at approximately 3:45 P.M. He will be met by the Vice-President, who will welcome him home on behalf of everyone. This is designed to keep the President from having to shake hands with the many well-wishers and personal friends who will be around. It is expected that all Cabinet members, members of the Diplomatic Corps, and all Administration and Congressional personnel who are in the city will be at the airport. The President's personal staff will be present also.

In his bubble car, he will drive across Memorial Bridge, where two fire trucks on either side of the road will be stationed with their aerial ladders forming an arch through which his motorcade will pass. A sign reading: "Welcome Home, Ike" will be hung from the arch. He will then proceed down Constitution Avenue, around the Ellipse, through East Executive Avenue, up Pennsylvania Avenue past the White House and down West Executive Avenue to the southwest gate.

The White House Staff and personnel from the Executive Office Building and their families will line West Executive Avenue to greet him. I have been put in charge of arrangements for the welcome there and have met with the Secret Service and the head of the White House Police to iron out security details.

November 10, 1955

AT LUNCH today I was shocked by Bernard Shanley's announcement that he had just resigned as Appointment Secretary and the news would be on the ticker from Denver any minute. Apparently his decision had been made three weeks ago upon his return from his visit to Japan, when he stopped by Denver to see the President.

Shanley stated that he thought this was a good time to get out. It would be many months before the President could return to his usual routine of office, and this would mean that the Appointment Secretary's duties would be practically nil. He felt he could not afford to hold a position that, at the moment, was purely honorary.

The talk at our table, among Rowland Hughes, Dr. Arthur Flemming, and Roemer McPhee of Dr. Gabriel Hauge's [1] office, indicated that this was a good time in the history of American government for a complete change in the concept of the President's duties. It was felt that altering procedures of office could save the lives of many future presidents if some serious thought and action were given to easing the tremendous burden of signing papers, reviewing courts-martial, and greeting thousands of foreign and native citizens.

It was recalled that as far back as the Hoover Administration there was not even a fence around the White House and that every day at noon President Hoover would greet all the callers who happened to be there. His office was run with a mere handful of people, and there was not the frightful strain of today's steady stream of callers. It was recalled that the budget at that time was some $6,000,000 and that during the Coolidge Administration the President was able to dictate and sign replies to all incoming correspondence. Today's mail often runs to 50,000 letters at a given time.

1 Hughes, Director of the Bureau of the Budget; Flemming, Director of the Office of Defense Mobilization; McPhee, Associate Special Counsel; Hauge, Economic Adviser to the President.

Dr. Flemming suggested that the American people should buy the President a home in one of Washington's residential sections where he could live with more privacy. The feeling was that the White House should be used only for official and state functions. At the present time it often takes on the aspect of a funeral parlor, with thousands of people pouring through it every day.

It is wondered whether the Shanley spot will be filled by anyone else. The President has been anxious to retain him in some other capacity, but there is no available position of comparable importance that could be given him without loss of prestige.

We are all apprehensive as to how the press will treat this resignation. It well could indicate that the President will not run again and that because Shanley is an inside member of the official family he has some advance notice of this. The press might also take the tack that there has been a rift in the official family and that Shanley has been asked to leave or is resigning in a fit of pique.

There are unconfirmed rumors that Sherman Adams and Shanley have not always seen eye to eye, but if this is true I have no knowledge of it. At any rate, it's the kind of situation in which politicians can speculate loud and long and unfriendly newspapers can have a field day with any interpretation that appeals to them at the moment.

November 11, 1955

I WENT over to the Vice-President's office at one o'clock today to escort him to the Willard Hotel, where the National Council of Negro Women was holding its convention luncheon.

There had been a great deal of confusion in trying to arrange a suitable time when Mr. Nixon could appear. His schedule was jam-packed, with the President due in from Denver this same afternoon, and it was a question of how quickly we could get into the Willard and say hello and leave.

We arrived at the hotel and were met at the door by the manager, who whisked us into a private elevator and up to the dining room. The inevitable photographers were there en masse, and the hauling and shoving and talk of "one more" picture began. I virtually had to shove the Vice-President into the room in order to make sure he could keep to his time schedule.

He gave a charming and effective ten-minute address. He told the women that it must be pleasant for them to meet in the nation's Capital now, when every possible facility was available to them without restrictions based on race or color. He congratulated them upon working so earnestly toward the same goals in human relations that the Administration is working for, and thanked them for their moral support in the never-ending struggle of the Administration to make first-class citizenship available to all Americans.

He touched briefly upon his trip across the world last fall, when he and his wife had discovered, in the Near East and the Far East, that all people—regardless of race or religion—have the same human frailties, ambitions and hopes and that a friendly smile and a warm handshake produce the same results in that part of the world as they do here in America or in any other civilization.

He thanked them for their concern about the health of the President, and said he must be off to the airport to meet him, and was sure that if President and Mrs. Eisenhower knew that he was there to greet the council, they would want him to extend thanks and best wishes to each and every member. The applause was warm and spontaneous. The Vice-President was pleased that he had appeared. Many of the women at the luncheon tables made a rush toward him as he left the dais, and again he had to fight his way out of the room to get to the elevator. Again the photographers swarmed around him, and there was much to-do as many of the women tried to get their pictures taken with him.

He dropped me off at the White House, and before he left, inquired about my golf game, asking me where I played in Washington. I told him that I had not played in Washington the two years I had been here because the private courses were not available and the public courses were too crowded. I said that when I could get off on weekends, I went back to New Jersey, where I played at the Riverdale Country Club. He seemed honestly surprised and taken aback that a member of the President's staff was unable to play on some golf courses in Washington. He said: "Well, as soon as this pressure permits, I'll get two or three of our gang together and we'll play at one of the local clubs."

DECEMBER 5, 1955

TODAY'S *New York Times* has an article by James Reston which states that Sherman Adams is among the prominent "dark horses" for the Republican nomination, in the event that President Eisenhower decides not to run. It says that Adams is the only person outside of the President who knows what the Presidency is all about.

This is an interesting speculation. I don't believe that Sherman Adams could ever get the nomination. Professional politicians dislike his austere personality and ruthless honesty. Here is a man who is not interested in deals of any kind or in any sort of skulduggery that will enhance the position of the party. He has no patience with incompetence or with apple-polishers. He has made a good second man for President Eisenhower because he is completely dedicated to the cause of good government and the ideals for which the President and his Administration stand. I am certain he would make an excellent President, but under his regime the professional pickings would be so lean that they would wither and die.

Mr. Adams usually holds court in the White House mess about 1 P.M. when he is in Washington. He generally has as luncheon guests many of the prominent and distinguished visitors, foreign and domestic, who have come to see him or the President on business. Most of the members of the White House staff try to get to lunch about one o'clock, in order to see and be seen. Any recognition by the Governor during these periods is much prized by staff members. A nod of the head, or when he is leaving, a touch on the shoulder or an abrupt "Come into my office as soon as possible," indicates the importance of the person involved. Also, if staff members have business with him, this is a good hour to determine his mood. If he appears to be sharp, caustic, and extremely cool, it is perhaps wise to put off the engagement as long as possible!

This man runs the White House with an iron hand. He is familiar with and briefed on every single detail of operation, and few decisions of any importance are made without him.

I have been fortunate enough to see his human side. From the very beginning—our meeting on the campaign train in September 1952—he has always shown a fatherly interest in me. A collector's item in Washington is the picture of my swearing-in ceremony, where the Governor is looking up into my face with a broad smile. Few people ever see him in this kind of pose.

Whenever I meet him, no matter where or with whom he may be, he always makes it a point to speak and to inquire about my well-being. If it is in the White House staff dining room, he gives me a warm clap on the shoulder, or a playful rap on the head.

However, this indication of friendliness merely means that your performance to date has been acceptable and that you are expected to continue in the same vein.

I watched this man take over the Eisenhower campaign train from the very beginning and run it according to his own plans. There were many who would like to have challenged his leadership and authority, but none ever successfully dared to brave the chill of his withering glance and authoritative manner.

December 8, 1955

THESE are difficult days for me as I contemplate what is happening in Mississippi in the aftermath of the Till kidnap-

murder case.[1] My memorandum to Max Rabb expressed my
fears that we are on the doorstep of a horrible racial conflagra-
tion in this country. I am convinced, more than ever before,
that the ignoring of this matter by the Republican party will be
a serious stumbling block in next year's presidential election.

Governor Adams spoke to me at lunch yesterday and asked
what the Party would have to do in order to win the Negro vote.
He had noticed that the Gallup Poll showed the Democrats still
running far ahead in the matter of Negro political support.

This question has been asked me many times since I have
been in the White House, and there is great disappointment
topside because Negroes do not seem to be reacting favorably to
the unprecedented Eisenhower actions in the field of civil rights.

I have had a hard time trying to assure the people here that
the Negro's principal concern is economic. The Democrats have
just about convinced him that when they are in power the little
man gets a better break jobwise than he does when the Republicans are in. The Democrats have had more than twenty years of
this philosophy, and it has done its job well.

There is a strong belief among Negroes that the Republican
Party represents great wealth and is not really concerned with
their general welfare.

It is things like the refusal of the Republicans to issue any
kind of fear-allaying statement on conditions in Mississippi that
contribute to the Negro's thinking that the Republican Party
deserts him in crises. It is true that none of the avowed Democratic presidential candidates are saying anything either. This
would alienate the South, and it would be difficult for these
candidates to get the nomination without the South's support.
The fact that the President has been operating on a program of
first-class citizenship for all Americans would appear to make it
simple for a member of the top command to issue some kind of
statement deploring the breakdown of law and order in Mississippi, stating that it is un-American and undemocratic.

---

[1] Emmet Till was a fourteen-year-old Negro who was visiting relatives in Mississippi. He was acused of wolf-whistling at a white woman in a store. His trussed
and mutilated body was found in a river. This case infuriated the entire Negro
population of the United States.

However, there seems to be complete fright when such action is suggested. I believe there is still a false hope that some part of the South may lend support to the next Republican effort. This seems to me to be childish thinking, for we know that the desegregation issue and the Supreme Court decisions have so infuriated the South that no Republican presidential candidate, including President Eisenhower, could count upon any active support south of Washington.

Today's *Courier* came out with a startling headline and an open letter to President Eisenhower stating: SEND U. S. TROOPS TO MISSISSIPPI. It is frightening to sit in this rather high spot and realize that bloodshed can result from this present impasse.

December 19, 1955

MAX RABB called a meeting in his office today with some of the prominent Negro members of the Administration to talk about the problem of civil rights, about mob violence in Mississippi in regard to the aftermath of the Till case, and the results of the latest Gallup Poll, which indicated that the bulk of the Negro voting still is in the Democratic column.

Max was very upset. Undoubtedly he has been feeling great pressure from various factions within the Administration for his strenuous activity in behalf of a forthright statement in the President's annual message to Congress on this explosive issue of civil rights. He is a thoroughly unhappy man, and he let us know it in no uncertain terms.

At the meeting were James Nabrit, Secretary of Howard University; Val Washington, Director of Minorities, Republican National Committee; J. Ernest Wilkins, Assistant Secretary of Labor; [2] Samuel Pierce, Assistant to the Undersecretary of Labor; Joe Douglas from the Department of Health, Education and Welfare; and Scovelle Richardson, Chairman of the Federal

[2] The first Negro to hold a sub-Cabinet position.

Parole Board. We were unanimous in feeling that the Republicans missed the ball when no prominent member of the Administration spoke out against the handling of the Till matter and the subsequent intimidation of Mississippi Negroes, as well as the economic sanctions recently imposed upon them.[3] We argued that the time had come when the President, or some designated member of the Administration, must take notice of the inhuman conditions in Mississippi and at least deplore them, if nothing else.

It is one of the several things that has weakened the party with the Negro voter. I pointed out that every Negro north of the Mason-Dixon line has relatives in the South, and whatever happens to them becomes an emotional problem to those in the North. Their attitude toward the party in power is conditioned by the welfare of their relatives in the South.

Rabb outlined the difficulty he was having in trying to get prominent members of the White House staff who are close to the President to go along with him on the matter of civil rights. He said he had a tremendous job in trying to convince the Cabinet that a forthright stand should be taken. It is my observation that there seems to be some uncanny fear that to alienate the South on this matter of race will be disastrous as far as any southern support of prominent Administration matters in Congress.

This is an absurd position as far as I am concerned, but apparently some of the members of the staff, as well as the Cabinet, are utterly conservative on the matter of race and are not completely convinced that the Administration should do any more than it has done on this explosive topic.

Meanwhile, the NAACP and other organizations are beating on our heads mercilessly, and they will continue unless some statement is forthcoming from the Administration.

Governor Howard Pyle,[4] former Governor of Arizona, came into the meeting to listen to our observations and to make some

---

[3] Stores in the South were cutting off credit to Negroes (who, through economic necessity, had to pay their bills weekly, particularly their food bills) in an effort to "starve them out."

[4] Administrative Assistant to the President.

himself. In colorful and forceful language he blamed his recent defeat at the polls upon the fact that despite all he had tried to do for the Negroes in his state during his terms of office, they had not been loyal to him at election time and had assisted in his defeat. He was not so much bitter about this as reflective and puzzled. He felt that the Gallup Poll indicated this same situation as far as the present Administration was concerned. That is, that the President had bent over backward in the field of civil rights, and yet every poll taken indicated that the Negroes were not grateful and were still clinging to the Democrat banner. He felt that we must get out into the field and preach loyalty to those who are not loyal to us.

We intend to have more meetings of this kind to exchange views, but since we have no desire to be tagged with the terms "kitchen cabinet" or "Negro spokesmen," we will do all we can to keep these meetings and the matters we discuss a secret.

JANUARY 17, 1956

CHARLIE MASTERSON came in to see me today to discuss my memorandum to Sherman Adams regarding his inquiry as to the Gallup Poll taken in December that indicated the bulk of the Negro vote was still with the Democrats. I had replied to the Governor's inquiry with observations of my own (given in another section of this book), and apparently the Governor had passed my memo on to other staff members for their observations and discussions.

Mr. Masterson, as an assistant to Howard Pyle, had been delegated to discuss both my memo and a similar one that Sherman Adams had received from Val Washington in response to the same query.

Charlie had made some very intelligent notations on the memo, and these raised questions that needed clarification for everybody concerned. We discussed the situation at length and arrived at decisions that will be transmitted to Sherman Adams, Governor Pyle, etc.

Charlie is nearer my age than most members of the staff, and this gives me a feeling of rapport with him. He has been listed as one of the ten best tennis players in this country, is equally alert mentally, and has a pleasing personality. I can ask him questions that I have not asked other staff members because of my life-long training to never presume anything with anyone at any time.

I told Charlie that whether the President ran for office or not, and whether or not a Republican won in November, I probably would not be willing to sign on for another four years in Washington. I have no political aspirations, and as far as I am concerned, this is my zenith in public life, so I must go from this position to one of comparable importance in civil life. I will wait until the President makes his announcement, and give whatever assistance I can to his candidacy or anyone else's, up to and through November. Unless the President is a candidate and wins, it is my opinion now that I will turn a completely deaf ear to any demands to remain in Washington.

Masterson told me that he could not make another sacrifice here; that he had given up a position paying more salary than his present one, simply because of his tremendous faith in President Eisenhower. There are many men holding thankless jobs in this Administration who have been fired by the same imagination and dedication. If the President does not run again, most of these loyal people will return to private industry.

We deplored the fact that the National Committee had been so weak in pressing the Republican cause among Negro voters. In his memo to Sherman Adams, Val Washington had outlined one of the reasons why the party has failed to attract Negro votes, stating that the budget for his office is less than $30,000 a year. This is a very small amount, and it seems ridiculous that the Director of Minorities for the Republican Committee should have to assume the responsibility of trying to cover forty-eight states and make any kind of impression on approximately 18,000,000 [1] Negro voters. He should have a staff of eight or ten alert, able young men who would spend their entire time organizing, spreading propaganda, and building goodwill—especially in our country's heavily populated cities.

Charlie indicated his alarm over the entire operation of the National Committee office. He felt that on the whole it was inept, understaffed, and that there were too many persons in high places who were not very knowledgeable, politically or otherwise.

I told him the story of my delayed entrance on the Washing-

[1] Today's census figure is a little over 18,000,000, but knowledgeable Negroes know that the true figure is closer to 25,000,000. A fairly substantial portion of the difference can be attributed to those of our race who are "passing" as whites.

ton scene due to some kind of chicanery within the White House staff, and that to this day I do not have the complete facts about the situation. The story fascinated Masterson. He had not known of it before and said that I must have a feeling about what it pointed to and about those who had handled it.

January 25, 1956

THERE was an early and serious staff meeting this morning, held to review questions that might be asked the President at his press conference at 10:30 A.M. today. It is more or less customary, when many controversial issues are abroad, to have the staff attempt to decide on the manner in which the President should handle difficult and "loaded" questions.

Jim Hagerty presided at this morning's session, framed the possible questions, and in some instances outlined what he thought the answers should be. Sherman Adams, of course, is always the final authority, and after the staff has offered various suggestions, the Governor usually crystallizes the whole idea and puts it down in terse form.

One of the most nagging questions that might arise today concerns the Powell Amendment to the School Construction Bill. I was pleasantly surprised at the staff's reaction to the amendment. Everyone knows Adam Clayton Powell, the flamboyant Congressman from Harlem. The effect of his proposed amendment would be to deny Federal funds for school construction in those areas where segregation prevails, in opposition to the Supreme Court decision outlawing segregation in secondary schools.

Hagerty stated that there was only one stand the Republican party—the party of Lincoln—could take, and that was support of the Powell Amendment. He felt that, since the Supreme Court had spoken on the matter of segregation, the Administration should indicate that it was for enforcing this amendment in every aspect of American life.

I had had no idea Hagerty felt so strongly. On the other hand, Mr. Adams felt that any expression from the President would have to include the realistic as well as the philosophical aspect of the question. He felt that certainly the President should indicate his great moral belief in the necessity of giving every American equal opportunity for development in American life. That was the philosophy of this Administration, and it would never deviate from this belief. However, he said we would have to deal with the reality of the situation too. Classrooms were sorely needed in every section of the land, and he felt that nothing should be allowed to interfere with providing them for the nation's students.

A general discussion ensued, including Harold Stassen,[2] Max Rabb, and Howard Pyle, indicating that this was an explosive situation. It was stated that the Powell amendment would get through the House but come to grief in the Senate, where the southern senators would filibuster it to death. Gerald Morgan [3] pointed out that the President could be placed in a very difficult situation should he come out in wholehearted support of the amendment. Morgan said that the President could be accused of insincerity, because in the past he had also indicated his deep concern for the classroom shortage. He could not now ignore this shortage in favor of the great moral principle involved in the Powell amendment.

The discussion on this went on for thirty or forty minutes. Time was getting short, and it was necessary to conclude the meeting rather abruptly. It was felt that the President would handle the question adequately and that we would point out only the pitfalls to him, hoping that he could avoid them successfully.

Last year, at a press conference, the President had used the term "extraneous" when asked a question about his attitude toward Powell's amendment to the education bill. The Negro press and public have never forgotten this, and it is generally agreed that the use of the term by the President was most unfor-

2 Presidential Adviser for Disarmament.
3 Special Counsel to the President.

tunate. At his press conference this morning he will probably be asked if he considers the Powell amendment to be "extraneous" as far as the School Construction Bill is concerned. He has been advised to avoid the use of this term, and also not to mention the proposed amendment by the term "Powell," because this will merely give Congressmen another item to use from public platforms at a later date in some foray against the Administration.

I have just returned from luncheon at the White House mess, where a tape recording of the President's press conference of this morning was played back for the staff to hear. He did his usual able job. The inevitable question did come up, and the President forthrightly stated that he believed in equal opportunity for every American citizen, that the Supreme Court had spoken, and that he would always support his theories of equal opportunity for all and the decision of the Supreme Court in any area. He acknowledged, however, that the situation was not that simple. He said that there was a great need for classrooms. He therefore recognized the inevitable conflict between his belief in the moral rightness of the Supreme Court decision, and his objections to denying needed classrooms to American school children because of the fact that in some sections of the land segregation—contrary to the Supreme Court decision—would prevail.

He stated that in handing down this decision, the Supreme Court had recommended to lower Federal courts that areas be given a reasonable amount of time to implement the decision. The President recognized the need for this element of time before there could be complete elimination of what he called "the deep roots of prejudice and emotion." He said that he hoped this would be taken into consideration in any determination made on the bill; that classrooms are necessary now, and he wanted school construction now. He added that he felt that every measure and issue proposed by Congress should be voted up or down on its own merits, and should be proposed in a single bill and not encumbered by additional legislation or additional matters that could becloud specific issues. In other words, what he meant was: Let's vote on the School Construction Bill on its own merit and then let the matter of civil rights be proposed and voted upon in another bill for that purpose.

Many members of the staff watched me intently as I listened to the playback of the President's voice. I felt that he had handled a difficult situation well, and it was to my satisfaction. Jim Hagerty kept looking at me and asking whether I approved.

I know that there are many of my group who will consider me a traitor for being willing to accept anything less than complete victory in a matter of this kind. However, I am very close to the scene, and I know and understand the innate honesty of the President and have complete faith in his judgment. As long as he and the principal members of his staff are agreed on the principle of equal opportunity for development in American life for all citizens. I have no fear that there will be any turning back in areas that affect Negro citizens.

I also know that this measure proposed by Congressman Powell has not a whit of a chance to pass the Senate, and at a critical time like this in American life—when the social and political thinking of Americans is being changed by Supreme Court decisions and by the very moral attitude of the President himself—it is a dangerous thing to insist upon the impossible, thereby alienating the friendship of those upon whom we must depend in really vital and serious matters. I am pleased that the President spoke out so that the whole world could hear that he is striving for equal opportunity for every citizen regardless of race, creed, color or previous condition.

During my lifetime I have never known of any other President who made such a statement publicly, with such complete conviction, and wholly without reservation.

January 26, 1956

SHERMAN ADAMS presided at staff meeting today and spoke of matters regarding the Administration. The significant part of the meeting was Jim Hagerty's warning to the staff to stay clear of any discussion concerning the possible contents of the note the President received yesterday from the Russian Ambassador. There is a great guessing game going on among Washington reporters as to its contents. Hagerty's statement to the press yesterday merely indicated that the President and the Russian Ambassador had been corresponding from time to time ever since the Geneva Conference and that the present note was simply a discussion of matters pertaining to world peace. But the warning to the staff to steer clear of discussion of this note indicates that it is a very significant one.

It's never certain what kind of mood Sherman Adams will be in when he comes to a staff meeting. At last week's session he walked in and announced that: "Today is a very significant day in the world, and this staff should start off this day recognizing this fact and doing something unusual to make it stand out in our minds. It is the birthday of the deputy assistant to the President [General Persons]." Mr. Adams immediately launched into singing "Happy Birthday" to General Persons, with the staff joining in. He has an excellent baritone voice and carried the tune beautifully.

FEBRUARY 1, 1956

I HAVE just returned from a five-day trip to the Middle West, where I spoke at the Kansas Day celebration in Topeka. Kansas Day is a colorful annual affair, commemorating the day President Lincoln signed the bill admitting Kansas to the Union. It is also the time when officeholders make known their intention to run for re-election, or political aspirants file notice of their intention to seek office. Kansas is a Republican state, and therefore most of the competition is between Republicans opposing each other in the primaries. Kansas Day turns out to be a Republican celebration, and the various banquets and dinners offer opportunities for speeches by local and national figures who extoll the virtues of the party.

In past years it has been customary for Negro Republicans to have a separate affair rather than participate in the big celebration completely. When I was first requested to speak to the Negro group, I made it very clear that I would not, under any circumstances, go to Kansas to address a segregated meeting. It would be ironic for me, as a member of the President's staff, to condone, aid, or abet the perpetuation of a vicious system of separation in party matters. I was assured that every effort would be made to have an interracial meeting at which I would speak in the municipal auditorium at 2:15 P.M. on Saturday, January 28.

I arrived in Topeka the previous day and was met by Governor John Hall's limousine and a Negro representative from his office, Arthur Fletcher, and was taken to the Kansas Hotel, which in itself was quite an event. It was told that I was the first Negro to be admitted as a guest in this hotel.

That evening the Governor held a reception for those who had come to Topeka for the celebration. He gave me a very warm welcome. It was the usual dragging affair, with hundreds of people passing through the receiving line to shake hands with the Governor, his wife, the staff, and high-ranking officials.

Later in the evening I was standing around, balancing a tea-cup, when one of the female guests came running up to me and said: "Boy, I am ready to go now; go outside and get me a taxi." I was stunned, but Arthur Fletcher did some quick thinking and immediately informed the lady that she was speaking to one of President Eisenhower's assistants. She was overcome with remorse and embarrassment.

February 17, 1956

THE past few weeks have been trying ones for all staff members as we await the President's decision on a second term. Our concern is not so much with our own jobs and what will happen to us as it is with what will happen to the party, to the Eisenhower idealism, and to all the goals that have been set for the Administration during the President's tenure. I have not been party to any secret sessions held to discuss this matter at any time, or have I done any speculating with any members of the White House team. I am keeping to a rigid policy of not choosing sides on any matter or participating in any schemes or projects to promote anything at any time.

The first question I am always asked by newsmen and others when I am on speaking tours is for my personal opinion as to whether the President will run. I always dismiss the question with a polite "No comment."

As a matter of fact, officials in the White House know less

about what is happening in this respect than a lot of people outside profess to know. Few of us discuss the matter, and again, the majority is reluctant to try to estimate what the President will do. Personally, of course, I hope that he will seek re-election, because I have visions of a terrific vendetta among aspiring Republicans as they run roughshod over each other, trying to get the nomination for themselves or for someone in whom they are interested. It is difficult for me to think that the President might not run.

Mr. Nixon is obviously a leading, if not *the* leading candidate, but there seems to be such a terrific anti-Nixon feeling in this country—even among Republicans—that I think some of them would conspire to defeat him if he were nominated. This is most unfortunate. I have discovered that Richard Nixon is a very capable, qualified, dedicated young man, and I feel he has the maturity of mind, purpose and vision to do a good job. However, to mention his name in circles outside of one's own household is like throwing gasoline on a smoldering fire. I often wonder what this resentment springs from, and feel that much of it goes back to the 1952 campaign, when he had to go on television and radio to explain the funds that had been collected in his behalf for his campaign to secure his Senate seat. I can only think of the old adage that "Truth can never catch up with a lie," and no matter how capably and vigorously he attempted to defend himself against the slurring accusations of the 1952 campaign, many will never accept his explanation.

I do not believe that Senator William Knowland of California could secure the nomination, but he too reminds me of the fable of the dog in the manger who could not eat the hay but would not let anyone else get close enough to try it. This leaves a sad picture for those of us who are earnestly concerned with the future of our party, and these are indeed dismal and nerve-racking days as we sit here hoping, waiting and praying for the President's decision.

February 23, 1956

IT has been rather shocking to my friends and acquaintances that since I've been on the White House staff I have divorced myself completely from any kind of social life. My friends argue that this is ridiculous, because I need these social distractions to relieve the tension and strain of the daily job. They chide me for being so completely unrealistic about social relations.

It is difficult for me to explain my reasons for living such a hermitlike life. In the first place, I am a pioneer in what I am trying to do, and whenever one is a Negro pioneer, he has the severe responsibility of doing the kind of job that will open opportunities to others of his race without their having to go through all of his difficulties.

Unfortunately, most of my life has been spent in pioneering endeavors, as were the lives of my father and grandfather. My grandfather, an ex-slave who was tutored by an Oxford don along with the son of his master of the same age, went to college at forty, leaving my dad at home to take care of and support a mother and a family of six children. Grandfather later became an outstanding Presbyterian minister and educator. During the Reconstruction, he was run out of North Carolina by the Ku Klux Klan for teaching other Negroes to read and write. He demanded much from his own children and grandchildren and would never permit us to shy away from difficult situations. He also had the philosophy that, since we had been gifted with a normal degree of intelligence, and this intelligence had been cultivated by good schools and colleges, we had a sacred obligation to those less fortunate members of our race who could not fend for themselves.

As long as I can remember, I have been involved in situations where it was necessary for me to fight for the opportunity to be part of the endeavor and to make the kind of impression that would erase the resentment aroused by my original efforts to belong. This was true in grammar school, in high school, in prep school and in college. It has certainly been very true since I came to Washington.

Naturally, my every move is open to observation, and being a bachelor adds to the inherent dangers of this position. I cannot attend social affairs with a young lady without having some significance attached to the occurrence. It is not possible to have female friends come to my apartment to visit me without having eyebrows lifted and significant comments made by nosy people of both sexes. Whenever my staff comes to see me, I have them come in pairs—to protect themselves as well as me.

I avoid social functions, because even the most innocuous question asked me about the White House will find its way into print in some gossip column the following week. If I were to attend a cocktail party and happen to stumble on the way out, there would be veiled remarks that "the President's assistant is not very discreet and cannot hold his whisky."

So I have cut myself off completely from any kind of social life, and the only indulgence I permit myself is to get to New York weekends when I am free, to play golf with my long-time companions Arthur Logan, Richard Carey and Howard Reckling.

This should indicate that the way of a pioneer can be lonely and full of sacrifices. It is also very expensive. No matter what financial demands are made on me, they must be met, because I am pioneering and have to make the best possible impression so that it can be acknowledged that I am no different from anyone else in a similar position. Most of the men in these high positions in the Adminstration are men of personal wealth, and it is not so difficult for them to maintain the prestige that goes with their office in this matter of financial responsibility.

For example, the Community Chest, the Red Cross, social service organizations, political affairs, etc., all expect substantial financial backing from Adminstration officials. There are also personal gifts and birthday tokens for associates. I can never plead that I am perhaps the poorest member of the Administration. I am expected to play my part, and I do, no matter what the cost. I shall leave Washington a poorer man than when I

came here, but must chalk this up as part of a determination
to represent my race well whenever I have that privilege.

A Fight For Freedom, a film shown at staff meeting this morning, pointed out the necessity for keeping Radio Free Europe
alive, and we were asked for staff contributions for this worthwhile project. It was replete with Russian propaganda, spread
throughout the Iron Curtain countries, showing the United
States as a center of violence, greed, prejudice, poverty and confusion. The constructive side of the film proved the great effect
that Radio Free Europe broadcasts are having on people behind
the Iron Curtain.

When the film was finished, Sherman Adams observed that
some of the agencies and newspapers in this country practiced
the Soviet method of distortion and lies in order to put over
certain propaganda. He referred to one morning paper which
had carried a story about him and the White House which he
said was completely manufactured and mainly made up of lies.
He also spoke of a well-known columnist who has a daily feature
in the Washington *Post and Times Herald,* and gives the impression of having inside information as to what is going on in
all the agencies and institutions in government, and particularly
inside the Cabinet and the White House.

One of these columns reported on a Cabinet meeting at which
the gas bill was supposed to have been discussed, and the columnist put words in the mouth of Postmaster General Arthur
Summerfield which indicated that he favored a veto of the measure. It indicated that Secretary of Defense Charles E. Wilson
also favored a veto. Governor Adams pointed out that the story
was completely false. In the meeting referred to, Summerfield
had not opened his mouth and Wilson had not even been
present!

It is this kind of reporting that does distinct damage to men
high in government circles and also to the Administration. However, there seems to be little that anyone can do to prevent this
odious type of keyhole reporting.

February 27, 1956

I WENT up to New York Friday to see Fred Friendly, associate of Edward R. Murrow, who produces *See It Now*. Friendly wanted to talk to me about doing a documentary on *See It Now*, depicting the highlights of the current racial tension in the South. Their men have been there for several weeks, filming events and interviewing whites and Negroes prominently involved in the Montgomery bus boycott matter. Talking to some of Friendly's associates, off the record, it appeared that CBS would like to do the film but wondered whether it might not inflame passions rather than allay them, and whether the desire to perform a good reporting service could succeed or would CBS be accused of fomenting strife and confusion.

I also gathered that the network did not want to become known as one that constantly engaged in controversial issues. Ever since Murrow took on Senator Joseph McCarthy and did a program on him, I believe the network has had trouble getting sponsors for this program. Then recently Murrow did a documentary on the explosive farm issue, and ran into difficulty with Secretary Ezra Taft Benson. While the race situation is top news at the moment and under ordinary circumstances would receive top treatment from a program of this kind, it is easy to see why these gentlemen are gun-shy at this point.

February 28, 1956

THESE are heart-heavy days for me. The tense situation in the South is making headlines in all the papers, and the pressure put upon me by outside groups to have the Administration speak out forcefully on this matter is wearing me down.

This contention is bound to become a political football, and Democratic candidate Adlai Stevenson is already capitalizing upon the fact that the Administration has not made any announcements on the matter—except the President's statement at the last press conference—deploring the display of violence at the University of Alabama against a young Negro woman, Authurine Lucy, who sought admission there.

Today's *New York Times* carries a front-page story stating that last night Stevenson proposed that President Eisenhower form a meeting of southern Negro and white leaders in an effort to allay mounting racial tensions. Stevenson said that he had been very much disturbed by the mounting tensions in the South, and in order to avoid the possibility of further disorders or futher damage to the nation's reputation abroad, he felt that the time had come when the President's influence should be used by calling such a meeting.

In a memorandum to Governor Adams on December 16, 1955, commenting on the Till case and upon the situation in the Deep South generally, I made a recommendation that a conference of a dozen or more leading ministers, white and Negro, be called together, under the auspices of the Administration, to discuss what could be done. I suggested ministers rather than laymen, so that such a conference would not give the appearance of being political or endorsing any kind of philosophy in the field of race relations. My suggestion was vetoed by higher authority in the White House.

The Stevenson recommendation has put the Administration on the spot. If the President does not call a conference, it gives the appearance—particularly to disheartened Negroes—that the Administration is not interested in their plight and that the President has abandoned them. If the conference is called, it indicates fear on the part of the Administration and the embarrassing fact that the Democrat suggestion had to be acted upon to get the President out of a difficult spot.

In my distress this morning I went to talk to Howard Pyle about the matter. His political judgment is greatly respected in the White House. I asked him point-blank what we should do now, and what our approach to the situation should be.

He said that we should not be panicked by the Democrat maneuver, which at the moment appeared to be part of the contest between Stevenson and Senator Estes Kefauver to secure Negro support; that each was jockeying to put the other in a hole. We also recognized that Stevenson was in difficulty with Negro voters because of an earlier announcement to a Negro group on the West Coast that he would not use the Army to enforce the Supreme Court decision in the South, since it was such an action had brought on the Civil War; in other words, he had appeared lukewarm on the matter of enforcing civil rights. There was a great reaction from Negro leaders after his statement in California, and he had been trying to explain it ever since.

Governor Pyle said that our attitude should be that the President had beaten everyone to the draw by his suggestion in the State of the Union Message that a Congressional committee be appointed to survey the whole problem of civil rights and to come up with recommendations for action. Pyle felt that we should merely reaffirm this stand and request that, because of the seriousness of the situation, a commission take up the request of the President's Message immediately.

I then went to talk with Max Rabb, who often handles minority problems for the President. Max gave me a tongue-lashing on the Negro's attitude on securing his civil rights. He felt that despite what the Administration had done in this area, Negroes had not demonstrated any kind of gratitude, and that most of the responsible officials in the White House had become completely disgusted with the whole matter. He said that there was a feeling that Negroes were being too aggressive in their demands; that an ugliness and surliness in manner was beginning to show through. He felt that the leaders' demands were intemperate ones and had driven most of the liberals to cover. He said that Negroes had made no effort to carry along with them the white friends they had gained, and that what they were insisting on at the present time so far exceeded what reasonable white people would grant that he was afraid these white friends were becoming few and far between. He repeated that he had stuck his neck out on this matter before, and that while he would always be for what was right, he could no longer argue that Negroes would be an asset politically or that doing things for them would gain any support for the Administration.

In effect, he was telling me that I should walk softly from then on and ask fewer questions of the members of the Administration on this matter.

Here, really, is my deepest conflict: I am an appointee in the Administration, with loyalty to that Administration, to the party and the President, but I am also a Negro who feels very keenly the ills that afflict my race in its efforts to secure in one fell swoop all the privileges and responsibilities of citizenship that have been denied it for three centuries in this country. It is my responsibility to explain to white people how Negroes feel on this matter, and by the same token, explain to Negroes the Administration's attitude.

The time may come when I will find that these two responsibilities are incompatible, and that will mean that I will choose. Knowing myself as I do, I know that I would decide to retire from my present position.

It is difficult to make any white person understand that you cannot tell intelligent, loyal, battle-tested, young Negro Americans to accept gradualism with the hope that someday full citizenship will be theirs. Each Negro today wants first-class citizenship in his own time, and is not appeased by the observation that some future generation will benefit by his sacrifices.

MARCH 1, 1956

TWENTY-FOUR hours have passed since the President made his dramatic press conference announcement that he would seek re-election for a second term. He went on the air last night, on the radio and television, to inform the American people of his physical condition and tell them that he felt sufficiently able to retain the Presidency for another term.

It was a simple, yet dramatic, recitation. He is one of the most unpretentious men I have ever known, and this is one of the qualities that endear him to most Americans. I have seen the President twice today; he looked very well, and still has some of the tan he picked up during his Georgia vacation. He was alert and friendly and seemed to be on top of things.

However, this has not been a very happy day for me, because of reports on the situation in the South. *New York Times* newsmen who have just returned from Tuscaloosa, the seat of the University of Alabama, state that the atmosphere there is so tense that it is just a question of time before there will be a bloody outbreak. The papers today announced that the Federal Court in Alabama has directed Authurine Lucy's return to school at nine o'clock on Monday morning, March 6. Both townspeople and students have vowed that she will not be permitted to return. We obviously have the makings of a first-class race riot.

I spent a good deal of time today with Max Rabb, trying to make plans for the Administration's position in the event mob violence should break out in the South. Sherman Adams has asked what the Government would do if the people in Alabama defied the Federal Court's decision and did not permit Miss Lucy to attend. I suggested that Rabb call Roy Wilkins and ask what the NAACP's plans were. Wilkins told us that he had just received a call from Alabama, saying that the university officials had re-expelled Miss Lucy on the grounds that she did not tell the truth in the original suit against the college. She claimed that she had been expelled from the university because of her race. The trustees said that this was not true, that she had been expelled to save her life. It is on the basis of this alleged falsehood that the trustees based their second expulsion. It poses a neat legal question in my mind as to how the university could re-expell Miss Lucy four days before she submitted herself for readmission. It also poses a question of whether or not this action of the trustees is in defiance of the court. How will this matter be handled?

Here in the White House, word has come to me that Miss Lucy has become a sort of Joan of Arc to Negroes and a symbol of hate, frustration and arrogance as far as southern whites are concerned. It has been said that her arrival on the campus in a Cadillac convertible infuriated many whites. The story is now being circulated that she is "a plant" and is not really interested in an education, but is being used as a tool by the NAACP to crack the university. I have been told further that if she would withdraw, and within a few weeks some other student would seek admission in a quiet way, the other student would be accepted without trouble or strife.

Miss Lucy is in a very difficult position. If she backs down and does not return to the university, it will be a triumph for mob violence and the antidesegregation forces. If she returns, the possibility is great that she may meet death or physical abuse. What a lonely and disturbed young woman she must be.

Rabb and I have decided to sit down quietly with some of the Negro leaders such as Wilkins, Thurgood Marshall, A. Philip Randolph, and Lester Granger, to see if we can arrive at a solution, or barring this, at some agreement that we will proceed with good sense and judgment during these treacherous times. We are also recommending to Sherman Adams that if the Congress does not shortly act on the President's request for the appointment of a bipartisan commission to study the Southern situation and make recommendations on the same, the President appoint a committee of his own—made up of men of real stature of both races who can command respect from the American people—to investigate conditions and report to him on their findings.

We are also recommending that the situation be watched very closely by the White House, and at a propitious time the President issue a strong, ringing statement deploring the breakdown of law and order in the South and the ignoring of civil and human rights, and pledging his office to do what it can to restore sanity, decency, and order to this section of the country.

March 3, 1956

I AM not normally in Washington on Saturdays, but I am glad I was here today. Sherman Adams put in an urgent call for me to come to his office for a conference. I spent a half hour with him as he filled me in on the Administration's concern about the racial strife in the South.

Last week I sent Governor Adams a memo indicating my fears that the situation was getting out of hand and asking permission to go to Alabama to talk with the Negro leaders there to try to find out exactly what was on their minds and what they proposed to do in the future. I sincerely wanted to help the Administration to come to grips with this problem. I realized that it was fraught with political dangers, but I was anxious for the Negroes in the South to know that they have not been abandoned by the Administration and that they have the moral support and understanding of the White House.

Mr. Adams said he appreciated my memo and had given it a great deal of thought, but that it would be politically and personally dangerous for me to be sent into the situation. He obviously had the latest reports from the FBI on the conditions in Alabama, as well as reports on who and what were governing the outbreaks of violence and race-baiting. He said that the Communist influence in the situation was tremendous, and he was certain that none of the responsible Negroes involved realized the extent of this.

He said that the matter was so serious that it would be discussed in a Cabinet meeting and in the Security Council during the week, and that if it were proper, J. Edgar Hoover of the FBI would be asked to come and go over the matter with the staff, and the Attorney General would be invited to come in to brief us on what was happening. He said that he could appreciate my position as a Negro and as a member of the President's staff, but that I must not become deeply involved in the problem, because I would be a target for recriminations that could be bad. As a member of the White House family, he would see to it in the future that I was completely briefed on what was happening, and that I could be certain that the President would never shirk his moral responsibility in this situation.

Mr. Adams said that it had not become necessary for Federal agencies to act yet and he sincerely hoped that it would not come to a point in the future where troops would have to be sent in to restore law and order and to preserve lives and property. He ordered the President's counsels to sit down and do some serious thinking on all the possible situations that might obtain and be ready with answers to meet these situations if it became necessary for the President to act. In other words, all of us must give thought to this matter and evaluate a series of hypothetical situations and their solutions. For example, suppose Miss Lucy returns to the university and rioting results or she loses her life. What would the Federal Government do? What would happen if an all-out bloody race riot broke out somewhere in the South and the hysteria spread to other sections of the country and we had race riots in Chicago, Detroit and New York? What action would the Government have to take?

Adams concluded by saying that, since we had gotten over the hurdle of last week—and I imagine he meant the President's decision to run for a second term—the second greatest problem before the Administration at the present time was this matter of southern racial conflict.

This was evident in this morning's papers. *The New York Times* carried front-page and inside-page stories on the Lucy case and on Stevenson's speech at the University of Michigan yesterday in which he called upon the North to eradicate its own color lines and to stop pointing an accusing finger at the South.

I feel that we are in for rough seas in the next few weeks. I only hope that we can avoid bloody conflict and rioting and that it will not be necessary for the President to call out troops or to bring in any other executive power in order to stifle this flame that seems to be enveloping our country.

March 14, 1956

WE HAD our usual weekly staff meeting this morning and concentrated on the questions that might be asked the President at his 10:30 press conference. He is sure to be queried on this all-important matter of race relations in the South.

Yesterday some ninety members of Congress signed a "manifesto" which, in effect, castigates the Supreme Court for its anti-segregation decision as regards schools, and frankly asserts that the decision went far beyond the Supreme Court's powers to determine such an issue. This is bound to add fuel to the already raging fires, and reporters can bombard the President with questions as to his attitude.

Sherman Adams was not at this morning's session, having gone to New Hampshire for yesterday's primary election. Jim Hagerty was away on leave, so Murray Snyder, Associate Press Secretary, presided.

Jerry Persons said that he had read the manifesto and that "it didn't seem too bad, for Alabama!" This brought laughter from the entire group, but we all realize that this is a serious situation, and there was much discussion on how the President might handle it. The consensus of opinion seemed to be that he could suggest that Congressmen have every right, as individuals, to make statements of this nature and that the President, as a member of the executive branch of the Government, never sought to make observations about the conduct, attitude and actions of another of its branches. It was then urged that he reiterate his oft-repeated observations on his deep and un-bounded respect for the Supreme Court and its responsibilities, and emphasize that as long as he is Chief Executive he will never interfere with the duties and responsibilities of another branch of the Government. He should ask all responsible citizens to assess today's problems with calmness and common sense, and say that he believed that with this approach we would all, in due time, arrive at a worthy American decision.

Another question that came up was the possibility that again the President would be asked his attitude toward having Mr. Nixon as a running mate, particularly in view of the fact that Nixon got a large write-in vote in the New Hampshire primaries yesterday despite the fact that he was not on the ticket or running for anything. It was felt that the President might reaffirm his statement of last week on his high regard and esteem for Mr. Nixon and say he had stated before that it was up to Mr. Nixon to make his own decision on his political future.

At lunch today the tape recording of the press conference was played back for the staff members. The expected questions were asked, and the President answered them with dignity and good judgment. He appealed for level heads, and again asked Congress quickly to consider his request (in his State of the Union Message of January 5) to create a bipartisan commission to study this whole complex problem of race relations.

He pointed out that in the past ninety years the South had not been acting contrary to law, but had not been obeying previous Supreme Court decisions which had upheld the "separate but equal" theory; that the fact that the Supreme Court had now reversed itself and called for equality of treatment and opportunity for Negro citizens in the matter of education and otherwise would indicate that this overthrowing of many years of fixed attitudes and conduct would take time. He pointed out that integration in school systems had been successful in some southern states, which indicated that there was a large body of citizens in the South who accepted the Supreme Court decision with equanimity and were willing to abide by the decision and, as good citizens, would work toward its implementation.

When asked by a reporter if he had considered Representative Powell's request that he call together white and Negro leaders in the South for a conference at the White House, he indicated that he had rejected this idea, because mere discussion was not enough and action was necessary after that kind of discussion. The reason he wanted a Congressional committee to do the reviewing was that such a committee would have the power to subpoena and could therefore get reluctant witnesses to talk and present evidence vital to any effective determinations.

March 16, 1956

I HAVE just been given the responsibility of maintaining physical security in the Executive Office Building, and I am not happy about it. The architecture of this building does not lend itself to any kind of sound physical security without a great outlay of money. An off-the-cuff estimate of the amount necessary to make the entire building reasonably secure is in the neighborhood of $120,000. Apparently this subject has been broached before, and the Bureau of the Budget literally shivered at the amount involved and turned down the proposal.

The startling fact is that some of the projects in the building handle some of the most sensitive data in the Government, and any leakage could seriously endanger the security of the nation.

This matter of security is a very vexing problem both here and abroad, particularly in Russia. In some of the embassies abroad, ingenious listening devices have been uncovered that are not connected with wires but have just been slapped onto an object in a room. Through sound rays directed from outside, the instrument in the room can be agitated to such a degree that it will act as a microphone and transmit voice sounds to some instrument outside the embassy.

In a building as large as the Executive Office Building, with as many entrances and exits, it would be simple for an enemy agent to get into the building and spend the day in one of the lavatories or in one of the many dark corners of the upper floors, and at night—using skeleton keys or otherwise—wire the rooms in which sensitive material is dealt with during the day.

I am having the FBI "sweep" these rooms with various instruments to try to find whether there are any hidden devices in them. This will have to be done fairly frequently because of the three or four groups now dealing with explosive matters.

The papers this weekend are full of angry comments by spokesmen for a Negro social organization on my remarks to a group of newspapermen last week. The newsmen had told me that a member of the group had chartered a boat for a week's cruise to Bermuda, and that the cost would probably be between $10,000 and $25,000. I was aghast at this and said so, particularly in view of the tragic struggle of Negroes in Alabama and other places to maintain a boycott against bus lines for their rank inequality of treatment on buses. The people in Montgomery are in need of funds to keep their car pools operating and to buy food and clothing. And the NAACP or its legal fund is in dire need of money to keep the civil rights fight going throughout the country. This is hardly the time for a flagrant display of spending on the part of responsible colored people.

One spokesman made a vicious attack on me in the newspaper, suggesting that I had been duped into my statement by persons who disliked the organization. He also said that this was a bid by me—as a person just recently rescued from obscurity—for publicity.

March 28, 1956

I HAVE been doing a good deal of traveling in the past few weeks, carrying out speaking engagements I made last year before the press of business became so great. The problem is to develop new material for every speech. This is essential, since I am very much in the news these days and what I say is closely scrutinized by newspaper editors.

I have been continuing the theme that reckless and thoughtless spending on the part of Negro social organizations at this time is neither prudent nor defensible, and that this money would be a great asset to those organizations and agencies carrying on the civil rights fight in various sections of the country.

As I have pointed out before, a great howl has gone up over this theme in some places. Insulting letters have been written to the newspapers, and a hostile attitude is evident in the gatherings I address. There are always the angry few who accost me after the speech is over.

One of the encouraging features, however, is the fact that some persons in prominent places do express thanks for what I am saying, and have urged me to continue. I appreciate very much the letter received from W. Beverly Carter, publisher of the Pittsburgh *Courier,* America's largest Negro weekly, who congratulated me upon the speech made in Hampton before the Alpha Phi Alpha Fraternity, last Sunday, and implored me to keep it up. This I intend to do.

Our staff meetings continue to be concerned about the problem of race relations in the country, and there is a growing demand in the Negro press—and even daily editorials in some of the great daily newspapers such as *The New York Times*—urging the President to take a more forthright stand and leadership.

The question most asked me at my public appearances is why the President or the Administration does not take a firmer stand on the whole matter of civil rights. Most Negroes, of course, are against any talk of moderation, and the use of the term "gradualism" is fatal when addressing a Negro audience. Experience has taught Negroes that gradualism to the white Southerner means never, and that moderation means going at a snail's pace and never attacking the real crux of the situation with any fervor.

With the majority of Negroes it is all or nothing, and this makes a crucial situation, because white Southerners are equally adamant about retreating from the attitudes and customs they've developed over many decades.

Knowing the President as I do, I am certain that he will not be pushed into making any further statements on the matter. He has urged moderation but steady progress, and I am certain that that will continue to be the pitch of the Administration.

Of course the Democratic candidates for the nomination are capitalizing upon what, in some quarters, is felt to be a Republican weakness of not speaking out fully against southern indignities heaped upon the Negro. Senator Kefauver is particularly vocal in advocating carrying out to the letter the Supreme Court's decision and upholding the Constitution. Mr. Stevenson's attitude is that of the President as he, too, urges moderation and refuses to promise anything that he knows he would not be able to carry out if he were nominated and elected. Senators Herbert Lehman of New York and Wayne Morse of Oregon have made masterful speeches on the Senate floor, deploring the lukewarm attitude of the Administration toward Negro rights and suggesting a more forthright policy in dealing with the disturbances in the South.

Senator Lehman is highly regarded as a liberal, and since he is a member of a minority group himself and from the melting pot of New York, his attitude is understandable. Senator Morse is also a liberal, but a highly unpredictable individual who unquestionably gets great delight out of embarrassing his former Republican colleagues. However, the work of these two men has been very effective, and their pleas have been used as examples by Negroes when protesting the moderate attitude of the Administration.

APRIL 2, 1956

YESTERDAY was Easter Monday and the day of the traditional egg rolling on the White House lawn. The President said hello to the crowd from a White House balcony in the morning. Today's papers report that 20,000 people took advantage of the opportunity to walk, play, sit and eat there. I was struck with the completely democratic atmosphere which prevailed. It is startling to see thousands of people streaming over these well-cared-for grounds which are rarely trespassed upon. Unless you are a personal friend of the President's family or a staff member with duties on the grounds, you do not walk there. I strolled through around noontime and shuddered at the litter of picnic papers, cracked eggs and other debris. This means a tremendous clean-up job for the National Park employees who care for the grounds.

There was one scene that struck me as being worthy of *Porgy and Bess* or some other Negro musical. Three Negro women, a man and two children were sitting on a blanket. The children were busy eating sandwiches and cake. The adults were engaged in a loud and vigorous game of cards. They were all completely oblivious to everything around them. Obviously they had not merely come to roll eggs; they were spending the day in a pastoral setting in which they could relax and enjoy themselves.

Walking from the East Wing, I ran into Kevin McCann,[1]

---

1 Special Assistant to the President.

whose office is there, and he asked me if I knew the name of the former dean of Storer College at Harpers Ferry, West Virginia. Storer was a small Negro college that was closed last year because of lack of funds. Kevin, who is president of Defiance College in Ohio, said that he remembered that this dean had a Ph.D. in chemistry, and that he, Kevin, needed a chemistry professor at Defiance. It was his feeling that this Negro dean was not only well qualified, but would be pioneering in this position and not likely to be lured away by another offer.

I was quite surprised by this. It is one more indication that color barriers are crumbling in the professional world and that ability is becoming the overriding factor in many instances and places. Kevin said that it was his personal feeling that the time was ripe for him to have a Negro on his faculty. I promised to do everything I could to locate the missing dean. This is an opportunity that should be used immediately.

April 3, 1956

TODAY was a very exciting day in the Executive Office Building. A female firebug set two fires in two of the ladies' rooms of the building, and earlier in the morning she touched off a small one in the Red Room of the White House. She was finally caught and told Secret Service men that she "had a lot of trash and wanted to burn it!"

April 4, 1956

WE HAD our usual prepress conference staff meeting this morning, presided over by Jim Hagerty. He had prepared an agenda of possible questions the press might ask the President. The matter of the disturbances in the Middle East [2] seems to be of paramount interest at the present time, and several minutes were spent on how the President might handle questions dealing with this.

Yesterday was primary day in Wisconsin, and the Democrats had made every effort to have this primary appear as a sort of popularity contest between Senator Kefauver, Democratic candidate, and President Eisenhower. This primary is important, because it may give some idea as to how the farmers feel about the Republican program; any unusual turnout for the Democrats could be interpreted as a repudiation of the Republican farm program.

Early returns indicated that Senator Kefauver got 44 percent of the ballots cast, but that early this morning the President had a 64,000-vote lead. The President's strength appeared to be mostly in cities, villages and the more prosperous farm areas of southern and central Wisconsin. It also indicated that Kefauver was leading in districts in the far north, where there are many fringe farmers whose incomes have been cut considerably due to lower milk prices.

Another possible question might be what the President's reaction is to Sherman Adams' public characterization of the present Congress as a "Do-Nothing Congress." It was felt that the President would, as usual, refuse to comment on individual statements, but that he could easily point out that Congress has not acted on major portions of his program.

Some minutes were given to discussion of the suggestion made by Governor LeRoy Collins of Florida that the President call a meeting of southern leaders to discuss the segregation issue. This of course has been suggested by both white and Negro persons of prominence, as well as by editorials in the Washington *Post, The New York Times* and other leading newspapers. The President's position remains that he has asked Congress to investigate this matter and to make recommendations to remedy it.

To those of us who have gone over it thoroughly, there *are* some valid objections to such a meeting. There is the question

[2] There had been an outbreak of fighting between Arabs and Israeli along the Gaza border.

of who should be invited. No matter what names were decided upon, there would always be those who would resent not having been included, and members of the public who would feel that those who had been invited should not have been.

April 25, 1956

AT THE weekly staff meeting this morning one matter that caused a great deal of concern was the Supreme Court decision in a South Carolina case brought by a Negro woman against the South Carolina Electric and Gas Company which runs the buses in Columbia, South Carolina, where the court stated that the separate but equal doctrine no longer applied, in light of the Supreme Court's decision outlawing school segregation.

The case arose in June 1954, when the woman boarded the bus in Columbia, and because the Negro section was crowded, entered a section reserved for whites. According to her brief, she was ordered from the section and was struck by the driver before she finally left the bus. She sued for $25,000 civil rights damages in the United States District Court, contending that the South Carolina segregation laws were unconstitutional. The District Court dismissed the case on the grounds that the state laws were valid under the 1896 Separate But Equal Facilities Doctrine. She appealed to the United States Fourth Circuit Court of Appeals, which reversed the decision and sent the case back to the lower court for retrial on the grounds that the Separate But Equal Doctrine no longer applied in light of the Supreme Court's decision outlawing segregation.

The bus company then appealed to the Supreme Court the decision ordering a retrial. In dismissing that appeal, the Supreme Court upheld the United States Fourth Circuit Court of Appeals.

Some circles hold this decision as ending segregation in intrastate transportation. The morning papers indicate that the Virginia Transit Company yesterday announced that it was discontinuing segregated seating in Richmond, Norfolk and Portsmouth. However, Georgia and Alabama have indicated that they will oppose any desegregation move by all possible legal means.

Once again we are face to face with an explosive matter. It will be difficult for the President to answer a question on this or kindred subjects directly. It was indicated in our meeting that he was disturbed about the Court making decisions concerning intrastate matters; it was suggested that he be guided, so that he would not make any public statements that would indicate his personal views. This could be a disastrous situation. These discussions in staff meeting always have hard going because of the conservative nature of many of the members and the fact that Jerry Persons, while a "liberal Southerner," is obviously deeply affected by and emotional about these sharp changes in southern customs decreed by the Supreme Court.

The most vocal person in the group, who always insists that the party of Lincoln must stand for the truth at all times, is James Hagerty. We did not arrive at any solution this morning as to what the President is to say if asked his reaction to this latest Supreme Court decision. I feel a sense of apprehension enveloping the conservative staff members; they feel that maybe this "race" business is going too swiftly to be digested by the average American.

There is another item that has made all the papers this morning. A meeting of seventy Negro leaders in Washington yesterday set up a racial steering committee to work by all practical means to speed up the process of school desegregation. They forthrightly reject "gradualism as an approach to economy of civil rights." They have petitioned the President for a meeting with him. I suggested to Max Rabb that we ought to discuss that and determine whether or not the President should see them. However, this was ignored, and the meeting adjourned without any discussion on this subject.

I came back to my office feeling very blue. I know that if the wrong answers are given on either of these matters there will be another hassle in the Negro press, and again people will ask why I am sitting by and apparently approving these decisions by the Republican Administration. I can only hope that foreign affairs will occupy so much of today's press conference that these vital questions in the field of racial matters will not be asked. I will know in a few hours, when the tape recording is played in the dining room at lunch.[3]

3 We were fortunate in that this was exactly what happened.

MAY 2, 1956

BEFORE the start of this morning's staff meeting, Hagerty came in to announce that we would not discuss possible press items. The President had called off his press conference in order to attend the funeral of Senator Alben Barkley.

I had lain awake during the night, thinking how admirable it would be if the President would attend the funeral of this outstanding statesman, rather than send some representative. Barkley's life is an inspiration to any young American born in adverse circumstances. His story is much the same as that of Lincoln, and he fought in the true style of a rugged Kentuckian. His life is the kind that always makes me realize the great privileges that abound in a democracy—the possibility of rising from poverty and obscurity, purely on the basis of character and ability.

We spent the time this morning in talking about matters that seemed of great importance to Sherman Adams. We had more than a half-hour discussion of the role that young Republicans should play in next fall's election, as well as in developing a strong Republican party for the future. The national president of the Young Republicans had been to see Mr. Adams, and apparently had expressed dismay at the minor role the group was playing, both in the Administration and in party circles. As one who came up through the ranks in the Young Republican movement, I was happy to note this new interest in the aspirations of these young Americans.

Some of the most frustrating days of my life were spent as an officer in the Young Republican movement in New Jersey, trying to convince the leaders of the party that we were not children and that we had a legitimate interest in the party's welfare and activity. There was always a tendency to treat us in a patronizing way. It discouraged many young people from participating, because roadblocks were thrown in our way at every step, and our enthusiasm soon cooled to a sluggish trickle.

Sherman Adams advised the staff members to spend as much time as possible speaking to young groups, with particular emphasis upon college groups. A recent poll taken among colleges in a certain section of the country had indicated an overwhelming majority in favor of the Eisenhower policies.

This was an interesting observation, because three fourths of the speeches I have made since I have been on the staff have been before young people—paticularly on college campuses. This is a vital area. College students are in their formative years, are questioning individuals, and are groping for a philosophy that will carry them through life. It is true that, politically, many of them are molded completely in the image of their parents, and that others in an academic atmosphere fall under the spell of the political philosophies of their professors. The Republican party has not been very successful in interesting the intellectuals or "the eggheads" who, for some time, have had a leaning toward the Democratic banner. The fact cannot be denied that Mr. Stevenson, Democratic candidate for nomination to the Presidency, has a greater influence on the intellectuals than does the Republican party. He speaks their language in an erudite manner, and his ability to handle the English language stands him in good stead in this campaign. We must give some thought to this weak link in our armor and see if we cannot develop within the party an allegiance from the intellectuals that will overcome our tendency to ignore or to sneer at this segment of the population.

Later this afternoon Dr. Gabriel Hauge called a meeting in his office with the younger members of the staff to continue our discussion on this matter of interesting young people in the philosophy of the Republican party. We will hold periodic meetings and try to develop a blueprint that we can pass on to the National Committee with our ideas as to how this problem should be attacked.

I am very much impressed with the brilliance of Dr. Hauge. He approached every problem with the finesse of a scholar. He has a keen analytical mind, and it is a fascinating thing to watch him carve out an idea and make it a living, breathing thing for all to see and understand.

May 4, 1956

WE had a very important staff meeting this morning prior to the President's weekly press conference. It was a rather charged gathering. The morning papers had been full of the testimony given before the Senate Investigations Subcommittee yesterday by Los Angeles attorney Murray M. Chotiner, who testified that some of his law cases were referred to him by a convicted jury tamperer, while others were expedited by presidential aides in the White House.

Chotiner said he had Charlie F. Willis, Jr., Assistant to Sherman Adams, and Max M. Rabb place phone calls and make appointments with other Government agencies for him in behalf of his clients.

Chotiner also told the committee he had never once traded on the influence of Vice-President Richard M. Nixon, his close friend and the man he served as 1952 campaign manager.

Rabb tried to treat the matter lightly, and he was teased in a friendly way by other staff members. It was obvious to me, however, that he was nervous and deeply concerned, and when Sherman Adams came into the room looking grave, it was apparent that this was not a laughing matter. The Governor stated that never again did he want any staff members going outside of his own area of responsibility, seeking to assist or inquire into the status of any cases pending before government agencies. He said that that was the responsibility of the President's

Counsel, Gerald Morgan, and he added very emphatically that only he and Gerald Morgan were responsible for handling matters of this nature and that they would be held responsible and take the blame for any blunders that might be made. Obviously both Rabb and Willis had gone outside their areas of responsibility to give a friendly assist in a matter that did not concern them.

It is very easy to become involved in situations like this in the White House. Generally, people who come to see you in its offices are people who are highly recommended by responsible friends or government officials, and it is the natural thing to try to be courteous and friendly. It is easy for me to see how Rabb and Willis became involved in this matter without realizing that it could boomerang.

It has become necessary for our office to refuse to intercede in behalf of anyone looking for a job or asking for recommendations or asking us to make inquiries about the status of anything, anywhere, since there is always the possibility that someday, despite our original innocence, this kind gesture will crop up in a manner that will cause us headaches and heartaches.

An interesting discussion arose over the possibility that the President, at today's press conference, might be asked a hypothetical question based on the appearance of Alger Hiss before the Clio-Whig Society of Princeton University last week. Hagerty felt that a question might be asked in this vein: *Mr. President: What would your attitude be if you were still at Columbia and the student body invited Alger Hiss to appear before it?*

The staff room was immediately in an uproar. Hagerty felt that colleges were for students and that they had the right to invite whomever they pleased to address them on any topic of the day; that colleges were to develop thinking individuals, and it could be very dangerous for a faculty to place restrictions upon the kind of things that students should be permitted to hear.

Bernie Shanley, Appointment Secretary, pointed out that the Catholic priest at Princeton had been very upset at the appearance of Hiss and had spoken out bluntly against it. He said that the entire Catholic sentiment in New Jersey was against it and that there should be a flat condemnation of it on the part of the President.

It was my feeling, along with others, that the question was a hot one. Since it was hypothetical and very iffy, the President should refuse to answer it. It had nothing to do with his present responsibilities as President of the United States. I believe this was the view that was accepted as the one that should be used if the question did come up.

May 16, 1956

THIS has been an eventful day for me. The Administration rolled out its biggest red carpet for Indonesia's President Sukarno, who is making a state visit. He was entertained by President Eisenhower at a state luncheon today, and I was fortunate enough to be one of the invited guests. It was my first time for such an occasion, and it made an indelible impression upon me. I am pleased that the President picked this occasion to have me as a guest, because the visit of President Sukarno is of deep significance to colored people everywhere. He is president of the third largest democracy in the world, consisting of 82,000,000 people, and the friendship of his country is vital to the United States in this time of international unrest.

Not only that, but if President Sukarno needed any proof that this Administration has put its own house in order by advancing the cause of integration in the executive branch of the Government, he had first-hand evidence of it in my presence at the luncheon.

Since this was a state occasion, all the elaborate trappings were in evidence; the red-coated Marine Band played behind potted palms inside the main entrance hall. Guests were escorted by air officers to a desk where they were given cards indicating their positions at the guest table, and then were taken to the entrance of the East Room where another officer announced the name of the guest over a loud-speaker to those already inside the room. After all the guests had been assembled, including the Cabinet officers and various aides of President Sukarno, the Marine Band struck up "Hail To The Chief," and President Eisenhower and President Sukarno came in. The guests then filed past, giving their names to a military aide who in turn announced the names to the President. The guests were then introduced to President Sukarno.

It was an imposing delegation that filed by the receiving line. In addition to President Sukarno's party and the Indonesian Ambassador, there were Vice-President Nixon, Chief Justice Earl Warren, Speaker of the House Sam Rayburn, Secretary of State John Foster Dulles, and the United States permanent representative to the United Nations, Henry Cabot Lodge.

Cabinet members included Secretary of Commerce Sinclair Weeks; Secretary of Labor James P. Mitchell; Secretary of Health, Education and Welfare Marion B. Folsom. Also at the luncheon was Director of the Bureau of the Budget Percival F. Brundage; Senators Walter F. George, H. Alexander Smith, William F. Knowland and Lyndon B. Johnson. From the House of Representatives came Minority Leader Joseph W. Martin and Representative Walter H. Judd. In addition, Chairman of the Joint Chiefs of Staff Admiral Arthur W. Radford, and Chairman of the United States Atomic Energy Commission Admiral Lewis L. Strauss.

I was pleased when the presidential aide announced my name to the receiving line and President Eisenhower said, "Hello, how are you?" and introduced me to President Sukarno as "one of my staff." The Indonesian president gave me a very warm smile and handshake.

The State Dining Room is a magnificent room and the table was arranged in the shape of a double horseshoe, for about sixty. Its flower arrangements were exquisite. The gold table service was used for this occasion and it is indeed beautiful. The Negro waiters served the food expertly. The main course was squab with boiled potatoes and fresh asparagus.

At the conclusion of the luncheon, President Eisenhower stood and simply and sincerely paid tribute to President Sukarno and the Republic of Indonesia. He said that Indonesia was in its eleventh year of independence and that it was experiencing all the growing pains and difficulties that attend the birth of any new enterprise. He said that in the eleventh year of the independence of the United States our President was John Adams, and his wife Abigail had hung her laundry in the East Room where we had assembled, and that he mentioned this to show that we, too, had been poor and struggling with problems in our early years and that we had sympathy and understanding for any nation striving to govern itself and be free. He then asked everyone to stand and join him in a toast to the president and Republic of Indonesia.

President Sukarno responded, saluting our country and our President and he, too, asked everyone to stand and join him in a toast to President Eisenhower. The wine was champagne.

My feelings on this affair can be summed up by part of my conversation with one of the guests who was commenting on the strides that American Negroes have made in this country in the past ninety years. He cited my presence on this occasion as indicative of this progress. Here, again, came to my mind the wonder at why—when there are 18,000,000 Negroes in this country—the Almighty had seen fit to give me the rare privilege of being part of the official family of a President of the United States. For here I, the grandson of slaves, had sat today as a part of a state function honoring the head of a government that has just wrested its salvation from another country. This sort of thing could only happen in a democracy, and no matter what this country's failings are, I never lose sight of the fact that privileges are available for all its citizens to work within the framework of the Government for freedom, self-respect and self-expression. It is the recognition of this that has and always will keep Negroes loyal to America.

We returned to the East Room for coffee, and I was able to circulate and shake hands with some of my friends including the Vice-President, Admiral Lewis Strauss and Henry Cabot Lodge. I left with a light heart, profoundly appreciative of this historic day in my own life and in the life of a new government aiming to succeed as a democracy.

May 21, 1956

TODAY the President had his annual garden party for hospitalized veterans in the Washington area. The south lawn of the White House was bright with colorful summer dresses and a sprinkling of resplendent uniforms.

The President and Mrs. Eisenhower stood under a canopy and shook hands with all the servicemen. It was heart-rending to watch at times. Some of them had lost an arm or a leg, others were in an obvious state of shock or had various physical handicaps. Then there were the veterans of earlier wars—bent with age but very proud to be received by the Commander in Chief and his wife. As usual, Mrs. Eisenhower was charming to them and moved about the lawn with her husband, speaking with special interest to those in wheelchairs or on stretchers.

The high-ranking officers on duty at the Pentagon were in attendance, particularly the chiefs of the various services, as well as the Vice-President and Mrs. Nixon. Members of the President's staff helped to make the guests feel welcome and comfortable. Refreshments were served, and the red-coated Marine Band played appropriate music.

The President was relaxed and in a happy mood as he talked with "his boys." He always seems especially at ease when he is with men in uniform.

May 23, 1956

THE usual prepress conference staff meeting this morning. Some time was spent on trying to set a position on the Russian announcement of the curtailment of its Army. Mr. Stassen and Secretary Wilson seemed to be at odds in estimating the effect of this announcement on the Adminstration's policy; Stassen appears a little more enthusiatic about the proposals for eventual peace than Secretary Wilson does.

Of course I realize that the newspapers like to enlarge a situation of this kind, but those of us on the staff know there is nothing to be alarmed about. It is Mr. Stassen's job to be enthusiastic at any evidence that progress is being made in the area of disarmament.

On the other hand, Secretary Wilson's job is to be ever alert and to see that the country is adequately prepared for any military eventuality. The staff felt that the time had arrived for the President to indicate to the press that he was in full command of any and all situations as regards the military and knowledge of our foreign policy, its development, etc.

JUNE 10, 1956

THE White House cars used by the staff on official business are conspicuous—despite the fact that they are in the medium price range—because of the double antennae on the sides, which enable the drivers to receive radio and telephone calls from the garage or from the White House radio office whenever an emergency arises. The drivers' uniforms are another distinguishing factor.

A few weeks after my appointment I was being driven to the Union Station to get the popular four o'clock Congressional express to New York. There is always a wild dash of taxis, private cars, and government limousines swirling about the station at this hour. However, when station police recognize a White House car, they normally give it preference and permit it to thread its way through the dense traffic to the unloading platform. This particular afternoon the crowds were heavy and the redcaps were busy with bales of luggage when my White House car pulled to a stop at the unloading platform. On seeing it, everybody stopped and stared. When the chauffeur opened the door to let me out, there were immediate screams from the porters: "Look, there he is; he looks just like his pictures; ain't he a killer!" Many of the redcaps farther down the platform dropped luggage that they were carrying, to go and see what it was all about, and before I knew it I was fighting my way through a crowd of admirers to get on the train!

In Pennsylvania Station I joined a long line of businessmen

who were waiting to place calls with the long-distance operator who was sitting on a high stool at a desk in the middle of the telephone room. When my turn came, I said to the operator: "My name is Morrow, and I want to call my office in the White House, with the charges reversed." She looked at me incredulously, dropped her pencil and put her hands on her hips, and looking me squarely in the eye, said: "And my name is Mother Goose—next number, please." I was completely confused for a moment. Then it suddenly dawned on me why this woman was a disbeliever. There had never been a Negro official in the White House before, and to one who did not read or perhaps did not know, it must sound ridiculous to have one say he had "an office in the White House." So I got in line again and once more made the approach. For the second time, I pleaded with her to place the call and see what would happen. This she did, reluctantly, listening to the conversation. When the operator said: "Oh yes, Mr. Morrow; we have been expecting your call, just a minute, please," I glanced over. She was red as a ball of fire, from the top of her head down to her neck. I left the telephone booth door open so that anyone could hear my official conversation. As I came out of the booth, with a definite glint in my eye, a Negro porter who had been feigning work while the conversation had been going on, whispered to me: "Daddy-O, you played that one real cool."

June 20, 1956

THIS long pause has been caused by several things, among them the fact that I took a week off to move into my new home in Teaneck, New Jersey, and that I have been on the road making commencement speeches.

I hope I will never have to move again. This effort was a nightmare. I have spent all my life in the family homestead in Hackensack, and had an accumulation of things from all those years that I had put aside under the belief that "someday I would get around to using them."

It was a time when a wide disposition had to be made, and even as the moving men arrived, I was ruthlessly casting aside objects, some of which had treasured memories. However, the task was finally accomplished, and I left the matter of arrangement in the new house to my sister [1] and some friends.

I made commencement speeches at the Norfolk Division of Virginia State College and at the Maggie L. Walker School in Richmond. Both affairs were well attended. I have discovered that commencement has an especially significant meaning in Negro institutions in this country. It is a great achievement for those who have climbed to this rung of the educational ladder, and parents and friends naturally make much of it. There were about 2,000 people in the auditorium at Norfolk, and better than 5,000 in the Mosque Hall in Richmond.

I always try to deliver the kind of address that will make the graduates aware of the challenges of the era in which they live and in those to come. The response was flattering at both places. I am pleased that the things I have been saying for some time are beginning to seem to make sense to some people. It has often been lonely and difficult.

I made another speech at the annual dinner of the White Plains Branch of the NAACP. One of my tablemates was Jackie Robinson, the famous baseball player. This was also a gratifying occasion. In his few remarks to the audience, Jackie said that I had expressed things that he felt deeply.

The past few weeks have been reminiscent of last summer and last fall when the President had his heart attack in Denver. While I was moving into my new house in Teaneck, the President had his attack of ileitis. I did not hear about it, because I had left Teaneck that afternoon to go to Richmond to make a speech. The news met me on my arrival there, along with a

1 Nellie K. Parker, another pioneer member of the Morrow family, was the first Negro schoolteacher in Northern, N. J.—a position which involved racial complications and even some violence at that time. Today she teaches in the Hackensack Junior High School.

telegram from the office from the indefatigable Hogan.[2] The telegram filled me in on the official diagnosis and the latest news of the President's condition.

This was helpful. It was inevitable that dozens of people at the evening meeting would be asking me about the state of the President's health. With an official statement from the office, it was possible for me to answer questions intelligently, and not say anything that would make headlines and get me involved in any delicate controversy.

I went back to Washington after the graduation exercises that night, because I wanted to be on hand early the next morning for what I knew would be a special staff meeting.

Sherman Adams did call one at 8:30 A.M. the next day, and it was a grave gathering of staff assistants who met in the old Cabinet Room to get the latest information on the President's health.

The Governor stated that the only thing we could presume from the doctors (who said that the President was doing nicely and things were going along in normal ways) was that the President would return to work as quickly as he was physically able. Mr. Adams made it very clear that no member of the staff or anyone else could estimate what the President would do in regard to running for a second term. He said this decision would be completely up to the President, and that no one could pressure him into making a decision until he was ready and able to do so. We would go along with our daily chores, under the assumption that plans had not changed, and that would have to be our attitude until we were notified otherwise.

It was apparent that we were not in a mood to discuss any other items of business. This was the second time within a few months that the Chief had been struck down, and again the outlook—if not completely gloomy—was certainly not bright.

It has surprised me that this illness, similar to the first one, has not and is not discussed among staff members speculating pro or con on what the future may bring. I don't know whether this is because we each feel that some imaginative soul among us

[2] Marjorie Hogan, my administrative assistant.

might say something that would cause us future discouragement, or whether it is a sort of tacit understanding that in situations like this there is nothing to be said. One can only hope.

This recent illness has made me think seriously about the future again, and what I shall do if the President decides not to run or if I feel it is not wise for me to remain in Washington for a second term.

These are days of burdens and confusion.

JULY 3, 1956

ON June 27 I went out to Ann Arbor, Michigan, to speak at the university there, on a special kind of program developed to point out the contributions of the American Negro to this country's life and culture. The summer school session is to be a series of meetings, and prominent Negro Americans have been asked to deliver lectures on various facets of American life.

Dr. Mordecai Johnson of Howard University will be one of the speakers, along with some outstanding Negro college professors from different colleges in the country.

My lecture kicked off the session and was a general recitation of the challenges in the field of human relations in the world today, with particular emphasis upon the problems that will beset Negroes and whites in this country if an earnest effort is to be made toward honest first-class citizenship for Negroes.

I spoke in Rackham Auditorium, which is one of the most beautiful and elegant I have ever seen on any campus. It was a delight to stand on that podium and address those interested students. I was pleased by the reaction, and Dr. Dorr, the director of the session, said that my talk was what it needed to get it off to a flying start.

These are still trying days around the White House. The President has just left Walter Reed Hospital for his farm to spend another two weeks recuperating. The papers are rife with speculation as to whether he will or will not run for a second term. Those of us on the staff still have had no indication one way or another as to what he will do. As a matter of fact, the same condition exists now that did during his heart attack in Denver last summer—those of us on the staff are the last ones to know what is actually happening, since we feel it would be presumptuous to discuss or speculate about the President's private affairs.

However, there is no doubt that it leaves many of us in a spot as to how to plan our own futures in the event he decides not to run. I console myself by believing that because it is so close to convention time and would be almost impossible to build up another candidate to any degree where he could tilt with a formidable Democratic opponent, an overwhelming sense of duty to country and party will convince the President that if he is physically able he ought to run.

July 12, 1956

THE National Federation of Colored Women's Clubs is holding its annual meeting in Miami, Florida, and it had hoped to secure either Harold Stassen or Howard Pyle as speaker. Quite a to-do has developed over whether either of these gentlemen should accept the invitation. Unfortunately, a staff assistant in the Stassen office had a security check made on the organization and its officers. It seems that during the 1930's, one of its officers belonged to several organizations that have been blacklisted by the Attorney General as engaged in subversive programs. It was a shocking thing for me to get this information, because, by and large, this group of women is one of the most outstanding civic groups in Negro life. It is only natural that such an organization consists of all shades of social, political, and economic thought. The officer who was named as having affiliated with Left-Wing organizations is an outstanding woman, brilliant and able, who has made a real contribution to American life.

Perhaps she was one of the thousands of both Negroes and whites who, during a period of the thirties when they were in college, or shortly thereafter, were swept away with characteristic youthful enthusiasm under the "do-good" philosophy of many of these organizations. It is particularly easy to understand how any Negro got involved with such groups during that period. It was the Depression, and the Negro—as the most downtrodden and benighted member of American society—was easily impressed by any group which professed to be interested in his plight and which gave him an opportunity to express himself in public or private forums. At that time many people were innocently duped into such membership and association and have found themselves damned for the rest of their lives.

I feel certain that this lady was one of them. However, when the information reached the White House, there was consternation on all sides and everyone let it be known at once that he wanted no part of the organization.

But the prominence of the federation makes it a power in national life, and I realized that to ignore completely the wishes of this group would serve no purpose. It seems ridiculous to me that this group of citizens should be denied the opportunity to hear a White House official merely because one of its officers had been called a Left-Wing sympathizer. I know scores of women in these local organizations across the country, and all of them are good, God-fearing mothers and wives.

I spoke to Howard Pyle and tried to persuade him to accept my judgment and go down and address the women, not as "Negro women," but as responsible citizens of the country interested in all the problems that beset the President and his Administration. Mr. Pyle said he would think it over.

He walked into the dining room the next day at lunch and told me that he had just talked to his good friend Governor LeRoy Collins of Florida on the telephone, Governor Collins had pleaded with him not to come there to speak, because Florida had its hands full with interracial problems at the moment, and did not want them heightened by a White House official coming down and giving the impression that the White House or the Administration had endorsed the program or the activities of these women in the field of human relations. Because Governor Collins is an old friend and because he had no desire to offend him, Mr. Pyle said he would turn down the invitation.

This reasoning literally shocked me out of my shoes. It seemed incredible to me that a Republican and a ranking officer in the President's official family would accept the pleas of a southern governor who had no sympathy whatsoever with the philosophy of the Eisenhower Administration in the field of civil rights, and that he would turn down an opportunity to strengthen the position of the party with Negro voters in an effort to appease a friend of an opposing political philosophy.

Same old problems! Many of the White House staff members pay eloquent lip service to the President's announced position on the matter of civil and human rights, but act intolerantly toward this philosophy whenever it is necessary to implement or employ it in practical situations.

We are going to have to come to grips with this problem someday. I hope it will be before the campaign and the election. The Democrats far outstrip us in astute handling of civil rights. Northern Democrats, for the most part, give support to a liberal point of view and are always able to place the defeat for this kind of legislation with the southern wing of the party. Republicans have no southern wing, and it makes their attitude of indifference stand out like a sore thumb!

It is maddening—frustrating. I am afraid it will lead to serious consequences in a close election.

July 16, 1956

IN THE past few weeks I have run smack up against the problem of color and decent housing. When I came to Washington in September 1953, I spent the first few days trying to find a decent place to live. I studied the newspaper ads—those that indicated that the rooms or houses were for rent to "Colored"— and I went from section to section, house to house, apartment to apartment, to discover that most of them were dismal, dark, dilapidated, unappealing rooms with falling plaster, ratholes, and signs of other vermin. This was long before any kind of emancipation had come to the city of Washington, so it meant that it was foolish to try any area outside the Negro community.

In the northeast section of Washington, I finally located a luxurious apartment house that had originally been designated for white occupancy. However, the development had been built with Federal assistance, and while it was in the process of being erected it was discovered that white housing built with Federal funds far exceeded the percentage of such developments intended solely for white occupancy. In order to keep Federal moneys which had built the project, it had to be opened to Negroes. The tragedy of it is that there were not enough Negroes in the high salary bracket who could afford the accommodations of this building. For a long time it was more than half empty. Several changes were made in managership, and each tried to fill up the the apartment house. As a result, the former high standard which had originally governed the screening of occupants apparently was dropped, and anyone who could come up with the rent was able to move in. Consequently, to my mind, many undesirable people had found lodging here. I have come home from work at night and found police cars outside, with policemen inside investigating situations, and very often the house sheltered many weird doings that I could neither fathom nor approve.

Because of the nature of my position, I needed the kind of living quarters in which I could entertain colleagues of the White House staff and return those social obligations that were a definite part of my job. It wasn't possible to do this under these circumstances, so I made up my mind that I'd have to find quarters elsewhere.

I asked my administrative assistant Marjorie Hogan to approach the managers of various apartment houses and hotels in Washington to see whether they would consider admitting me as a resident. Most of them were sympathetic, but pointed out that many of their old established residents would protest vehemently if the doors were opened to me.

I shall always be grateful to the owner of the luxurious Woodner Apartments at 16th Street and Northwest, who made a personal effort to get me into his building, but was stymied by the firm refusal of members of his board of directors, some of whom I understand were from Atlanta. According to my information, the Southerners of the corporation reached a compromise where they were willing to let me have an apartment, but I would have to promise not to use any of the other facilities of the hotel such as the dining room or lounge. I understand that Mr. Woodner was indignant over this suggestion and said he would deny me admission before he would be willing to subject me to such a humiliating request.

Other apartment hotels that advertised boldly and daily in the newspapers have also turned me down. It is indeed depressing that a member of the staff of the President of the United States cannot find a suitable place to live.

AUGUST 1, 1956

THE most important subject at today's staff meeting was the permission given to Harold Stassen to take a thirty-day vacation in order to promote the candidacy of Governor Christian Herter of Massachusetts for the Vice-Presidency. There was a great deal of mystery surrounding the Stassen position, but the matter is obviously dynamite and must be handled with kid gloves. The general feeling was that the President should more or less stand pat on his previous statements about the Vice-Presidency, and that he should state frankly his belief in an open convention and the right of every citizen to further the candidacy of anyone he wishes. Mr. Stassen, as a private citizen, has every right to promote a candidate of his own, and he was given this leave of absence so that he could do just that!

The delicate aspect of this situation is the possibility that some reporter may ask the President how he can remain friendly and calm toward Mr. Stassen in view of the President's statement to the press many months ago that anyone trying to drive a wedge between him and Dick Nixon would have as difficult a time as if he tried to drive a wedge between him and his brother. The apparent calm with which the Stassen situation has been handled by the White House does not give any outward indication of the President's personal attitude. Whether he is angry or not I do not know, but there are strong political possibilities and much significance in today's press conference.

There is great reluctance on the part of the staff even to talk about civil rights legislation. It is one of the most disturbing notes in the whole situation here, and I am greatly pained when the matter comes up and there is an immediate effort to squelch all discussion or turn the talk to something else.

When the question was raised this morning as to whether the President should make any suggestion or comment on the failure of the civil rights bill to pass, Howard Pyle immediately stated that he should ignore it, since it was a pro and con subject. The staff was ready to move on to something else when Max Rabb spoke up to say that it could not be ignored, that it was a vital part of the President's legislative program, and that some recognition would have to be given this fact. Sherman Adams said that it would have to be mentioned along with other bills that did not pass, and with this we moved on to a different discussion!

Another banana peel was thrown in the way today when Rabb told me that the President's Committee on Appointments had decided that it would not be wise at this time to see A. Philip Randolph and his committee, because it would incense southern governors and other persons who have wanted to talk to the President about the race situation and have been denied.

This puts me in an untenable position. Just a month ago, at the request of Rabb and Bernie Shanley, I went to New York to talk to Randolph about his request to see the President, and was authorized to tell him that a conference would be granted him as soon as the President was well enough. I asked him to bring a small committee—of which he would be spokesman— and told him that any information of the conference given to the press should be given by him after the meeting. Now I am faced with the knowledge that Randolph and his group will consider me utterly insincere, and that when this leaks out I will be the subject of much embarrassing editorializing in the Negro press.

The convention is less than three weeks away, yet to my knowledge there will be no part of any consequence given to Negro appointees or delegates. The Administration, in effect, has done very little to build up in the public mind the role that its top Negro appointees are playing in carrying on the business of the country. There has been very little publicity. Only a handful, white and black, is aware of the quality of the jobs these people hold and the importance of the work they are doing. It would just seem like good common sense to give these appointees an opportunity to participate in the convention, in order to show the entire world what the President has done in the matter of integration in his Administration.

I shudder to think what the Negro columnists are going to write when the convention goes on with none of the proper Negro members of the Administration either on the program or in attendance!

August 14, 1956

THERE have been many meetings about this question of the Negroes' part in the San Francisco convention, but no one seems able to come to grips with it, and it drifts on and on.

A few days ago, a staff member from the public relations office of the National Committee came to see me, and we talked about possible persons who might be used in a strategic spot—either to second the nomination of the President or to make an inspirational speech. We felt that the real need was for a dynamic Negro woman of poise, background and training, and one who would look unmistakably Negro on a television screen, rather than some light-skinned person who might be mistaken for white. I felt that Dr. Helen Edmonds, the professor of history at North Carolina College in Durham, fitted this bill perfectly, and I submitted her name for consideration.

Several days passed and I heard nothing about this until yesterday when I had a call from Sherman Adams' office asking me to phone Dr. Edmonds and find out whether she would accept the invitation to second the nomination of the President. I called her immediately, and she was both surprised and thrilled, and of course accepted.

I am very pleased about this, especially since Sherman Adams is responsible for the decision. This means that the idea has been settled at top level and that more than passing consideration has been given to it. It also pleases me that an idea of mine has been accepted. If this one pans out successfully, it may mean that some ideas in other areas that I have been breaking my heart about for the past year may eventually meet consideration.

This whole area of the Negro is a delicate matter here in the White House. There are so many places where one can get information that is needed, and each person at top level has his own personal source that he uses to advise him on what steps should be taken about the Negro. This means there are different ideas and opinions and each believes his source to be the best. This leaves an alien like me out in the cold. No matter how vigorously I may disagree in my own mind about certain top-level advice that has been given, it is not wise for me to interject my own ideas. I have to sit back and watch developments and deplore the fact that in my estimation a lot of these actions will lead to real difficulty.

I am certain that Dr. Edmonds would not be the choice of many Negro politicians or Negro party leaders. A plum of this nature would be used by the average politician to pay some debt or to curry favor with some individual. I know Dr. Edmonds only by reputation, but feel that her value in this particular situation will pay high dividends to both the party and the race.

Sherman Adams made another decision over the weekend. I am to go to San Francisco to participate in the convention. Here's another matter that has been kicked around for weeks without decision. I feel that many members of the White House team are reluctant to see me go, for various reasons. I think it finally occurred to Mr. Adams that my failure to attend could spark a brushfire of questions in the Negro press and elsewhere and that it would be an advantage to have me there.

I am not particularly overwhelmed by this decision. The benefits that can come to the party by my going have seemed so obvious that it has appalled me that top-level thinking has taken so long to grasp this. I don't know what my duties will be—if any

—and I have a horror of just milling around headquarters or some hotel merely to be able to say that I was there.

There is also the matter of expense. While my transportation will be paid by the National Committee, I am a member of the White House staff and will be expected to assume the social responsibilities that go with my title. This can be costly. For a new homeowner, it is not a cheerful thought.

REPUBLICAN NATIONAL CONVENTION
1956

I SPENT all of my time at the convention working in the White House office, assisting in the usual routine, and doing whatever chores had to be done to keep things moving. Only once did I get out to the Cow Palace. That was the evening the President made his acceptance speech.

Meanwhile the White House had been bombarded with telegrams and telephone calls from prominent organizations and citizens, pointing out the fact that I should be used on television during the convention or at least have the opportunity of making a short speech during one of the sessions, so that the country would know that I was on the President's staff. But nothing came of this. The only appearance I made was when Sherman Adams decided that I should be named to the committee to escort the President to the platform the night he made his acceptance speech.

I believe that the Republicans lost a million-dollar opportunity to capitalize upon my presence in the White House, but I gained a great deal of satisfaction from the fact that Dr. Edmonds made an excellent seconding speech on the President's nomination.

The North Carolina delegation was adamant against her appearance. It felt that this smacked of the kind of social equality that it was not ready to accept or abet. The papers stated that one member of the delegation said that they would walk out of the convention and go back home rather than have a Negro woman appear. Their intransigence created a difficult situation; but the White House stuck to its guns.

I was extremely disappointed in the fact that the Republicans did not take a stronger stand on the matter of civil rights. In view of the fact that the Democrats had pussyfooted on the issue, the way was wide open for the Republicans to make great headway in a forthright and unequivocal endorsement of the Supreme Court decision. However, the plank seems to me to be a shade stronger than the Democratic plank.

September 14, 1956

THESE are ominous days for the White House. We keep a close eye on the turbulent racial conditions in the South as many of the southern states defy the Supreme Court decision on school integration. The calling out of the National Guard in Sturgis, Kentucky, and Clinton, Tennessee, has focused the attention of the entire country on these troubled spots. Negro leaders are demanding that the President use his office to protect defenseless Negroes who are merely trying to exercise their rights as determined by the Supreme Court decision. The President has indicated that the states have the facilities to enforce law and order, and until it is clear that they no longer have the ability or the determination to do so, the Government will not be able to step in and take over.

The White House is plagued by many vital questions on this matter. For example, how does the Federal Government handle the breakdown of law and order in a southern state? Can you handle a mob merely by putting the leaders in jail or by sending United States marshals into action? Short of sending in troops to do the job, what other method is effective? Can the President stand by and see anarchy prevail in any of the communities of this country? Has the Attorney General a sufficient staff and adequate methods by which he can enforce Federal law? These are difficult questions, and ones that we hope will not have to be answered.

However, I realize that a race riot in any community in this country prior to the election could be almost fatal to Republican chances. In a situation of this kind, the whites would blame the Administration for its stand on integration and the fact that the Supreme Court decision was handed down during a Republican administration. On the other hand, the Negro leaders would probably point out that the President did not take a strong enough hand in the matter, it got out of control, and the mob took over and ran rampant. It is really vexing.

At our staff meeting the day before yesterday we were trying to determine how the President might handle questions on conditions in the South at that afternoon's press conference. It was generally felt that all he could do would be to stick to his previous statements that his job was to enforce the Constitution of the United States; if and when the states appeared to be unable to cope with the situation, only then would the Federal Government consider intervention. This of course does not take care of specific matters that could be asked, but it is the only manner in which this delicate matter can be handled in such tinder-box times.

After staff meeting I went to Max Rabb's office with Gerry Morgan, to try to prepare an answer to a telegram that had been sent to the President by an NAACP lawyer from Dallas, Texas. The telegram petitioned the President for assistance in helping several Dallas Negro students to enter a junior college that the Federal Court had opened to them in that area. They had tried to register, been met by a mob, and one of them was reported to have been beaten up. The telegram said that law and order had broken down; that State Rangers were in the area, but their orders were to help only members of the white race; and that the Negroes felt helpless and deserted by their state government.

Here again we faced the question of what kind of telegram could be sent from the President's office without putting him in a position of being pilloried and castigated by one or the other side of the controversy. I suggested that the President's reply should indicate that he had continually deplored violence in any form between citizens of this country and that he would instruct the Attorney General to look into the matter, if he had not already done so, and to keep him advised as to developments.

Max and I realize the vital necessity of the President's making some kind of gesture at this moment, in order to prevent Negroes from having the impression that he is lukewarm on this matter of violence and denial of civil rights and that they will be left to the mercy of disinterested state officials.

The White House has consistently turned down any suggestion by Max and me that a meeting of whites and Negroes be held under the auspices of the White House to discuss this problem. However, we are moving into a difficult and important election and it is freely acknowledged that Negroes in the border states may very well hold the balance of power in a tight election. In an emotional situation such as we face today, it is only natural that whatever ills beset this group would be placed at the feet of the Administration in power. Some kind of gesture must be made by the White House to assure Negro citizens they have not been forsaken by their President.

Max has come up with another idea that perhaps a meeting of southern educators, white and Negro, could be held under the auspices of the White House, where they could sit down in an effort to arrive at some kind of intelligent solution. Again—how far we will get with this decision I do not know, but time is running out and the situation is desperate.

OCTOBER 1, 1956

I HAVE been unable to write anything for the past few weeks due to the pressures of the campaign. At the time of the convention, it appeared that all the Republicans had to do was to wait until Election Day and go to the polls and re-elect the President, but I have been quite alarmed as I have gone through the country, to notice the apathy of Republican leaders and workers. Anyone who reads must know that the Democrats have made phenomenal inroads into the Republican vote. The CIO has done one of the most intensive jobs in political history of getting into every neighborhood and community where working people live. They point out, with some effect, that the Democratic party is the party of the working man, and that the Republican party can hardly have their interests at heart when the Cabinet and the prominent leaders are very rich men.

Also, there has been a sinister campaign against Vice-President Nixon. The Democrats have subtly used the fact that if the President does not live out his term, Nixon will become President. In some quarters Nixon has never recovered from the effects of the 1952 campaign. He has been a target for the opposition ever since, and unfortunately this attitude has communicated itself to certain Republican leaders and voters throughout the country. Many have pointed out that Nixon is the albatross around the neck of the President and that he could very well pull him down to defeat. This is another reason why Republican leaders are dragging their feet and hoping that the President's personal popularity will carry the ticket across.

At the moment, the polls are very discouraging. They show a steady decline from the large margins that the President had in 1952. Crucial states like Pennsylvania, Ohio, Illinois, California, New York, and New Jersey, are still in the doubtful column. The loss of any of these states could mean defeat.

The key role in this whole picture will be played by Negro voters, and every poll indicates that 90 percent of them are Democrats. This is difficult to explain to the average white Republican, in view of the remarkable record of the President in the area of civil rights. But this generation of Negroes will never forget the desperate depression of the thirties, and the fact that the President at that time was Roosevelt, and that they were fed and given job opportunities through various work programs has caused them to be eternally grateful to him and to the party he represented. In his heart the Negro voter knows that Eisenhower has tried to advance his cause, but he is always aware that his economic position in this country is terribly insecure and that with the Democratic party he was given the opportunity to work and make a living.

One of the disturbing elements today is the fact that white Republican leaders have written off the Negro vote. Confidential reports have come to me from all over the country, and all of them indicate that little or no money is being spent in Negro areas and that those who have volunteered to try to line up Negro voters are disgusted with the lack of support—financial and otherwise—from Republican headquarters. I'm afraid it's too late for any effective work to be done in Negro areas. I have tried for months to make it clear to responsible officials that in a great many sections Negroes are the key to a successful Republican victory, but this has not been well received, and I have had to stop trying.

October 9, 1956

THE latter part of last week held one of the most exciting and meaningful events of my life. I was in Chicago for a meeting and at its conclusion was on the golf course playing with friends when I was paged to take a call from the White House. It was Sherman Adams, telling me that I had better catch the first plane back to Washington. The President wanted me to accompany him to New York the next day for the opening game of the World Series.

This good news really startled me. I had no idea that I would ever be summoned back to the White House to accompany the President on a purely social trip. Both my friends and I were incredulous.

I got a night flight out of Chicago and arrived in Washington about three in the morning. I was met by a White House car, and got to my apartment about four. This meant that I had only two hours' sleep before getting up to go to the White House to try to clear my desk before the *Columbine* took off for New York at 10:30 A.M.

It was the first time I had even been on the *Columbine,* and it lived up to all the adjectives that have been used to describe it. I felt as if I were in a luxurious small apartment rather than in a plane. The quite spacious living room forward was beautifully furnished, while aft there was a small but impressive dining room and galley. The plane carried a crew of about nine and lacked nothing in comfort and elegance.

The others in the party were: The President, Mr. O'Malley, John Foster Dulles, George Humphrey, James Mitchell, Arthur Summerfield, Marion Folsom, Kevin McCann, Major Puglisi, Murray Snyder, Francis Stephenson, Major John Eisenhower and Dr. Howard Snyder.[1]

1 O'Malley, President of the Brooklyn Dodgers; Humphrey, Secretary of the Army; Mitchell, Secretary of Labor; Summerfield, Postmaster General; Folsom, Secretary of Health, Education and Welfare; Puglisi, an Air Force aide; Stephenson, President of the White House Correspondents' Association.

As soon as we were airborne, we were served a steak dinner, since it would not be possible for us to eat at the field. It took us about an hour to land at La Guardia, where we were met by a huge police escort and motorcade to take us to Ebbets Field in Brooklyn. It was about noon, and a surprising number of people were along the road to wave to the President. This was not an organized effort, but the road that the cavalcade would take had been printed in the papers the day before. The President received a tremendous ovation when his car entered the field, and he drove up to home plate where the Yankees and Dodgers were lined up, and shook hands with every player. The President and his party were guests of Mr. O'Malley. Our box was in a strategic spot between home plate and first base, and we had a fine view of every play. It was an exciting game, which the Dodgers won, and the President could not hide his delight when they came up with a sparkling play or were able to get a run.

He told me the next day he was a little peeved that the newspapers had tried to make political capital out of the fact that he stood up and cheered when the Dodgers made a spectacular play. After all, he was the guest of the president of the team, and even if he had been unbiased in his attitude, he still had to be polite and show his host how much he appreciated his hospitality.

Just before the game got underway, there was a flurry of excitement when Governor Averell Harriman of New York, his wife and friends, entered the box directly opposite us. Governor Harriman, of course, was a candidate for the Democratic presidential nomination, and since the convention he had been out in the country, stumping for candidate Stevenson and saying some pretty tough things about the President and his Administration. However, when the Governor's presence was called to the attention of the President, he immediately stood up, glanced over in the direction of the next box, and said: "Hello, Ave," and stuck out his hand to the Governor. Later, Mrs. Harriman was brought over to shake hands with the President.

We left the field immediately after the last out in the ninth inning, and motored back to La Guardia. There was a goodly number of people along the return road also. The *Columbine* took off immediately after we had boarded, and we were back in Washington an hour after the game. It was a delightful flight with good companions, and I shall always be grateful for the opportunity of seeing my first World Series game under such friendly and unusual auspices.

The next day a very colorful personality came to the White House to see the President, and I was asked to accompany her into his office. She was Mrs. Portia Washington Pitman, the daughter of the late famous Negro educator, Booker T. Washington, founder of Tuskegee Institute.

Mrs. Pitman had come to pay a courtesy call on the President. It had been her custom to call on each President ever since her father had first brought her to the White House for this purpose. This was her first opportunity to meet President Eisenhower and to pay tribute to him for his endeavors in the field of human rights.

The President was in a good mood and was eloquent in what he said to Mrs. Pitman. It impressed me so much that after the interview I hurried right back to my office to put it down. As nearly as I could remember, he said: "Mrs. Pitman, I am very glad to see you. I have always admired your distinguished father and his remarkable work."

Mrs. Pitman replied: "Mr. President, I am honored by this opportunity to pay tribute to you. I just regret that my father did not live to see some of his dreams come to fruition."

The President said: "Most men who make a real contribution to civilization do not live long enough to see their work bear fruit. While they are living they have to get the satisfaction of knowing that what they are trying to do may sometime mean something to mankind."

He added: "Mrs. Pitman, the vital things that affect your race and others, where changes have to be made in the attitudes of mankind, cannot, in my opinion, be done by law. I like to feel that while we have to change the hearts of men, we cannot do it by cold lawmaking, but must make these changes by appealing to reason, by prayer, and by constantly working at it through our own efforts." The President also indicated that the best values of life are spiritual and that the important thing in life is people—human beings.

He went on to say that his father, who died a few years ago, had had three great personal disasters in his life—all of them financial. He said that his father, like all humans, had lamented the fact that things had gone so miserably, but that he had reminded him that money was not the most important thing in life and had pointed out that his most valuable asset was his family—his wife and five sons.

The President was obviously proud that these five sons had done so well, and said that he lamented the fact that his father had not lived long enough to see the contributions he was trying to make to his country.

I had only been back in my office about ten minutes when Ann Whitman, the President's secretary, called to say that he had a small memento for Mrs. Pitman. He had intended to give it to her while she was in his office, but had felt a little too bashful to do so, and wanted me to see that she received it. It was a set of earrings and a pin, with IKE on it. These were campaign objects that various novelty manufacturers throughout the country had sent to him, and he made a habit of giving them to those who came to see him. Mrs. Pitman came back to get them later and was delighted with them.

October 23, 1956

I HAVE been running around the country the past few weeks, making speeches, as a regular part of my campaign responsibility. In the past two weeks things look much better than they have at any time since the beginning of the campaign. I think this is largely due to the fact that the President has finally come out, swinging both fists against his opponent, and his television appearances have been vigorous and effective.

However, at this stage of the game I am certain that the Negro vote for the President will not be as large as we would like. There seems to be a ground swell for him among professional and middle-class Negroes, and it is very gratifying that many outstanding Negro ministers have come out for him. This shows that people on this level have a high appreciation for today's economic conditions and for the fact that salaries are high and upper-bracket job opportunities have increased.

On the other hand, the working-class Negro, which would include those laboring in factories and generally in the category called Labor, are still predominantly in the Democrats' column. This is because they have been worked on by labor leaders and because they characteristically identify themselves with the cause of labor. Whenever I am in barbershops or sitting on a shoeshine stand and the talk is about politics, it normally runs in the Democratic vein. This is also true when I talk to taxicab drivers, attendants in railroad stations, etc. The propaganda that the Republican party is a rich man's party has made a deep impression upon working-class Negroes. The Democrat party, assisted by labor, has done a fine job in this respect.

One of my principal difficulties when I am speaking at large banquets, such as the one held at the Sheraton Park Hotel here on the President's birthday, is the fact that neither the White House nor the party has done very much to build me up, and the people who run these meetings and banquets always look upon me as some unknown figure that has been foisted on them. Inevitably, the chairman of the meeting will come to me a few minutes before I am to speak, to urge upon me the necessity of making my speech very brief, since there are important people to follow.

At the Sheraton Park dinner the other night, Undersecretary of Labor Arthur Larson and I were to be the two principal speakers, with a smattering of local candidates and representatives of women's groups thrown in to make two-minute remarks. The dinner was to recess at nine o'clock, when the President was to speak over television. Around 9:30 he was to make a brief appearance at the dinner. The chairman of the dinner had misjudged the time, and it was necessary to cut down on speeches before the President's speech. Originally I had been asked to prepare a fifteen-minute talk. During dinner the chairman spoke to me two or three times and finally asked me to cut my speech to four minutes.

This threw me into a panic. Some of the speakers who had preceded me had gone on and on, with no effort to cooperate. Not only that, but I was called on while the waiters were clearing the tables, and the noise was deafening. In addition, one waiter dropped a tray loaded with dishes right at the climax of my speech. I had managed to stand up and say something, and apparently it had been effective, for the applause was enthusiastic and I was pleased by the comments from the audience afterward when I was leaving the auditorium. Members of the White House staff were especially complimentary. This was the first time any of them had ever heard me speak.

The chairman and several others on the dinner committee came to me with profuse apologies for the cursory way in which I had been treated. This usually happens, and I always try to be gracious about it. It occurred when I went to the Ohio state convention early this fall and in other states where I was representing the White House. It is still difficult for some people to understand that a Negro can be in a position of responsibility in the White House and that he can be sent out to represent the President. If Dwight Eisenhower is returned to office and I am still on his staff, I will have to insist that Republicans be indoctrinated about my exact status in the White House.

I went down to Birmingham, Alabama, last week to speak at Miles College, and had to go to the airline's office in a local hotel to change my return-trip reservation. I always dread entering the lobby of any southern hotel for any reason. Most Southerners are still un-Reconstructed, and there are obviously hostile glances from both guests and employees. This time I stood in line, and when my turn came was completely ignored. I left the counter and sat down on a bench in the office and waited to see what the clerks would do. After about thirty minutes, I left and made the fifteen-mile drive out to the airport to get service.

One of my difficulties in being a member of the President's staff is that I must always keep myself under control in situations like this. Any hasty action could damage the President's position and is strictly taboo.

But when I got back to Washington, I wrote to Captain Eddie Rickenbacker, chairman of the board of Eastern Air Lines, telling him of the embarrassment and frustration I had felt in Birmingham. He replied immediately and thanked me for writing him. He said that he was naturally not familiar with the facts, but that he would make a point of getting them in detail, because any such action on the part of his employees was entirely out of order and not in keeping with Eastern's policy. He offered me his personal apologies and said that copies of my letter would be sent to all of his department heads to prevent this happening to anyone else.

This is one of the few times that I have ever used the prestige of my office to try to rectify a situation that could affect a whole racial group.

October 25, 1956

I HAVE just come from Val Washington's office, and have asked him to send a letter to Sherman Adams, informing him of the great harm that the speeches of Howard Pyle are doing us. The other day, in a speech in Virginia, Pyle said that the people of the South had little to fear from the Eisenhower Administration on civil rights, because the President was a temperate man. He indicated that as a white Southerner, he would take his chances and support Eisenhower rather than Stevenson. The whole implication is that with the bulk of the Negro vote indicated as being Democratic, Southerners could vote for Eisenhower and be confident that civil rights would not be a major issue in his second term, and that he would not try to force it down southern throats.

This kind of sabotage is heart-rending to those of us who have labored so hard to show that the Eisenhower record on civil rights is a moral and honest one.

I showed Val clippings from newspapers, white and Negro, that carried the quotes from Mr. Pyle's speech. In addition, I am told that at a meeting in New York City the other night Mayor Robert F. Wagner used the Pyle quotes to embarrass Attorney General Jacob Javits, the Republican candidate for Senator from New York.

Val sent a very strong note to Sherman Adams, saying that it was discouraging to have all our hard work torn down by the unfortunate remarks of a member of the White House staff. He went on to say that if we wanted to remain the minority party, we were certainly going about it in the right way. He asked that Pyle either be "muzzled" or relieved of his White House post.

NOVEMBER 6, 1956

I HAVE been giving all of my time to campaigning. My last few speeches were made in Memphis and Nashville, Tennessee; Durham, North Carolina; New York and New Jersey. In all these places I found a regular ground swell in favor of the President. It was interesting to see that a great many Negroes are eager to be convinced that Eisenhower is the man they should support.

One of the most outstanding gatherings was that of workers and precinct captains called by George Lee, a prominent Negro leader in Memphis. I had spoken to the Omega Psi Phi fraternity at its annual awards celebration on Le Moyne campus that afternoon. Later that evening Lee called this special meeting of his workers so that I could give them a pep talk. It was a really fantastic gathering, organized in a matter of a few hours. Lee was able to round up over 600 workers, in the Elks' clubhouse, and to provide refreshments for them after the meeting. It was a most enthusiastic group and gave me a fine reception. This was probably the highlight of the campaign for me.

Another interesting meeting was held on a dismal, rainy night in New York's Harlem at the Theresa Hotel. A gigantic outdoor celebration had been planned for that famous corner at 125th Street and Seventh Avenue—the crossroads of the world for this black metropolis. Sound-wagons and trucks, vans and searchlights had been assembled, but shortly before the meeting a tropical storm hit the city and washed out all hopes of an outdoor affair.

An active committee moved the rally into the ballroom of the hotel. Duke Ellington played, and by nine o'clock there were at least 1,000 people in the audience. The platform group was a distinguished one and included Helen Hayes and John Roosevelt.

My role was to introduce Attorney General Jacob Javits, a candidate for the United States Senate, and Vice-President Nixon. He had been delayed by a stormy trip from the Coast, but he and his wife arrived around ten o'clock and were given a thunderous ovation.

The Vice-President was at his best that night. In his seemingly effortless manner, he gave one of the most dynamic speeches of the entire campaign. He electrified the crowd, and his whole manner and attitude gave the lie to the derogatory statements that have been issued about him during this campaign. Many Negroes were convinced by his logic and intelligence.

Even at this late stage in the campaign, there was some question as to just how close the election would be. Some of us still had no inkling that the President would be elected by a landslide.

Election day was cool and clear. I flew home to vote in New Jersey, then returned to my office in Washington to wait for the returns.

There was an outward calm in the White House, but every staff member was on edge, waiting for the outcome. Most of them assembled with their wives in Suite 200-D in the Sheraton Park Hotel for the television returns. This suite had been reserved by the White House for the use of the staff only, but the usual mob of freebooters and celebrity-hunters was on the prowl for free food and drink. When I got there around ten o'clock, there were so many strangers that I thought I was in the wrong place.

There were numerous later victory celebrations, of course, but I had traveled so many thousands of miles in the past weeks that I went home to bed.

November 7, 1956

THE enormity of the victory was surprising. It is apparent to me that the American people voted for Eisenhower and not necessarily for the Republican party. The Republicans won neither house of Congress, and perhaps even at this early date we may anticipate a tough term for the President, with a Democratic Congress.

I was pleased that Sherman Adams gave me a smile and warm handshake, saying, "A job well done, son." He was referring to the fact that thousands of Negroes across the country broke their ties to the Democratic party for the first time in twenty years and voted for the President. I believe the concentrated effort we made in the last few days of the campaign paid off. I also feel that the fact that a great many prominent ministers came out for Ike reassured Negroes. A deep moral issue was involved, as far as Negroes were concerned. It had seemed incredible that the great majority of Negroes could go along with Adlai Stevenson, despite his estimable qualities. The southern wing of the Democratic party controlled the party and would control the Congress. It would be the same old story: a Democratic President, able to give eloquent lip service to human ideals, but unable to translate this into action because the southern wing of his party controlled the committees and refused to get these ideals into bills and out on the floor for votes.

The events in the South in the past months were first-hand evidence that the South did not intend to comply with the Supreme Court decision. And despite the prating of Democratic candidates in the field of civil rights, the southern wing of their party had demonstrated that it did not approve any constructive strides in this area. This meant that even Negroes who talked vociferously about Democratic candidates and platforms publicly, when alone in the voting booth with only their consciences, probably voted for Ike. This attitude has been detected in the results at the polls in a great many of the black belts throughout the country. The outcome is gratifying to me and to all of us here at the White House.

November 27, 1956

ONE of my most annoying and daily time-consuming problems is that of providing space for the scores of activities that go on in the executive offices. Each presidential assistant has a staff consisting of anywhere from three to five people, with consultants coming in from time to time to add to the problem. These people must have suitable office space to work in, and because of the tremendous growth of the executive branch of the Government in the past twenty-five years, there just isn't any space left to take care of its multitudinous activities.

Consequently, a game of musical chairs goes on—moving one group from one office to another in order to squeeze some other group into the space just vacated. Some of these people work under incredible conditions which would not be tolerated for five minutes in private business, but most government people are dedicated public servants and try to make out as best they can.

However, there are often prima donnas coming in from private enterprise, doing a short stint for the Government, and they refuse to accept anything but the "best" before they will even attempt to operate.

Many crises have arisen for me because some new person finds that his office is not as spacious or as luxuriously furnished as his counterpart in some other department or agency. I am then faced with demands that the situation be corrected or the person cannot serve his country.

An interesting but difficult situation arose early in my time in the White House. Two retired Army generals, then top-flight executives in private companies, were appointed by the President as special assistants. I believe that one, whom we shall call "A," was of higher rank in the Army than "B." However, "B" was a stronger personality and came from a more powerful corporation. "B" got to Washington a few days ahead of "A" and secured a very desirable suite in the Executive Office Building. When "A" arrived and found that his suite did not compare with "B's" and particularly that his offices did not contain a fireplace and mantelpiece where he could display his trophies, I had a first-class feud on my hands. I sat these two gentlemen down in my conference room and with logic, persuasion, and finally with anger and disgust, told them off. "A" consented to take the suite that we had selected for him, provided we could do a refurbishing job and get new rugs and furniture.

There has never been any realistic planning for the Executive Office Building. This means that each new project—the Bureau of the Budget, for instance—has been placed willy-nilly in the building and few projects have contiguous space. Part of a project may be on the first floor and the other half in the attic. This causes real confusion as far as telephone lines and messenger services are concerned, and just plain chaos for the business of the project. It has been a headache for many years, and it has grown progressively worse during the Eisenhower Administration.

The enigma of the moment is that of trying to rearrange certain elements in the Executive Office Building so that those groups that need to work together will be close to each other. None of the groups wants to give up the space it now has and move into any other. Each project head can only give reasons why he cannot move, and is not interested in cooperating in a program that may make his burden easier. Sherman Adams had jumped into the middle of this and has ordered a blueprint on his desk within the next forty-eight hours that will show how this gigantic move can be accomplished over a weekend!

DECEMBER 19, 1956

WE HAVE finally located headquarters for the Hungarian Refugee Relief Committee, and things have been more or less quiet in that direction for the past two or three days. However, I have been somewhat surprised at the violent Negro reaction to the part the United States is playing in welcoming Hungarian refugees to this country, in going all-out to see that they are properly housed, clothed, fed, and given jobs commensurate with their skills. Many Negroes are bitter about this. They point out that they are citizens, indigenous to the soil of this country, and yet in many areas of the nation they are not given this red-carpet treatment in any of these avenues of life.

I was in Chicago over the weekend and talked to a few social workers employed by the city welfare board. Their observations were similar: Negro clients in dire need of relief often experience great difficulty in having their needs met and in finding benevolent and sympathetic treatment, yet in the past weeks these same agencies have bent over backward to administer to the needs of Hungarian aliens.

It is difficult to reason with people on an emotional question such as this. Deep down, Negroes are sympathetic to the plight of any downtrodden and benighted people, but it is the same question that arises so many times during the life of the average Negro. How charitable can one expect him to be when he so seldom experiences this kind of charity on the part of others?

I remember this problem during the early stages of the last

war, when separate racial outfits were the vogue in the Armed Forces. After I became an officer, most of my time was spent in trying to give Negroes the incentive to be good soldiers and to develop the will to fight abroad for something that many of them had never known. Their question was: Why were black soldiers expected to go 3,000 miles across the sea to fight and perhaps die for a way of life for others that they themselves had never experienced in their own country?

Therefore, during these past weeks of working hard to assist in locating the Hungarian Refugee Relief Committee, there has been real irony in my devotion to duty. As a member of the President's staff I was obligated to work earnestly and honestly on this, yet underneath—all the time—were these rumblings from friends and associates who could not wholeheartedly contribute to this cause mentally, spiritually or financially. Conflicts like this can cause great anguish.

Jackie Robinson came down from New York today to have lunch with me in the White House staff dining room. It was a pleasure to have him, and the staff was eager to meet him and learn more about his recent sale to the New York Giants by the Dodgers. Jackie is an interesting and modest person, and talk with him is never tiresome. He was shocked by his sale to the Giants and said that even his small son had taken the news very badly.

When Jim Hagerty asked him point-blank about his experiences in overcoming obstacles during his initial entrance in big-league baseball, Jackie explained that the good common sense and fine leadership of Branch Rickey [1] had made it possible. He also said that Peewee Reese, the captain of the Dodgers, who is a Southerner, had done a great deal to make his life easier; Peewee's main concern was not a man's color, but whether he knew the game, could play it, and would give his best to his team.

Robinson and I have a rather close relationship. He understands my pioneering in my present job and in others I have had. Because of this, I asked him—in front of the rest—if he

1 Former manager of the Brooklyn Dodgers.

hadn't found that whenever the top man is decent, honest and democratic, this makes it possible to do a creditable job. He agreed very definitely.

I have felt this keenly since being in the White House. I realize that if the President did not have the character, decency and courageous spirit that he has, it would not have been possible for me to be here in the first place or to have remained.

This has been an eventful week. Colonel Andy Goodpaster, Staff Secretary of the White House, has been promoted to Brigadier General by the President. Because Goodpaster is a straightforward and decent person and has been my friend in many ways during my time here, I bought two silver stars for him, hoping they might be the first he would receive.

Yesterday I went down to National Airport with other members of the staff to see the Vice-President off on his trip to Hungary, where he is to make observations for the President and report back on the needs of the Hungarians and on the increased possibilities of admitting more of them as refugees than the quota now allows. It was a colorful sight at the airport as the dignitaries gathered. We stood on the ramp near the plane while photographers took their inevitable pictures, and at a crucial moment in the activities Governor Stassen emerged from the crowd, shouldered his way to the Vice-President, grabbed his hand and pumped it vigorously as he wished him well on his trip. Nixon's features did not change at all, and he accepted the wishes with a smile. To some of us in the crowd, however, this was an ironic moment. A short three months ago Stassen had done everything in his power to bring about Nixon's defeat at the Republican National Convention in San Francisco. Some wag in our crowd suggested that perhaps the Vice-President owed a deep debt of gratitude to Stassen for causing Republican delegates to stand together as one and nominate the Vice-President by acclamation. I can never cease to marvel at the gall —some call it courage—of Mr. Stassen. He refuses to be humbled!

December 20, 1956

THE Christmas spirit officially entered the White House today. This afternoon at five o'clock the President made a short address and pressed the electric switch that lit the huge Christmas tree on the Ellipse, signifying the official opening of Christmas festivities in the nation. It was a thrilling affair, and I was able to see it from the south portico of the White House, along with other staff members and Cabinet personnel and their wives who had been invited for a social hour after the President returned from the ceremony.

We entered the huge State Dining Room, where fruitcake and eggnog were served. A short program had been arranged and it was a hilarious one. Philip Young, Chairman of the Civil Service Commission, was master of ceremonies. Phil owns a fine collection of English hand bells, and for two days had been trying to train seven members of the President's staff to play Christmas carols with them. Several of the bell-ringers could not read music, and this added to the difficulty as well as to the hilarity. For example, Jack Martin, Administrative Assistant to the President, is not only tone deaf but cannot recognize a single note of music and would only ring his bell after Gabe Hauge either kicked him in the shin or nudged his elbow. This meant that Jack's note was always a delayed one. The expression on his face was something to behold.

In addition, the group was composed of both short and tall men. Phil Young, Gabe Hauge, Andy Goodpaster and I stand over six feet, while Jack Martin, Roemer McPhee and Gerry Morgan are rather short. They were wedged in between us giants, and it added up to a ludicrous picture.

Phil Young gave a very funny introduction, telling the President that bell-ringing was one of the undeveloped areas in the country, but since his staff had been practicing for two days, the area was no longer undeveloped, but "underdeveloped." The President and Mrs. Eisenhower were in good spirits and enjoyed the Young humor.

Our first offering was "Joy to the World." My job was to ring a B-flat bell whenever that note appeared in the score. Gabe Hauge handed me a bell, saying, "Fred, this is yours." I didn't check it in the candlelight and assumed it was the right one. We were moving along smoothly when all of a sudden a B-flat note appeared in the score and I promptly gave my bell a resounding shake. A blatant and discordant note pealed out— it was certainly no B-flat!

The President and Mrs. Eisenhower broke up completely, and I followed suit. The other members of the group were convulsed, and Gerry Morgan had trouble restoring order. The program went on without further mishap, and we played two encores, "Silent Night" and "O, Little Town of Bethlehem."

After the bell-ringing, Young presented the Eisenhowers with the staff gift—a pair of candelabra for the dining room at their Gettysburg farm. They were delighted.

There was chatting and more eggnog before we went through the line to thank and say good night to the President and his wife. I joined the line rather sheepishly, realizing that I would be kidded about my boner. When I got to the President, he laughed and said, "I really didn't know that you were a musician." I replied, "Sir, after that dismal performance, your doubt is still sustained."

The next morning there was a general party in the White House for the entire staff, including clerical, domestic, police and military personnel. The usual coffee and buns were served, and the Eisenhowers circulated among the crowd, extending holiday greetings. Each one of us was given a signed photograph of the President and the First Lady.

JANUARY 7, 1957

SHERMAN ADAMS came into the staff dining room today, and instead of going to his usual table, sat down with Andy Goodpaster and me and proceeded to take charge of the conversation.

He always twits me about New Jersey; he thinks that New Hampshire is the only place in the world to live. I kidded him about New Hampshire. I had spent a few days there recently, and it had rained constantly and the morning mist and dew had been so heavy that it was difficult to start a round before noon. He said he'd done some skiing during the holidays, but couldn't get up to his New Hampshire ski lodge often because of the pressure of business here in Washington. He said the lodge was expensive to maintain and that he had thought of selling it, but that some of his friends were able to enjoy it from time to time.

Adams asked me if I knew how the Pittsburgh *Courier* was doing; he understood that it was in financial trouble. He was interested in that paper, because he considers its president and owner, Mrs. Jessie Vann, a distinguished woman. This led us into a discussion of the Negro press, which had come into being in the days when white newspapers did not carry Negro news. Today, even in the Deep South, all newspapers are beginning to carry it. At one time they ran only the derogatory kind, presenting Negroes as criminals and irresponsible citizens, but today their achievements as well as their shortcomings are given space. This means that the market for Negro newspapers is shrinking. Now we buy Negro papers merely out of sentiment and habit.

This country has two dailies which specifically cater to the Negro—the Chicago *Defender* and the Atlanta *Daily World*. The latter has done well for many years, but whether the *Defender* will be able to meet the competition of the great Chicago dailies is not clear at present; it has only been in operation about a year.

The whole point is that when integrated life becomes a reality, many facets of Negro life will go down the drain because they are no longer necessary for the Negro's welfare, comfort, enlightenment and pride. The Governor agreed with my concept of this, and we both felt that it was a good thing despite the fact that any progress always means that someone suffers.

January 10, 1957

THIS was an exciting day. The President went to Capitol Hill to give his State of the Union Address. He had appeared there only a few days ago to request greater latitude in coping with sudden emergencies in the Middle East, and apparently was not enthusiastic about a second visit within so short a period, but Congressional leaders had urged him to do it.

I joined several staff members in our guest seats in the rear of the House. It was exciting to watch the dramatic events. The Chamber stood and applauded when Mrs. Eisenhower came in with her brother-in-law Milton Eisenhower and they joined Mrs. Nixon in the guest box in the gallery. The galleries were crowded with dignitaries, guests and the press. The whole occasion was televised and broadcast on radio.

Before the President's entrance, ambassadors and foreign representatives marched in together to take their seats in the well of the House. They were followed by the Senators and Justices of the Supreme Court. The Vice-President was on the dais with

Speaker of the House Sam Rayburn. Mr. Nixon suddenly rapped his gavel. The doorkeeper announced: "Mr. Speaker, the President of the United States." The entire audience stood and applauded as the President walked to his place on the stand.

His address was one of the shortest on record and more or less philosophical in tone. He recommended that a commission be appointed to make a thorough study of the monetary system. He stressed his hope that Congress would pass legislation increasing classrooms for all of the children of this country, without regard to creed or color. He urged enactment of legislation to protect the civil rights of all citizens. He expressed the need for maintaining military strength—not to project war, but to prevent it and maintain peace.

I felt that it was a sober and thoughtful address and was not flamboyant, demanding or boastful, but the Congress that heard it was not enthusiastic. (Later that day I met Ray Scherer of NBC and he asked me if I had any idea why Congress had been so lukewarm in its reception, but of course I had no comment to make. My guess is as good as anyone's as to why Congress evinced this reaction.) It just does not seem to be a Congress that wants to do anything about civil rights.

At the conclusion of the session we were rushed to our waiting cars by Congressional officials and driven back with a flurry of police sirens and motorcycles.

January 15, 1957

I went up on the Hill today to talk to the Vice-President about my alarm over the situation in the South. Negro homes and churches constantly are being bombed and destroyed by disgruntled whites who are determined that the Supreme Court decision on bus transportation and schools shall not be carried out. There is great Negro indignation about this situation. I was in New York over the weekend at the home of friends who literally gave me hell for the Administration's apparent indifference to the plight of the defenseless Negroes in the South. A sore point with all people with whom I talk is the same fact that the Administration is giving so much attention to the plight of Hungarians. There are blatant editorials in the Negro press, pointing out the similarities between the Hungarians and the Negroes, both of whom are refugees from oppression, and stating that the Hungarians seem to be getting a better break in their efforts to find freedom and succor. The Vice-President is honestly concerned. His office has been flooded with letters and telegrams from distressed Negroes. They are asking him to come down to make a survey of their conditions, just as he did when he went to Hungary for the President. But I imagine that if he did, the Senate of the United States would literally blow up in his face.

January 17, 1957

STAFF meeting this morning was devoted to a report on the President's trip to the drought-stricken Southwest. Jim Hagerty gave a heart-rending report of the terrible destruction nature has wrought on some of the most prosperous farms in this country. He felt that the President had benefited by this trip and that his presence had given a lift to the farmers' flagging spirits. Jim said that the trip had been completely devoid of any political ballyhoo or campaign tricks; this was the President of the United States visiting fellow citizens, trying to get a first-hand knowledge of their ills and problems, and offering to do whatever he could to help them out of their difficulties.

Hagerty said that the President had not found these farmers bitter or overly discouraged; most of them were determined to stick to their farms and try to bring life back to them. He also said that they are not just sitting and waiting for the Federal Government to rescue them; they are thorougly self-contained men who want to stay that way, and they are interested in merely the barest minimum of Federal effort to help them get on their feet. What they need is rain, and there is little else that can help. It is futile to widen, deepen or extend dried-up river beds.

January 20, 1957

I received an invitation from the Reverend Doctor Elson, Pastor of the New York Presbyterian Church, which the President attends, to be present at a special pre-Inaugural service to be held in the church today. It is scheduled for nine o'clock, and I asked my fiancée Catherine Boswell,[1] who is visiting relatives in the city, to be ready at eight, since all guests have been asked to be there by eight-thirty.

When we arrived, there was a long waiting line in front of the church—visitors who hoped to find seats or standing room after the guests and the members of the church had been seated. The center portion of the large auditorium was roped off for members of the President's family, friends and staff. When we entered, an usher met us and scrutinized our admittance cards for a long time. He was obviously in a dither, and hurriedly called another usher, who seemed to be in charge, to make a decision. It was apparent to us that they found this an unexpected emergency. Apparently it had never dawned upon church officials that Negroes would attend the ceremony. In a very cool and impersonal manner, we were ushered to a rear seat across the aisle from the roped-off section.

It was interesting to sit there and see the distinguished persons in the auditorium. The guest list was studded with great names in American life, members of the Cabinet, the Vice-President and his family. The President and Mrs. Eisenhower, with their

1 Mrs. Boswell and I had met in Chicago, where she was a medical social worker, about a year and a half before this. We had been engaged for two months, and were married in the fall of 1957.

son John and his wife Barbara, arrived about three minutes before the start of the service.

The service was an impressive one. All the favorite hymns of the President were sung, and the choir was one of the best I have ever heard. The minister's sermon was short but meaningful, and except for the unpleasantness when we entered the church, I was happy that we had come.

I had hung my coat and hat in the little vestibule off the main auditorium. As we were edging toward the door I left Mrs. Boswell standing just inside the door of the auditorium until I could get my coat. She was flushed with rage when I returned. Two women members of the church, ignoring all propriety, had discussed our presence within her hearing. They had speculated about us, and one had made the caustic comment: "He must be a high Government official, because if he were not, he would never *dare* enter *our* church."

The whole thing seemed ironic to me. My paternal grandfather was a prominent Presbyterian clergyman, and served for many years as a member of the Board of the National Presbytery. My own father, who started off as a Presbyterian clergyman, broke with the church over its policy of "race" and became a Methodist minister. Here, some fifty years later, I found myself involved in a battle of "race" in the number one Presbyterian church in the nation. I said to Catherine that surely even God must have a difficult time finding a place in this church.

I looked about me and saw the faces of several colleagues— men with whom I work every day. They ignored me or looked over my head, with no sign of recognition. This often occurs when these men are accompanied by their wives. Perhaps they feel they may have to introduce me as a colleague, or perhaps they are embarrassed to speak to me before a group of people, for fear it might indicate some kind of personal relationship. I don't know, but afterward I never trust them again.

January 21, 1957

I WAS about to leave my apartment for the President's Inaugural ceremony when the phone rang. It was Ann Whitman. She informed me that the President wanted to honor me by having me sit in his box after I had finished the parade route as a marshal. She also invited Catherine.

The guests in the President's box consisted of his family, close personal friends of many years' standing, Cabinet members and their wives, and a handful of ranking presidential assistants who had come to Washington to work without compensation and to head various special committees.

The box was closely guarded by Secret Servicemen and White House police. Though I am known to all of them and they know my position, even they were uncertain as to whether I was correct in thinking that I was to be a guest there. But Ann Whitman had thought of every eventuality and had fortified me with the coveted gold tickets of admittance.

I left Catherine there and went to take my place in the parade. This was another "first." No other Negro had ever been honored by being a marshal of one of the divisions of an Inaugural parade. As my aide for this occasion, I had Air Force Colonel Thomas Thorne, who had thoughtfully provided fleece-lined flying boots for my feet, two heavy blankets to wrap myself in against the chilling air, and a five-gallon container of hot coffee. The most difficult part was waiting in line at the Capitol for our division to form and enter the parade. We stood in the cold for two hours. I was tremendously grateful for Colonel Thorne's coffee.

The only difficulty about being in a parade is that you never get to see it. However, since several of the divisions formed at the Capitol, we could see a small part of it. I rode down the historic parade route in an open car. The thousands of Negroes along the route were particularly enthusiastic, and I was pleased that my being there gave them a lift and a feeling of belonging.

When we passed the presidential box, I raised my hat in tribute to the President and Mrs. Eisenhower, and he gave me an enthusiastic wave, as did the Vice-President.

I had the car turn off the parade route, and we entered the White House grounds where I left the car and joined Catherine in the President's box.

Later that night we attended the Inauguration Ball at the Armory. This was a brilliant affair, with beautiful women, beautiful gowns, and scores of Army officers in full-dress uniforms, as well as thousands of men in white tie and tails. A real effort had been made to make the Armory beautiful, but I have never seen any effort that has succeeded in disguising the utilitarian features of an armory. And the floors, scuffed by thousands of marching feet and military vehicles, are never conducive to good dancing.

We stayed for an hour, and then left to attend a late party. I fell wearily into bed at three-thirty, and got up again at eight to come down to the office to work. I shall be glad to see night follow this day!

January 29, 1957

THE Stassen operation was moved out of the Executive Office Building several weeks ago to 700 Jackson Place, which is diagonally across the street from the White House and the Executive Office Building. However, Mr. Stassen retains his own office and that of his deputy and two aides in the EOB. This move was necessitated by the need of bringing the Operations Coordinating Board over to the EOB on the same floor with the National Security Council, so that all these operations dealing with matters of extreme secrecy could be behind security barriers and receive twenty-four-hour protection from guards. This move, of course, has not made anyone very happy, and the needs of the Stassen group—both in personnel and office furniture and equipment—seem to double daily. It was originally thought that the disarmament staff would be a very small one, but it has ballooned into more than forty-three persons on the payroll at the present time, not counting part-time consultants and advisers, and there are continual requests for more secretaries, more messengers, more equipment. . . .

What particularly peeved me today was the request sent to me to approve more than forty hours overtime for Mr. Stassen's personal chauffeur. I do not even know whether it is legal to do this, because I think that there are certain disagreeable factors inherent in a chauffeur's job and that he is expected to drive the boss whenever and wherever necessary. I often see this chauffeur sitting around in the anteroom, waiting to be called, and at other times—when Mr. Stassen is out of town—he seems to be taking things very easy. However, I am told that he has to drive many hours at night and to many affairs, but this still seems to me one of the "occupational hazards" in this kind of job.

Stassen is in the news again today because of an appearance he made on a television program the past weekend when he again dragged Vice-President Nixon's name into a discussion on the loss of several Congressional races by the Republicans in the last election. He theorized that the Republicans would have made a much better showing as far as Congress is concerned if Governor Christian Herter of Massachusetts had been the candidate for Vice-President instead of Nixon.

This has opened a lot of old wounds, and the question becomes pertinent again as to how long Stassen can continue this kind of conduct and remain on the President's staff. There is a great deal of speculation as to why he continues his discordant theme. Is it because it keeps him in the news and he needs the publicity to further his ambition? Is he trying to be fired in an effort to become some kind of a martyr to a cause?

The President is a very patient man in some respects, but I am certain that not even he will stand for this continual sniping at his Vice-President for much longer. Certainly in the last election Mr. Nixon did not prove any great handicap to the Eisenhower candidacy, and both men were elected by an overwhelming landslide.

I am making a private bet with myself that within the next few weeks some means will be found to ease Mr. Stassen out of the official family. His views are becoming almost untenable and are causing considerable unrest among the staff.

A significant thing happened this afternoon when I went to General Goodpaster's office to tell him about my indecision on approving the overtime for Stassen's chauffeur and the numerous requests for staff additions and office equipment. We went down the hall so that we could talk privately. Goodpaster was very cautious in approaching this matter and felt that we should play along with the situation a little while longer. He said that the possibility of some kind of change in that operation was in the offing. I can only assume that soon there will be a new head or that the operation will be curtailed severely. At any rate, here's a new straw in the wind as far as my own thinking is concerned.

One of the great difficulties of the Stassen group has been the fact that he was formerly head of Foreign Operations Administration where he had millions of available dollars to spread around. Many of his present staff members were with him during that and previous operations, and it has been difficult for them to learn how to function within the limited means at our command in the White House. Every time we develop a new budget for a fiscal year, we have trouble with this outfit. They always visualize their needs as "tremendous"; they are always on the threshold of some great operation—so nebulous it cannot be defined—which we are assured is absolutely essential. I am certain that a lot of these demands are not those made by Mr. Stassen himself, but are merely suggestions on the part of those around him, who think that he would be happy if these things were accomplished. However, it keeps our two offices at odds at all times, since his staff feels that we turn down many of their requests just to be difficult.

Another frustrating moment occurred today when a female member of the Stassen staff who was formerly connected with the President's staff protested my request that she give up her parking space on West Executive Avenue for one outside the gate on the Ellipse. This request was necessary because there have been several new presidential staff appointments, and these persons—because of their positions—are entitled to parking positions on West Executive Avenue. This handling of parking permits is the most irritating part of my job. Out of the 1,500 people connected with running the White House in some manner, almost all of them drive cars, and with about 250 parking spaces available, it is very difficult to satisfy even a small percentage.

One of the first jobs I had when I got here was to make a survey of who parked where. I came up with a lot of odd situations. Some people who had no connection with the White House at all but had offices in the vicinity had been given the special privilege of parking on West Executive Avenue. These persons were indignant, and they, too, used a great deal of pressure to remain there. I have made it a rule to issue these parking permits on the basis of need and on the basis of the hours one works and the distance one has to come to work, but politics enters into even this little performance, and the people go to all ends to get a parking sticker near the White House door.

I have been able to resist these pressures fairly successfully until today, when the lady on the Stassen staff was able to have a direct order issued to me from the staff secretary's office that her permit be returned to her. There are many elements involved in this case that I cannot write about here, but I have definitely "lost face" in this incident, and it may interfere with my performance of duty in this area. If it occurs again, I will have no alternative but to ask to be relieved of this responsibility. It is not my nature to yield to pressures, no matter from what quarter or in what form.

FEBRUARY 14, 1957

THERE has been much excitement in the Negro world over the birth of the new nation of Ghana, on the African Gold Coast. Ghana is to be established officially on March 6. The United States will be represented by the Vice-President and an official delegation made up of members of Congress and other persons designated by the Secretary of State. The new Prime Minister, Dr. Kwame Nkrumah, attended a Negro college in this country—Lincoln University—and has many friends here. Large private delegations are planning to go to his inauguration, and great pressures have been put on the White House and the State Department by prominent Negroes, asking to be named to the official delegation from the United States.

A few days ago I suggested to Max Rabb that it would be politically wise if I were named to the delegation to accompany the Vice-President. Nixon had gone to many colored countries in the world before without a Negro member in his group, and I felt that the presence of Negroes would make his visits much more effective. Each time the Vice-President had made one of these trips, the Negro press had asked why he was not accompanied by some Negro official.

Max was less than enthusiastic about the project. He reminded me that just a few weeks ago I had been a marshal in the Inaugural Parade and that there was such a thing as "overdoing it"! I was a little miffed. I had not sought to be a marshal or to participate in the Inauguration in any way, and I have certainly never tried to push myself into any of the official festivities of the White House or the Administration. I had no way of knowing whether this was an official attitude or something dreamed up by Max to discourage me from making any other efforts to go along on the trip.

You can imagine my surprise the next day when I entered the dining room and Sherman Adams called me over to his table—which was filled with visitors—to say: "Fred, how would you like to go to Africa with Dick?" I fumbled for an answer, and the Governor smiled and said: "Maybe you'll find some of your relatives over there." I had to laugh at this quip and quickly retorted: "I hope not, sir. I have enough trouble with my blood relatives in this country." He dismissed me by saying: "I think you ought to go, so call the Vice-President's office."

At this writing I am in the process of taking the dozens of medical shots necessary for the trip, and collecting gear and clothing for that area of the world. I must begin a daily routine of taking two tablets to combat yellow fever, and am now on a search for a special kind of mosquito repellent that will be a very important part of my wardrobe.

MARCH 1, 1957

WE LANDED in Rabat, in Morocco, to find a tremendous reception at the airport. A color guard had been drawn up, and a Moroccan band played loud martial music. The diplomatic corps was out in force, and the Crown Prince of Morocco was there to extend the official welcome.

A brilliant scene indeed! The Vice-President went down the line to review the guard, and then shook hands with all the members of the diplomatic corps. The area set aside for the ceremonies was gay with bunting and flags of all the nations, and scores of gorgeous Persian rugs had been laid on the ground for the VIPs to stand on. There were thousands of citizens in the background.

After the ceremonies at the airport, we drove into Rabat. Thousands more enthusiastic natives lined the roadway and cheered as we passed. We could not help but be appalled by the scenes of overwhelming poverty and dirt and the obvious lack of sanitation.

Moroccan women have a queer throaty yell that they give whenever the Sultan or members of the royal family or visiting dignitaries pass by. It is a kind of warble that makes a weird piercing noise. This is their manner of paying homage to a VIP. It is all the more notable because the women are veiled, and even if you look right at them, there is little evidence of how this sound is made. This was my first experience of seeing veiled women. I wondered how a man could tell *his* wife from anybody else's, since most of them dress alike and look alike.

The cavalcade was led by the Sultan's motorcycle corps, a kind of elite guard riding German motorcycles which are fast and light and are driven through the narrow streets at breakneck speed. It seems to be customary in this part of the world that all rulers have motorcycle corps that race them through the countryside.

A stop was made at the entrance of a small community, where the traditional ceremony of welcoming a visitor with goat's milk and honey was observed. I felt sorry for the Vice-President. Americans are not too keen about warm goat's milk, and to get it down with over a tablespoonful of thick, sickeningly sweet honey—in all that tropical heat—must have been a real problem.

We entered Rabat, and drove toward the Imperial Palace, where we were to meet the Sultan. The scene was right out of the *Arabian Nights*. The palace is a gigantic, sprawling structure covering many acres, and inside the huge white walls are superb gardens and tropical fruit trees. The roadway leading to the palace was lined with mounted guards on sleek Arabian horses. The royal band was playing Moroccan music outside the gate, and the mounted troops were brought to attention by French officers in command, who had trained them.

We entered the gate and walked under trellised arches into the building where the Sultan was waiting in the summer throne room. This was a gorgeous building with one side completely open and facing on the royal gardens. It was of marble, and its wide interior was filled with fine fresco work and detailed carvings. The floors of the vast throne room were covered with Persian rugs piled a half-foot deep on top of each other.

The King was seated on the throne, and there were two seats on either side of him reserved for the Vice-President and Mrs. Nixon. After handshakes all around, the Sultan spoke through his interpreter. The Vice-President responded, and this in turn was interpreted to the Sultan. The two men talked for a half hour, and then we retired to take our places outside in a stand across from the palace, where we were able to observe the King ride from the palace to the mosque to pray. Thousands of people lined the street, from the palace to the temple, to see this unique sight. The procession was led out of the palace gates by a band, followed by a squad of cavalry, and then, in a magnificently decorated carriage drawn by Arabian horses, came the Sultan. Beside the carriage and behind trekked the elders and the religious leaders of the court. Bringing up the rear, in a flashing brand-new Cadillac, was the Crown Prince. As the Sultan rode by, the women gave their throaty yells, and general ecstasy prevailed!

Incidentally, women in Morocco have no status at all. They bear children and act as servants. Whatever position they have comes only from what the men decide to allow them. In most of the countries we visited, the women always acted as beasts of burden, while the men walked serenely along the streets with them, carrying nothing but the clothing on their backs.

The Crown Prince seems very pompous. He returned from the mosque in his Cadillac, came up to the stand where the Vice-President was sitting, and proceeded to put on a very royal display of himself. He was resplendent in a pristine white uniform with medals and all other accouterments, and acted completely oblivious of the awed thousands who viewed him. It was at this point that the Vice-President and his wife, in typical American fashion, left the stands to mingle with the people. The Vice-President shook hands with scores of them, and Mrs. Nixon patted babies on the head and finally picked up a very dirty infant to cuddle on her lap. The crowd literally went crazy over this display of friendliness on the part of the "VP" and his wife, but it seemed to make the Crown Prince very uncomfortable. The Nixons were to do this same thing many times during their visit in Morocco and elsewhere, and newsmen later indicated that they knew both the Sultan and the Crown Prince would be glad when we left. Royalty does *not* mingle with peasants, and this display of American democracy at work could very well put queer ideas into the people's heads.

That night the Prime Minister held a lavish reception and dinner for us at Guest House. It was the kind of dinner that would be repeated many times on this trip: native dishes washed down with appropriate wines, two- or three-hour meals; positive exhaustion!

March 3, 1957

WE LEFT for Casablanca by car the next morning in a fast and furious motorcade, our way cleared by the elite motorcycle guard which went at lightning speed down the twisting, turning cement roads.

We made a tremendous entry into Casablanca. It was one of the greatest demonstrations I have ever seen, and I have seen many famous personalities return from exploits around the world and take the traditional ticker-tape ride down New York's Broadway, and I saw the parade given for Ike when he returned from Europe after World War II. But for sheer numbers and enthusiasm, I have never seen anything like the demonstration put on by the people of Casablanca when the Vice-President's cavalcade arrived.

Police estimated that more than 200,000 delirious, cheering people took part. They crowded every rooftop, every tree, every telegraph pole, every square inch of the city, to get a glimpse of Mr. Nixon. The local police and the Secret Service men accompanying us were nervous wrecks. The Vice-President's car was slowed to a halt as the people scrambled around it to shake his hand or to cheer him, and at several points he got out of the car to circulate and greet them.

After a tour of the city, we went to a luncheon given by the businessmen of Casablanca at the city hall. It was easy to understand why business shuts down for four hours in the middle of the day. We were the victims of an eight-course luncheon in the searing heat, and it was almost unbearable. Here again we were confused by choice native dishes, and none of us was in the mood to tackle the huge meal. A particularly discouraging factor was a whole pigeon laden with sauces and creams. Since we were on a goodwill tour, it was not possible to ignore this hospitality, but it was almost more than my stomach could stand. I realized that a pigeon is not much more than the squab that we eat with such relish in America, and yet I kept thinking of our attitude toward pigeons in Washington—despoilers and nuisances that they are! However, the Moroccans consider pigeon a delicacy, and they showed great concern and dismay as we picked at our birds, in what I'm afraid was a finicky manner.

The first pleasant surprise to meet us in Accra was the beautiful and modern hotel that the Ghana Government had erected for the delegates and visitors to the Independence Celebration. The *maître d'hôtel* was a German, but the waiters and other functionaries were natives. The manager told us that six weeks before our arrival the African employees had never seen a hotel, been inside of one, or had any knowledge of any of their tasks. He and his wife and a small staff had organized them so that they could function the day the hotel opened—about a week before we arrived. There were some snarls of course, and it was difficult at times to make the servants understand what we wanted. We discovered that an African servant never says, "I do not understand." He may make a dozen tries to come up with what you want, but in his efforts he is always smiling and shaking his head with a vigorous nod to show that he understands!

March 4, 1957

I WENT with the Vice-President to meet Prime Minister Nkrumah at Government House early today. I had not expected the government buildings to be so large or so modern. A prominent area of Accra had been staked out for the various ministry buildings, and in the center of these modern structures is Government House, a magnificent building of marble and native stone.

Even at this early hour in the morning, the custom of serving all guests with glasses of champagne was being observed. All members of the diplomatic corps were present, as were the official delegates from various countries around the world. Prime

Minister Nkrumah was obviously glad to see the Vice-President, who, upon being presented, immediately introduced me as his assistant. The Prime Minister expressed great delight at my presence, and as soon as he could get away from his other guests he led me into a corner and immediately launched into a discussion of the significance of the occasion.

Nkrumah is an inspiring man, humble, and a little bewildered about what has happened so suddenly in his country—but impressed with his great responsibility to make this new endeavor work. He congratulated me upon my position on the President's staff and agreed that we both had something in common, since we were both pioneering in difficult fields. He urged me to come back to talk again, and said that after six months he hoped to be able to travel and looked forward to coming to the United States at an early date. We promised to keep in touch.

That afternoon we went out to the enormous athletic stadium, where a celebration was being held. It was one of the largest gatherings I had ever seen. The stadium was lined with soldiers, both cavalry and footmen, and with representatives from the scores of tribes in the country who had come to Accra for the celebration. We were treated to a colorful review by the troops and by tribal dances from the many tribes represented.

At the appropriate moment in the ceremony there was a flurry of trumpets, the movement of cavalry units through the gate, and in a long black Rolls-Royce—with footmen and outriders— her Royal Highness the Duchess of Kent, representing Great Britain, made her entrance into the stadium. The scene resembled a Coronation Parade in London, when the newly crowned monarch rides from the Palace to the Cathedral for the ceremony. It was indeed an inspiring sight, and the thousands of people in the stadium cheered, screamed, and shouted as her Royal Highness, who is very regal looking, but vivacious and attractive, waved from the royal limousine.

She entered the stands and took her place in the Royal Box with the Prime Minister, who had walked down to meet her.

March 5, 1957

THE first thing on the program today was a convocation at the University College. I was pleasantly surprised by the physical appearance of the college, which is located on a hill several miles outside of Accra. The buildings are white stone and stucco, and very attractive.

The academic procession was indeed impressive, with the regalia of the officials in the line of march and the multicolored hoods of professors from various colleges in England and Europe. The college staff is predominantly white, and it appeared that most of the professors had been recruited from countries abroad.

The Vice-President, Mrs. Nixon and I joined the crowd pouring into the auditorium, and we had some difficulty finding seats until we were rescued by an official usher. We were in the center of the hall, and it was stiflingly hot. We all hoped that the ceremony would not be long.

The candidates for graduation were presented to the Duchess of Kent, and her response, in the form of a short address, brought greetings from Her Majesty the Queen, and noted that it was a glorious day both for the mother country and for the young men and women being graduated here.

On our way out we ran into Reverend and Mrs. Martin Luther King of Birmingham, Alabama, who had come out to Africa for the celebration. This was a coincidence. Reverend King had been trying to see the Vice-President for many months back in the States, and here—several thousand miles away—the two men met face to face. The Vice-President invited Reverend King to call upon him during his next visit to Washington. (This meeting, of course, made headlines in the Negro press, because Reverend King was a current hero in Negro America, having successfully led the bus boycott in Montgomery, Alabama.) I was grateful for the Vice-President's ease of manner in handling the difficult situation. Anything less tactful could have made derogatory headlines for the Republicans in the Negro press back home.

We have made a visit to a native village high up in the hills. The only way to describe this experience is "terrific." The paramount chief, the subchiefs and the whole village turned out to greet us. It was like the scenes of villages in the heart of Africa that one sees in the movies. We were taken inside the compound and given seats of honor under huge colored umbrellas. The natives then proceeded to dance our welcome.

The Vice-President spoke to the people of the village, and his words were interpreted to them in their native dialect. They were so overjoyed by the friendliness of the group that even the paramount chief danced to honor the Vice-President! This was unprecedented. Paramount chiefs maintain all the dignity and regal bearing of any ruler of state, and to see this kingly man leave his throne, push aside his attendants, and begin one of the delirious African dances, was really something to behold.

About nine that night, I got into a white dinner jacket and accompanied the Vice-President to the out-of-door reception given by the Speaker of the House on the spacious grounds of Accra's Parliament House. They were crowded with people. Colored lights placed in the flower beds added a glow to the crowds of dignitaries from all over the world. It was a beautiful sight. The Vice-President presented the Speaker with a gavel made from the old wood from the White House.

At midnight, Ghana became a nation. The Union Jack was hauled down from the staff on top of Parliament House at the stroke of twelve, and the red, yellow, and green national flag of the new nation was raised in its place. "At long last," Kwame Nkrumah shouted to a crowd of 12,000 rapt Africans, "the battle has ended; Ghana, our beloved country, is free forever. Let us pause for one minute to give thanks to Almighty God." For sixty seconds the crowd stood silent. Then a mighty roar shook the air: "Ghana is free!"

I was awakened later by the blowing of taps which marked the end of colonialism in Ghana and the beginning of a new independence. I could hear the thousands of cheering voices, and it was a strange and stimulating feeling to lie there in the darkness and realize the significance of this moment in the history of man.

March 8, 1957

THERE was a formal dinner at the American Embassy in Liberia tonight, given by Vice-President Nixon for President William V. S. Tubman. The Embassy is beautifully located on a cliff overlooking the ocean, and makes an imposing picture for miles around. The details of the dinner and its preparation had to be handled by the Embassy staff. Ambassador Richard Jones' wife was in the United States, so the wife of the Counselor had to supervise. She made a real effort to succeed, but it was a terribly ordinary meal, served with no sign of formality or flair, and it was pitiful and rather embarrassing.

The respective toasts were made by the Vice-President and Mr. Tubman, but the affair was really dead. We were all happy that it was over by ten o'clock.

At ten thirty that night I received a telephone call at President Tubman's guest house, where I was staying, from Mrs. Inez Maloney, an old friend from Washington, who was working in one of the banks in Liberia. I had forgotten she was in the country, and it was good to hear her voice. She came by the guest house to take me for a ride through Monrovia. We visited two night clubs, one near the Embassy, overlooking the ocean. This particular club was in a garden, and under the tropical African moon, with the ocean lapping the sandy beach at our feet, we sat and listened to the music for about an hour.

March 10, 1957

WE LANDED at Entebbe, Uganda, around ten o'clock in the morning. It was a scenic flight, coming into this lush little area right on Lake Victoria, the third largest and one of the most beautiful lakes in the world. There was the usual band playing martial music, and a contingent of black ceremonial troops commanded by British officers.

The Hotel Victoria, where I was lodged, was a fascinating place. It was loaded with black houseboys and waiters, flunkies who moved about the hotel barefooted, some in long white gowns with green sashes and red fezzes—others in less stylish garments which looked like brown denim rompers. The barefooted waiters would slog around in the banquet and dining halls, and houseboys polished the hardwood floors by standing on rags in their bare feet and going around in circles to rub the polish into the wood. They spoke in several dialects, so it was difficult to understand them and to make them understand me. The hotel is run by the English, and run very well.

In the evening a white-tie dinner was given by the Governor General and Lady Crawford at Government House—a typical spit-and-polish affair. The Oxford diction was a yard thick, and all the guests were highly educated and interesting people. A black police band in handsome uniforms played good dinner music. It was one of the most interesting evenings of the trip. The food and drink were good—the conversation stimulating.

As seems to be the custom in this area of the world, the British had put Government House on top of the highest hill, overlooking the town and the lake. It is a majestic-looking place, towering over the city.

Entebbe is a garden spot of Africa and one of the most beautiful places I have ever seen. The British have done their usual job of making themselves comfortable and developing a splendid civilization in this unique area of the Dark Continent. Despite my extreme dislike for colonialism and everything it denotes,

I cannot deny that the British really benefit any place into which they move. They provide all the preliminary essentials such as good roads, fine water systems, functional hotels, and the ever-present golf courses.

Sunday afternoon the Governor took a party of us out to Victoria Falls Dam, about fifty miles outside Entebbe. These falls are at the beginning of the Nile River, and the dam is a colossal one, but it cannot compare with some of the gigantic efforts in the United States.

March 11, 1957

WE LEFT Entebbe at 1 P.M. for a four-hour flight to Addis Ababa, Ethiopia. On the plane we changed from street clothes to cutaways, striped trousers, and high hats, for the official arrival in the Ethiopian capital. We landed at five and were met by the Crown Prince, heir apparent to the throne, and other high Ethiopian officials. We piled into smart European cars and went directly from the airport to the Jubilee Palace, home of the Crown Prince, where the Nixons were to stay. The rest of us were quartered at the Ghion Hotel, diagonally across from Jubilee Palace, and an excellent hotel with all modern appointments.

Promptly at five thirty, we drove to the Imperial Palace for an audience with his Imperial Majesty, Haile Selassie. The ride to the palace was fascinating. There were thousands of poor bedraggled natives outside the huge gates, watching our procession enter. We proceeded up the long, winding drive to the top of the hill where the palace sprawls over several acres. There were soldiers on guard every inch of the way up the drive, and the stone steps at the entrance leading up to the palace were crowded with dozens of flunkies, top brass and functionaries. We were escorted through a long hall to the door of the throne room. When this door was opened, we looked into Fairyland. The King and Queen were on throne chairs in the gorgeous setting of a room a block long; the floors were smothered in costly rugs, and brocaded draperies hung to the floor from windows more than thirty feet high. All about were fabulous treasures. Man-sized vases and urns stood in corners all over the room, and gold bric-a-brac was in evidence at every turn.

The King and Queen were flanked by three royal highnesses and a niece. The aide-de-camp introduced the Vice-President and Mrs. Nixon to His Royal Majesty, and after a brief chat, the Vice-President introduced his staff. We all made low bows from the waist and shook hands. The King gave me a double handshake and whispered, in perfect English, "I am glad to see you." This was startling to me, because in the United States word was that Ethiopia was not kindly disposed toward American Negroes, and not until very recently were they acceptable in Ethiopia in any capacity.

The legend is that Ethiopians do not want to be identified with the lowly plight of the American Negro. The Ethiopian is brown in color, but his features are the chiseled ones of the Arab or Hamitic race. But my reception was warm and sincere, and I had a feeling that these scores of impeccably clothed and highly educated court functionaries were not only surprised but rather proud to see a brown man in the Vice-President's entourage.

I could look out of my hotel window and still see the thousands of people who had lined the streets to view us as we came from the airport to the palace. They were still standing in the cold rain, and they looked wet, bedraggled and defeated. They shuffled about in colorful dress and costume, in streets that were clogged with two-wheeled carts pulled by donkeys or spavined horses.

Other than the large cars in the Emperor's fleet, most of the cars seen in Addis Ababa were small foreign models that one would see in the hilly country of Europe. There is utter chaos in the streets of Addis Ababa. Traffic goes in all four directions at the same time, without any pattern and without any policemen to direct it. It is worth one's life to drive, ride, or walk in this confusion. There is the constant honking of horns, braying of donkeys, and shouts of pedestrians—utter bedlam.

We were astonished by the backward appearance of the country. Ethiopia, high up in the mountains, was inaccessible to most of the world until the invention of the airplane. There is much poverty and illiteracy and few of the ordinary comforts of life that are universal in our world. True, there is the pageantry and color of the royal family, but the great mass of people is poverty-stricken. I wondered whether democracy could thrive and grow in a country that has lived like this for centuries. The only thing these people have ever known is worship of the Emperor. Perhaps it is possible to give the Ethiopians more privileges of citizenship, but I doubt very much if the average American idea of democracy could be transplanted easily in this ancient country.

The formal state dinner was scheduled for eight o'clock at the Imperial Palace. Upon arrival, the Vice-President's party was escorted to the throne room to await a summons to the upstairs reception room where the Emperor and the Queen would receive the guests. The diplomatic corps had been assembled in another room for the same reason.

Soon we were escorted up a beautiful winding stairway to the second floor, and entered a gigantic room in which the Emperor and Queen were standing on a royal rug. The Emperor was resplendent in formal dress uniform, and his imperial staff, bemedaled and standing stiffly at attention, formed a dramatic background. The Vice-President and Mrs. Nixon joined the Emperor and Queen, and the rest of us stood to their left, just beside the Emperor's staff. After this maneuver, the royal announcer went to the door at the north end of the room, pulled back a heavily brocaded curtain, and beckoned the diplomatic corps to the door. He announced the name of each ambassador and his wife. Each couple walked forward ten steps; the women curtsied and the men bowed. They would go another ten steps and do the same thing, finally reaching the royal rug. Again they would curtsy and bow, shaking hands with both the Emperor and Queen, and then move slowly backward into the royal dining room to find their places at table.

Some of the women's dresses were so long and close-fitting that when they went to curtsy, they almost fell on their faces.

These were tense moments for me as I stood there watching this endless line of foreign representatives and their wives go through this ritual, hoping each time that they would be able to get up to the royal rug and away without disaster. I was interested in the Russian Ambassador and his wife. They walked in, stolid and unsmiling, but went through the ritual like everyone else.

After this procession of ninety or more people, Mrs. Nixon took the Emperor's arm, and the Queen the Vice-President's, and behind them we entered the royal dining room.

The dining room was at least two New York city blocks long, gorgeously decorated, and the floors covered with rugs piled at least six inches deep. The table, placed in the center of the room, ran the entire length of the hall, seating 125 people. The room was ablaze with light from gold candelabra, gold vases filled with every conceivable kind of flower, and the gleaming reflections from the gold table service. Everything in the room was gold. Even the chairs and table had the royal crest emblazoned in gold.

There were scores of waiters and assistants. The waiters wore white gloves, green velvet cutaways, red knee breeches, white stockings, and black patent-leather slippers with silver buckles. The head butler wore the customary formal dress of white tie, while his assistants wore blue uniforms with red trousers, and on the shoulders of their jackets were gold epaulets. Out of sight, somewhere in the courtyard, a string orchestra played softly during the meal. The menu was written in both Amharic and French.

I sat between two medal-laden Cabinet members. They spoke Amharic, also Italian, Spanish, and French. With my limited French, we exchanged a few pleasantries, but state dinners are a strain for me in any foreign country because of the language difficulties. At an appropriate moment champagne glasses were raised by the Emperor to toast the Vice-President and the President of the United States. The Vice-President rose to return the toast.

I downed the native foods with great difficulty. Each time a white-gloved hand would offer me a dish of some weird concoction, I would have to copy the actions of my tablemates and take whatever portion they took. I did not think I was going to make it.

After the last course, the women went to a drawing room and the men to a large hall for cigars, demitasses, and liqueurs. By this time my stomach was queasy and I was scared stiff that I would disgrace the Vice-President, my country and myself. I endured a miserable half-hour in the midst of a hundred strange tongues as I listened to the growls of my stomach and felt all the panic that goes with that kind of signal.

On the long drive back from the palace to my hotel I got very ill and tried to open the car window for air. This did very little good, and I am sorry to say that I left part of my dinner in the royal car. I was, to say the least, embarrassed, and upon arrival at the hotel I gave the driver a generous tip. (He was so pleased with his good fortune that every time he drove me thereafter he gestured, inviting me not to worry about getting sick in the car again.) By the time I reached my room, I was very sick and beginning to have chills. I finally got to bed. I was a miserable man!

March 12, 1957

THE royal palace sent an American doctor over to see me this morning, and I am feeling much better. My temperature is lower and my blood pressure is up a bit, but this is probably because of the extremely high altitude of Addis Ababa. I won't take part in any of the activities today, so that I will be in good enough shape to leave for the Sudan in a few days, and this means that I will have to miss lunch with the Crown Prince.

March 13, 1957

EARLY breakfast at the Ghion Hotel this morning consisted of French rolls, horrible native coffee and native jam. It
was very difficult to get down, but we had a long flight ahead
of us and I felt I should eat something.

There was the usual official procession to the airport in a
cavalcade made up of members of the royal household and various Ethiopian dignitaries. By nine o'clock we were en route to
Khartoum, Sudan.

After a flight of several hours we landed in Sudan without
incident. The Sudanese are a very reserved people, and their
welcoming demonstration was less noisy and uninhibited than
those in the other countries had been. They have enjoyed freedom for only a year, and they are wearing it with dignity and
a deep sense of responsibility.

We were given lavish quarters in a great palace which had
been the headquarters for French governors for many years.
It was an incredible mansion, overlooking the Nile, and apparently had also been used as a barracks to house both French and
native troops during the long period of occupation.

Shortly after our arrival we began round after round of teas
with the chiefs of small communities in the area. A huge one,
staged that afternoon on the grounds of the palace where we
were staying, was a fantastic sight. We mingled with thousands
of Sudanese in colorful dress and met powerful chieftains from
the many tribes which had come to pay their respects to the
Vice-President of the United States.

We were particularly awed by our first formal meal in the
palace as guests of the Prime Minister. The principal course was
fish, which was placed on the table in its original size, approximately that of a small whale. It had been baked whole, and each
guest was permitted to cut his own piece. We were given native
tools to do this: the knife was the size of a sword; the utensil
used to place the fish on one's plate was the size of a small kitchen

shovel. The fish was delicious, but it had lots of bones, which made precarious eating for us unskilled Americans. However, the atmosphere was friendly, and we were able to glimpse the intelligence of this young nation's top men.

March 14, 1957

WE WERE airborne at 9 A.M., en route to Tripoli, Libya. The stewards aboard the plane had been thoughtful enough to prepare coffee, fruit juice and toast, and a few minutes after we were aloft we were enjoying this light American breakfast. We were crossing the great Sahara Desert again, and it was an awesome sight as we looked down from 12,000 feet to see nothing but endless miles of sand. You couldn't help wondering what it would be like to land in this eternal waste of sand.

We were flying blithely along, chatting about our hours in Khartoum, when all of a sudden one of the starboard motors backfired and then quit completely. This was startling. We all looked at each other, not so much in fright, but with stunned surprise. We could feel the plane lose a bit of altitude, and were conscious of the effort to restart the motor. Even before word came back to us from the pilot, we were aware of the fact that we were circling to start a crippled flight back to Khartoum.

As soon as we had made the circle, an announcement by the pilot over the loud-speaker requested the Vice-President to come forward right away. After a few minutes, Mr. Nixon returned to tell us that possibly we could have limped into Tripoli on three motors, but the pilot would rather not take this chance, and felt it was better to return to Khartoum for repairs. We would be flying at a lower altitude on the trip back to Khartoum, but there was every reason to believe we would make it safely. The pilot had wired ahead to the airfield to inform the Prime Minister that we were returning.

Despite this assurance from the pilot and the Vice-President, we put in an anxious two hours on this return flight. All of us were beginning to get a little jittery. There were still many harrowing miles ahead of us before we would reach home, and we began to wonder whether we should risk crossing the Atlantic in this plane, despite the fact that it was one of the most plush jobs in the Air Force. Since it was a personal plane of Admiral Radford, Chairman of the Joint Chiefs of Staff, there was every reason to believe that it would be completely safe and reliable.

Another problem was the fact that a tremendous celebration had been prepared for us in Tripoli, and the newsmen, who had already left an hour ahead to record our arrival, would sense a great story in our failure to arrive on time. It was possible that they would send it out via cable and wireless, which could alarm our families and friends at home.

We made the trip back to Khartoum safely and an excellent landing, despite our crippled motor. An auxiliary plane loaded with spare parts and mechanics had been dispatched from the great American air base in Tripoli, and would arrive in a few hours. There was nothing for us to do but brave the 105° heat at this desert airport until our plane was repaired.

The Prime Minister came to take the Vice-President and Mrs. Nixon back to the palace, and the rest of us decided to buy souvenirs for friends in the small shops surrounding the airport. Haggling with the shopkeepers over prices was fun. All items went up 100 percent when we showed any interest in them—the usual hike when Americans are shopping abroad.

We waited around for more than four hours, but the plane from Tripoli arrived about noon, and its mechanics went right to work. Also arriving from another African base was a "rescue plane" which would follow us for the rest of our trip in Africa and on the European Continent.

We were ready to take off again around 2:30, and this time we reached Tripoli without incident, arriving over the city as darkness fell. It was beautiful to come into this ancient city just as lights were being turned on in the little dwellings below, and we zoomed down onto the runway of the great American air base located off the seaport that was once an operating area for pirates. The United States has built a massive installation in

Tripoli, and it is a genuine oasis in this faraway section of the world.

We were greeted with a typical American celebration, and it was thrilling to see numbers of American men and women after so many days of meeting only strangers of other countries.

We were hustled off to a barracks that had been provided for our use. The Nixons were given quarters at the home of the commanding general of the base.

Our first concern was getting our laundry done and our clothes cleaned. The Special Services Officer of the base had cleared the decks so that all facilities were at our disposal, and our laundry and cleaning were collected as soon as we were able to get them together. We were not so happy four hours later, when our laundry was returned clean, but with nearly all of the buttons shorn from the shirts. This posed a problem as to how we were to keep our garments on from this point. However, we were immediately issued GI sewing kits by the commanding officer, went to work at our sewing, and were soon ready to enjoy our short stay in this historic seaport town.

The next morning we were driven about and shown several places of interest. One could not help but be struck by the signs of great poverty and primitive living. Many of the natives were in rags, and it was obvious that the efforts to make a life in this impoverished area were difficult. Tripoli's government buildings are modern, and efficient.

We met the various officials of the city, and over coffee and native buns they were very hospitable and gave an earnest impression of deep concern about their responsibilities to give the natives a better way of life.

We had traveled many thousands of miles in Africa, across jungles and deserts, and yet we did not see our first camel until we reached Tripoli. It was not plodding across some wide expanse of desert, but was being used as a beast of burden by a native peddler hawking his wares on the hot asphalt streets.

While we were being taken on an official sight-seeing tour of the city I was startled when a young woman ran out of the crowd collected along one of the main streets, shouting my name. She waved for the driver to stop. When he did, she stuck her head in the car and I recognized her as a former secretary at the Republican National Committee. She had been spending the last year in Tripoli with her father, who was there on a mission for the State Department. This was a very pleasant surprise. Later that day she brought her mother and father to our quarters at the air base to have tea. I had a similar happy meeting with a former Army buddy who had remained in the service and was now a major and a jet pilot attached to one of the outfits at the Tripoli air base.

It was comforting to us to see and appreciate the need for these great air bases in various sections of the world. They are vital for our national security, and are equipped to do an effective job whenever they are called upon. All day and all night—as long as we remained at this base—jet squadrons were taking off for or returning from some important mission. The Air Force has done an excellent job in trying to give its men on these far-off bases most of the comforts and a few of the luxuries of home.

March 16, 1957

ONE of the highlights of our stay in Rome, on the first leg of the return trip, was the great state dinner at the American Embassy on the night of our arrival. It was apparent to me that the diplomatic corps and the titled persons present at the dinner were a bit shocked to see me in the official party. At first they were not quite sure whether I was some kind of servant accompanying the Vice-President or actually an official representing the United States Government. I must say that at every turn Mr. Nixon left no doubt in anyone's mind as to my role in the delegation. On this particular occasion I found myself doing something that I have had to do many times in my life at similar affairs. I had to make every effort to put other people at ease rather than be concerned about my own reactions.

After dinner we went into the large ballroom, where we

greeted more than a hundred more guests who had come in for an evening of entertainment.

During the course of the evening I was rather embarrassed to find myself the center of attention, because I felt that this honor belonged to the Vice-President, but naturally people were curious about my role in the delegation. I had a wonderful time, but decided that it would be smart for me to plead fatigue early and ask permission to retire to my hotel. I did this for several reasons. First, several of the very attractive women at the party were beginning to feel their champagne, and I did not want to be involved in any situation arising out of "champagne friendliness." I also felt that I had made my contribution to the occasion and that there was no point in staying any longer. I went back to the hotel and went to bed.

Two hours later I was awakened by three Negro newspaper people who had accompanied us on the trip and who, along with other American newsmen, had gone to the Embassy after I left, to cover the party. They came to report something that happened after I left.

An American woman at the party, obviously tight, had accosted them and asked if they had been on the trip to Ghana with the Vice-President. She wanted to know their impression of the country. She then added: "My husband is the American Ambassador Designate to Ghana. We are not very happy about going to this black country, but somehow we always get the dregs." She then went on to indicate in no uncertain terms that she had nothing good to say for black people. The Negro reporters fled the scene. They appealed to me to do something about this situation by reporting the incident to the State Department so that the Administration would not commit a blunder by sending this couple to represent us in Ghana.

I can report here that this controversy became a small scandal upon our return to the States. The State Department did make an investigation of the incident, and of course the lady categorically denied that she had made any such statements. I took no part in the controversy, because I was not present, but it was difficult to believe that three responsible newsmen would make up such a story. The ambassador was formally cleared by the State Department and sent to Ghana. I do not know whether Prime Minister Nkrumah ever heard the story.

The high spot of the visit to Rome was our personal audience with the Pope. I believe that this must be a stirring moment in any human's life, no matter what his religion or creed, when he comes into the presence of the man who is the symbol of one of the world's great religions. Certainly I, a Protestant, was visibly moved.

The Vatican is a tiny self-contained city. It is one of the most historic communities on earth, and one is conscious of this as soon as he enters the gates. It has retained all the tradition, pomp and ceremony of past centuries, and the Swiss Guards, with their extraordinary uniforms and ancient weapons, are like soldiers from a fantastic fairytale.

We were given the red-carpet treatment, and each of us in the official party was offered the privilege of shaking hands with the Pope and saying a few words to him. We were told that, since he was a very delicate man, we were to take his hand lightly and shake it gently. Since he could not speak very loudly, we were advised to keep as quiet as possible, and also not to take more than a very few minutes with him, so as not to tax his strength.

Mrs. Nixon had purchased a special outfit for the occasion, a floor-length black gown and a gorgeous black lace mantilla. The Vice-President's personal secretary, Rose Wood, was similarly dressed. We men wore morning clothes or dark blue suits.

When we entered the Pope's study, he was standing to greet us, and we were all surprised when he gave us each a firm, warm handshake, saying how glad he was to see us.

He read greetings from a typewritten page, expressing his gratitude for our visit and his deep respect for President Eisenhower, Mr. Nixon and the American people in general. Then he presented each of us with a beautiful silver medal embossed with his picture—commemorating the eighteenth year of his reign—and raised his slim, patrician hands to give us his blessing and benediction.

March 18, 1957

WE left Rome early this morning for Tunisia.

Tunisia is a tiny, poverty-stricken nation on the Mediterranean shore of North Africa. Its population is half that of New York City, yet it is playing an important role in Arab and world affairs. Free of France, which ruled it until a year ago, Tunisia has come to represent a nationalism friendly to the West.

We were met at the airport with the usual courtesies from the dignitaries of the country, led by Prime Minister Habib Bourguiba. Our motorcade left immediately for the palace of the Bey of Tunis, the last of the fabulous monarchs of that area. The Bey has become almost a mere symbol of past glories, since Tunisia is well on its way toward ridding itself of all royal prerogatives and becoming a practicing democracy. Even at this hour Mr. Bourguiba appeared to be "the strong man," and our information indicated that the Bey would probably be exiled in the very near future, and that Bourguiba would become the first president of the country.

At any rate, we were received in the Bey's palace with all the pomp and ceremony expected of a king, and again, as in Morocco, this was like a glimpse into an ancient story book. This is the land of fezzes and veiled women, and Western dress looks rather odd in this city.

The usual welcoming speeches were made, and the usual expressions of friendship tendered. The Bey gave the Vice-President a jeweled watch to be presented to President Eisenhower. We were told that it had cost several thousands of dollars and had been made especially for the President.

After our visit with the Bey, we were taken to the guest house where we were to be quartered—a fabulous palace overlooking the Mediterranean. The surroundings, appointments and furnishings of this palace made any we had seen in other sections of the world appear drab. It was certainly on a par with the royal domain of Haile Selassie. It was built entirely of marble, with huge winding staircases, and the floors were covered with fabulously valuable Oriental rugs. Our bedrooms were the size of small ballrooms, and each bed could easily have held four people. There were two or three male servants for each of us, and their garb was wonderful. They wore red fezzes, white mess jackets, red pantaloons, and odd shoes that turned up at the toes. They moved swiftly and softly about the house, and no matter where one might be in the castle, there was always a servant in the vicinity, ready to do one's bidding.

I can easily understand why so many of history's kings and members of royalty suffered and died from tuberculosis. Despite the 100° heat outside, these palaces are always cold and dank. After being in them for an hour or so, it is good to get out in the heat and get warm.

Every effort was made to give us all the luxuries of home. A bar where every conceivable kind of American drink was available was set up in a small downstairs room. The native bartenders could not understand us, and we had great fun trying to get them to serve us the drinks we wanted, and soon became very proficient in gestures and self-service.

We were located in Tunis, the capital city, and during our visit the country was at the height of celebrating the first year of its freedom. There were endless parades which kept traffic in a continuous snarl, and the people were in a jubilant and festive mood.

I begged off from the formal dinner given for us that night, because there were certain to be more of the bizarre native dishes that I had fallen victim to in Morocco and Ethiopia. I spent my first free evening sitting around the palace and socializing with some of the younger members of the American Embassy.

Later I went to the home of the Second Secretary of the Embassy, and it was pleasant to find that many members of the American colony had charming homes on the edge of this cliff overlooking the Mediterranean. It was a beautiful location, and they were able to run out of their homes, right down to the water's edge for swimming or boating.

One enjoys being the guest of Americans in far-off countries, because they make such a fuss over you; you are fresh from America and have the latest news. Americans living abroad are always eager to be brought up to date on what is happening back in the United States. I am certain that most persons serving our embassies make a real effort to be friendly with the natives and to cultivate neighborly relationships with foreigners, but on the other hand, it is inevitable that they have a tendency to hang together and to form closely knit groups of their own. This naturally has its drawbacks. It leads the officials of the country to believe that Americans are inherent snobs and that they feel superior to the local citizens. I don't feel that these accusations are entirely true, but I do think that we should make greater efforts to become friendly with the citizens of the countries where we serve.

Once my identity was established, I had a wonderful time in Tunis. People in this part of the world seldom see an American Negro, and certainly not one who has a position of any consequence in the United States Government. I also believe that American Negroes have the ability to make friends with foreigners, if for no other reason than the fact that they know what it means to be discriminated against. I found these natives eager and anxious to help me at every turn, and the servants in the palace were particularly pleased to have me as a guest.

My first night in these strange surroundings resulted in fitful slumber. My room opened out on a beautiful court, and with the windows wide open, a desert moon shone brightly into the room. In the stillness of the desert one can hear all the weird sounds of the night. The only difficulty about open windows in this area of the world is that if they are not screened (and they seldom are), the room becomes full of countless strange bugs and insects.

I awoke with a start about 6:30 in the morning, conscious that someone was in my room. The sun was streaming in brightly, and when I raised myself to full height in the bed, I was completely startled by the sight of four red-fezzed gentlemen in pantaloons, standing by my bed, watching me. I had no idea what this strange scene meant, and I had difficulty orienting myself. They were there merely to help. In Tunis, it is customary for one's personal servants to be present at the bedside in the morning when one awakens.

One of them held a tray with a silver coffeepot and service, ready to pour me a piping hot cup. Another was holding a gold tray laden with tropical fruits. The other two carried bath towels, soap, and a huge terry-cloth robe for me to wrap myself in when emerging from the ancient bath. They had no intention of deserting me, despite my protestations, and they stayed with me until I was completely dressed and ready to go downstairs for breakfast.

During the day, members of the embassy staff who served as our guides drove us several miles outside Tunis to view the ruins of a once glorious city. We later visited a very beautiful cemetery on a cliff overlooking the Mediterranean, where many of the heroic American soldiers who lost their lives in World War II were buried.

One of the most unique experiences of our visit was our trip to the Souks, the native area where hundreds of little shops, peddlers, and merchants are located. It is in the oldest section of the city, and is a *mélange* of dirt, confusion and poverty. The visit to the Souks was made doubly dangerous by the wild and drunken celebrants. They were tossing exploding firecrackers in all directions, and it was a wonder that many people were not injured. This caused Mrs. Nixon to cut short her shopping tour in this area, and it was with some trepidation that the male members of our group remained to try to find a few bargains in copper trays, scatter rugs, leather goods, etc. We were getting near the end of our trip, and were all looking for gifts to take back to relatives and friends.

We had three exciting and enjoyable days in this small desert country, but were happy when our planes pointed toward home, with our first stop in the Azores.

March 20, 1957

OUR trip to the Azores was uneventful, but it is an odd experience to be on a plane that is trying to pick out a small spit of land in the midst of a vast ocean. The plane's searchlights dance across the water, looking for familiar landmarks, and the uninitiated passenger is only aware of the dark water below. One sits at a window and strains his eyes to see exactly why the pilot is coming down to land where there apparently is no land at all. Not until you feel the familiar bump of the plane wheels on the runway do you have any sense of security.

The commanding officer and the ranking officials of the big air base at the Azores were present to greet us, despite the fact that it was 1:30 A.M. The Nixons were carried off to the commandant's home for breakfast, and the rest of us went to the officers' club.

The press plane had arrived a half hour ahead of us, and the correspondents were already busy stuffing handfuls of quarters into the dozen or more slot machines in the club. Others were trying to make last-minute purchases of a few bottles of whisky, which sold for two or three dollars less than in the States. Even though we were on special planes, we were rigidly held to the rules and regulations governing customs, and each of us was permitted to take back only three bottles of liquor.

The huge planes were refueled and we were ready to take off again in about an hour and a half. Weather reports indicated that we might find severe head winds, slowing our homeward progress, so the planes were turned toward Newfoundland, rather than Bermuda, since the weather reports in that area seemed better.

All I had to do was lie in my bunk and wait for dawn. It was thrilling to sight the frozen wastes of Newfoundland in the early light. We did not stop for refueling, but continued toward Washington. As soon as land was sighted, all of us seemed to feel much better. It was a jubilant, happy group that got ready for breakfast as our plane streaked across the coast of Maine.

We reached the airport at Washington about noon, and were given a heart-warming reception. We all posed for a final picture coming down the ramp, and it was with real regret that we said good-bye after four thrilling weeks of association in far-off sections of the world.

APRIL 11, 1957

In the past few weeks, many newspapers have speculated that I will be named Ambassador to Ghana or head of the new African desk at the State Department. I have no desire to be either. Val Washington asked me if I wanted to be an ambassador, and I told him, frankly "No!"

I feel that going to Africa with the Vice-President will prove to have been one of the most valuable events of my life. It gave me my first glimpse of that part of the world, and it opened new vistas that I was not aware existed. It also made me doubly anxious to be of service to my dark brother on this continent. I have resolved to return to Africa sometime and to talk at length with my new friends there. This visit has renewed my determination to be of service to people. I am discovering that this is one of life's most rewarding experiences.

I've been able to do very little writing in this diary during the past thirty days. Getting my office in running order again has kept me busy. But events are piling up, and some of them are significant.

I was slated to make a report on the trip to the staff this morning. Our meetings usually last only about half an hour, and today Sherman Adams used up over twenty minutes with odds and ends that he wanted to discuss. This left me with only ten minutes in which to describe a twenty-two-day trip, and I could only give a few episodes. The other staff members have requested a fuller report at another meeting, and many of my associates want to discuss it informally over coffee or drinks.

Many of the staff members seem quite surprised that I have a sense of humor. This amazes me. My sense of humor has gotten me into great difficulties at times, but the ability to find humor in even the toughest situation has often been a godsend.

This week *Ebony* Magazine came out with a picture story on my position here at the White House. It has excited a lot of attention, and I am getting telephone calls and letters from friends about it.

I know I should be happy that so many of the opportunities that I dared hope for in my early youth have come to me. But I am in the stock-taking frame of mind that another approaching birthday always provides and cannot help being soberly impressed by the responsibilities that go with my position. And I have no illusions that any public acclamation which I now enjoy will continue. All that I hope for is that I will feel secure and serene enough in my own soul to buffet the storms that are inevitable.

I honestly have no further ambitions for high position in government or elsewhere. I want to retire from public life as soon as possible. I'd like to have an ordinary commuter's job and be able to go home at night and enjoy my family life. I only want a big enough salary to let me live comfortably in modest circumstances, with a feeling of some security for the future.

April 29, 1957

THE past four days have been harrowing for me. On Thursday I left to go down to Austin, Texas, to fill an engagement at Huston-Tillotson College, where the National Alumni Association of Negro Colleges was holding its annual meeting.

Flying weather has been so uncertain lately that I thought it would be a good idea to go by train and get more rest. The trip turned out to be a nightmare. This has been a full season of tornadoes, floods and storms in the Arkansas–Texas–Missouri area, and we ran right into the middle of them.

The lands were flooded, bridges had been washed out, and for scores of miles along the Missouri-Pacific, gravel had been washed from the roadbed and the tracks were weakened dangerously. We dragged through the flooded terrain and arrived in Austin five hours late. The train had been due in at 10:50 Saturday morning, and my speech was scheduled for the luncheon at one o'clock. We did not get to Austin until 2:45, and I was supposed to get my return train at 3:50! Trains were delayed all along the line, planes were unable to take off, and there was much doubt as to whether the tracks would be open to let any other trains through to St. Louis.

I was rushed to the campus, spoke for twenty minutes, and was delivered back to the station in time to make the 3:50, which would probably be the last train headed north for some time. We just barely got through, and I was in the office Monday morning having spent—except for one hour—four solid days on trains.

I have noticed before that something happens to people who come to Washington to work for the President or in any of the top agencies. Prestige seems to be determined by the size of the office, its appointments, and the number of secretaries one has. If, in addition, a bathroom is available and an American flag— or a flag indicating one's position—this is the pinnacle of achievement. Any new gadget in someone else's office immediately becomes a necessity for the observer. Budget lines are thrown overboard, and the poor devil whose responsibility it is to see that economy is practiced is pilloried day and night.

One of today's most disturbing situations has shaken me considerably. It is very difficult to get really high-class, competent secretarial help that meets the requirements of the White House. Whenever we find qualified persons, we train them and try to keep them as long as possible. They are constantly being lured away by higher pay and greater incentives for future security. With new projects arising almost daily, I always try to have a small pool of them available.

For the past three months I have been trying to keep in the pool one secretary whose job in a former project folded when her boss returned to private industry. She's an A-1 secretary, intelligent and personable, and I had recommended her highly to a new presidential appointee. I was horrified to receive a phone call from the security officer of the highly secret project on which she was to work. He said that they did not feel that this young woman's personal record met the necessary security standards of the project. He came down to see me and proved that for some time, in a prior agency job, she had used an office telephone to place horse-racing bets with a local bookie. Her file also showed that her father and brother had once been arrested for gambling in their home town. While this may not seem to be a heinous crime, it does indicate a weakness, and financial stress can expose anyone to unscrupulous persons and their rackets. Naturally, we could no longer consider her for the new position.

The Negro press, through some of its reporters, has begun to take swipes at the President for his alleged refusal to recognize questions from Negro newspaper people at his weekly press conferences. These articles imply that the President has an aversion to answering possible questions on civil rights, and claim that many times in the past weeks, when Negro reporters have stood up and tried to get his attention, he has ignored them consistently.

This is the sort of thing for which the Negro press and other people expect me to have the answer. I do not believe that the accusation is true, but it is just one more headache for me. I've written a memorandum to Jim Hagerty on this, in the hope that the President will go out of his way to recognize Negro newsmen at his next press conference.

The President returns from his vacation in Augusta today, and there are ominous and pressing international problems that will engage his immediate attention. I do earnestly hope that war will not break out in the Middle East because of the present disturbance and budding civil war in Jordan, but from all indications, there are dark clouds looming over that part of the world.

MAY 21, 1957

THE Prayer Pilgrimage brought nearly 20,000 Negroes from all over the United States to Washington last Friday, and I am relieved that the ceremony went off without any untoward incidents. The city officials had been geared for possible problems, but nearly all are in agreement that this was one of the most orderly assemblages seen in the capital in recent years.

I don't know whether this ceremony will have the desired effect on Government officials and whether the President will see fit to speak out more strongly on civil rights or not. As I have pointed out, he has presented his views many times, and apparently can see no reason why he should utilize a special occasion to repeat them.

It is difficult for me to explain to my friends why the President will not accede to the wishes of Reverend King, Roy Wilkins, and A. Philip Randolph, and admonish the South on its outright flaunting of the Supreme Court's edict on schools. If I let myself, I'd be on the defensive every minute of the day, but I refuse to get into this position. All these people recognize the President's position, and know he has kindly thoughts on this matter, but they are so emotionally involved that they reject any attitude that differs from theirs.

Max Rabb and I have talked for months about the feasibility of a meeting of the President and American Negro leaders to discuss the question of civil rights legislation and the general mental and spiritual status of Negroes. But there has been a unanimous, continuous rejection of this by other presidential advisers. I was therefore taken completely by surprise today when I entered the staff dining room and Sherman Adams called me to his table and said: "Mrs. Ogden Reid, publisher of the New York *Herald Tribune,* was in to see me today. She said that the majority of Negroes in the country feel that the President has let them down on the matter of civil rights. She feels that something has to be done immediately to allay this feeling. What do you think?"

I assured him that Mrs. Reid was right. I said that on every public platform I had occupied I had been attacked during the question-and-answer period by people denouncing the President's apparent lack of interest in the welfare of Negro citizens. I felt that the time had come when some positive steps would have to be taken, and I suggested that the President, at long last, meet and talk with Reverend King and his committee.

Mr. Adams agreed, but he wanted to hold it until Congress had voted the President's budget up or down. At present, Congress is having a field day pruning the budget, and this is one of the most controversial matters ever to come up during the President's tenure in office. It has created a tense and unhappy situation at the White House. Last night the President went back on TV to make a fighting speech on behalf of his budget. All of us will be glad when Congress acts, one way or the other.

JUNE 11, 1957

THE past weekend has been one of the most interesting I have known for some time. While in Chicago on Saturday I was the guest of George S. May at his fabulous Tam O' Shanter Country Club. This place is really a wonder, and the goal of every golfer who is not a member is to play there. In all my travels about the world, I have never seen any place to compare with it. Literally millions have been poured into it to make it the ace of all such establishments. The clubhouse, inside and out, is a dream. Even the locker rooms have wall-to-wall carpeting! And almost any quick service you could ever want is provided, from shoeshining and dry cleaning on up the line. The course is cared for immaculately and is always maintained in a state of perfection. The whole place is almost unbelievable.

I had written George May a personal letter, asking him if he had any objection to my playing his course, explaining to him that I was a Negro and that I had no desire to deceive him or to establish any kind of precedent. I merely wanted the thrill of playing at Tam O' Shanter. He wired right back, saying he would be delighted to have me, so I went out and took three of my friends. We were given really marvelous treatment from arrival to departure, and Mr. May invited us to lunch, and spent more than an hour telling us of his fantastic life and adventures. He is truly one of today's great captains of achievement. He told us that Tam O' Shanter had grossed over $3,000,000 in the past year.

As I was leaving Chicago today a friend taking me to the station said, casually, that the President must be sick again. I had not read the morning papers or heard the early newscasts, so I was quite startled. He went on to say that he had just got the tail end of a newscast in the car, and the reporter mentioned something about the fact that the President had suddenly been taken ill last night. I had him turn on the radio, and we were able to get the last few lines of a broadcast announcing that the President had eaten something that had not agreed with him, had vomited several times during the night, and that Dr. Snyder had spent the night with him. Heart specialists had been called in as a precautionary measure.

When I returned, Hagerty's office reported that the President's condition was in no way related to his heart attack of last year or to his recent ileitis operation.

I was glad to get this official interpretation of his condition, because already wild rumors were flying about Chicago, and newspapers on the stands indicated that the stock market had dropped and that there was general concern throughout the world. It is apparent that from this point on any indisposition of the President will cause apprehension in every capital of the world.

I was happy to return to the office this morning, and at midday to discover that the President was back in his office and had put in over an hour at his desk. All indications are that he is making a speedy recovery from this temporary upset.

June 25, 1957

OVER the weekend I went up to Jackie Robinson's beautiful country home in Stamford, Connecticut, for a visit with him and to play some golf. We'd talked on the phone about where we'd play, and agreed that neither of us wanted to spend hours waiting on a public course. (Jackie had been invited to join a private club near where he lives, but subsequently two or three of its members had complained, and he had not wanted to join under those circumstances.)

Jackie called his friend André Baruch, radio-TV commentator for ABC, who invited us to be his guests at the swank Fenwick Country Club outside of White Plains. We had a wonderful afternoon there. André's wife, the former Bea Wain, made us feel welcome and at home. My golf was atrocious, but I got a big kick out of the whole deal and had lots of interesting conversation and good fun.

Carl Rowan, a house guest of Jackie's, had come on from Minneapolis with his wife to discuss writing a book about Jackie. Carl has made quite a name for himself as a writer and is one of the few Negroes in this country who is working as a feature reporter on a prominent daily newspaper. He is with the Minneapolis *Star*.

There has not been too much excitement around the White House the past few days. The President has been meeting with Congressional leaders at breakfast in an effort to become better acquainted with them and also to promote his legislative program. It seems to be a good idea, because even those of the opposite political faith are bound to be impressed when they are personal guests of the President.

Max Rabb and I are still trying to devise an acceptable method for a visit of prominent Negro leaders to the White House. Phil Randolph has just written the President a third letter, renewing his request for this, but he has now asked to bring sixteen other persons with him. Max has thrown up trial balloons on this matter with the presidential assistants, and they are not at all enthusiastic. In the first place, sixteen people are too many; in the second place, they feel this might not be a strategic time to hold such a meeting—when the civil rights bill is being cuffed around by Congress. The bill has already passed the House, and the southern members of the Senate are now engaged in delaying tactics to try to keep it bottled up until Congress adjourns. Any visit with the President by Negro leaders at this time could be interpreted by the Senators as pressure to make them act. There is also the problem that if we honor the request of these Negro leaders, it means that the White House will have to accede to requests of southern governors, southern attorneys general; Americans of Italian and Greek descent who want to talk about immigration; Jewish people on Israel; Hungarian and Lithuanian people on independence, etc.

The question has also been raised as to what these leaders would say to the press when they leave the President. They could not quote him, of course, but would they engage in provocative statements?

These are the usual summer "dog days" in Washington, and at times the heat is almost unbearable. I have started my annual exercise of looking for better living quarters. The newspapers are full of attractive offers of houses or apartments to rent, but none are available to me, because of my color. I am sorely tired of driving by and seeing the horrible ratholes and dilapidated houses that are advertised "For Colored" in the newspapers. This is one of the nightmares of a responsible Negro in almost any community in the country. He cannot, without struggling and fighting, find a decent place to live. No matter what opportunities are available to him in any other capacity, it is more important to him that he live in a comfortable, desirable place.

Here is also one of the major stumbling blocks to any complete integration in this country. The philosophy inevitably breaks down when it comes to Negroes and whites sharing the same neighborhoods. This is one of the most compelling reasons forcing me to think about leaving Washington.

Last night I went to the Liberian Embassy to a cocktail party for Vice-President William Tolbert, who is here on an informal visit. It was a very pleasant evening, and I saw many of those who had traveled with me in Liberia and numerous officials of that country who are in America for various reasons.

AUGUST 1, 1957

I HAVE been increasingly alarmed in the past few days by the apparent weakening of the Administration's stand on civil rights legislation. At a recent news conference, the President, inadvertently or otherwise, admitted that there were some phases of this legislation that he did not understand. This is shocking. It is an Administration bill that is being debated, and subject matter of this nature seldom goes forward without the President having been briefed on every facet of it. The opponents of this legislation seized upon this statement by the President to point out that this was clever legislation, designed to humiliate the South and so laden with secret gimmicks that even the President of the United States could not understand it. It has caused considerable embarrassment to many Administration officials.

I have been bombarded with telephone calls and letters from people all over the country who are holding me personally responsible for the President's equivocating attitude. They feel that my job is to keep him informed of the desires of Negro citizens in every avenue of American life, and when the President makes statements or takes action detrimental to their cause, they feel that I have been some kind of traitor or have gone "soft" since becoming a member of the Eisenhower staff.

I recently talked to Louis Martin, Executive Editor of the Chicago *Defender,* and in my estimation one of the best editorial writers in the field. The *Defender* is not favorable to the Admin-

166] BLACK MAN IN THE WHITE HOUSE

istration, but Martin is a thoroughly objective writer and can be fair when he has all the facts before him. It is his feeling that if the Administration—even at this late date—can get through some kind of effective legislation that will protect the Negro's right to vote in the South, it can gain back some of the ground it has lost in the past few weeks through weak leadership.

Another hassle arose a few weeks ago about Louis Armstrong, the great jazz musician, who was appearing in a week's program at the Carter Baron Amphitheatre. Great pressure had been brought on the White House to have Louis call on the President. He finally did get to the staff mess for lunch with two or three staff members, but he did not get in to see Eisenhower. Bernie Shanley called me to say that the State Department and others were putting tremendous heat on him to have Armstrong see the President, as he was soon going on a goodwill tour abroad for the State Department. Shanley wanted to know whether I thought the appointment should be allowed. I admitted that Armstrong has done a great deal for our country abroad, but I added that by no stretch of the imagination is he representative of the aspirations and hopes of our millions of ordinary Negro citizens. As a matter of fact, there are many people who resent Louis's clowning, and feel that while he is superior in the field of entertainment, this does not give him great ability in other fields.

I told Shanley that I did not see how Armstrong could be admitted to the White House for a personal visit to the President when we had tactfully refused to honor the requests of such stalwart Negro leaders as A. Philip Randolph, Martin Luther King, Roy Wilkins and others. It would be difficult to try to explain to the Negro press and Negro citizens how Louis Armstrong would have more priority on the President's time than these eminent and responsible Negroes.

August 7, 1957

WORD has just come down from the Hill that, by common consent on both sides of the floor, the Senate will shut off debate on the civil rights bill this afternoon and take a vote on the measure as it now stands. Predictions from competent newsmen indicate that the bill will be passed by a comfortable majority. It will then be sent posthaste to a joint House and Senate committee to iron out differences, and then on to the White House for the President's approval or veto.

It has been my position all along that an emasculated civil rights bill is worse than none at all; since the original version of the bill has been completely riddled by amendments, it is weak and will probably prove ineffectual if enacted. I sincerely hope the President will veto it. But I have just been informed at staff meeting this morning that certain executives of the NAACP are requesting civil rights supporters on the Hill to vote for this watered-down measure on the grounds that half a loaf is better than no bread at all.

This is shocking to me. For more than forty years the NAACP has been uncompromising in its attitude that human rights are not to be dealt out piecemeal to American citizens, or should there be legislation indicating willingness on the part of the Government to insure and protect only certain rights. Yesterday the *Afro-American* came out with an editorial supporting the half-loaf theory. Since Carl Murphy, the publisher of *Afro,* is one of the prominent board members of the NAACP, this would seem to confirm the information that has been given me that the association is in favor of a compromise. It is strange to see the NAACP agreeing with men of the South like Senator James Eastland of Mississippi, Lyndon Johnson, and Senator Richard Russell of Georgia! This in itself should be a warning that the bill has no substance. Great pressure is being used from all sides to get the President in the mood to sign whatever kind of bill comes out from the joint committee.

August 15, 1957

As SOON as I hit the office this morning there was a call from Max Rabb to come to his office right away. We are trying to assemble telegrams and letters from prominent Negro citizens who have urged the President to stand firm and not sign a watered-down civil rights bill. We have telegrams from Mrs. Jessie Vann, publisher of the Pittsburgh *Courier,* Jackie Robinson, several bishops, John Sengstacke, publisher of the Chicago *Defender,* and others. It is a promising response, and we hope that this is the beginning of an avalanche of protests against the half-loaf philosophy advanced early in the week by the NAACP and other organizations.

Val Washington has made calls around the country and talked with various people, and he indicated that after his talk with Carl Murphy, the *Afro-American* would run another editorial stating that the House must stand firm on its original version of the bill, that it pass, and must not accept weakening amendments or compromises from the Senate version. It would appear that despite Murphy's original editorial, he later realized that this position was not in keeping with his paper's solid reputation of fighting for complete and absolute citizenship rights for Negroes.

This activity, of course, has brought a torrid tempo into my life, and these are sleepless nights and heavy days. I am preparing a speech for delivery in Atlanta before the National Alliance of Postal Employees in a few days. This will give me an opportunity to hit this half-loaf theory hard. I am sorry that it will mean treading on the toes of some friends and persons for whom I have had high regard for many years, but in the area of human rights and simple justice I cannot permit anything to interfere with my conscience or convictions.

SEPTEMBER 10, 1957

THE past ten days have been tragic ones in which press, radio and television have revealed the bitter struggle going on in Arkansas, Alabama and Tennessee as efforts are made by Negroes to enroll in white schools in accordance with the Supreme Court decision of 1954. Governor Faubus has called out the Arkansas militia on the pretext of restraining violence and maintaining law and order, but the presence of these troops has seemed to encourage a disregard for law and human feelings. The newspaper pictures of Negro children being booed and jostled by enraged white crowds assembled around the schools are haunting.

The Mayor of Little Rock said that the Governor is making a political grandstand play, since there was no evidence that there would be violence or that common sense would not prevail in the city, as it had in the past. Faubus has been adamant in his refusal to withdraw the troops, and now a Federal judge has ordered the Attorney General to apply for an injunction against the Governor to prevent him from interfering with carrying out a court decree that Negroes will be admitted to Little Rock's schools. In Birmingham yesterday, a prominent Negro minister, attempting to enroll his own child and several others in the city school, was brutally assaulted, kicked, and beaten with brass knuckles and chains wielded by maniacal white men. He was taken to a hospital for treatment.

In Nashville, Tennessee—a normally calm and civilized city—

sermons of hate, spread by professional race-baiter John Kasper, have inflamed that city, and violence and distress are imminent. The latest radio reports said that one school there was destroyed by an explosion early this morning.

This whole situation has the President in a difficult spot. He has stated that he will use every legal means in his power to see that the Supreme Court decision is carried out. However, he had previously stated that he could imagine no situation where he would use troops to enforce the decree of the court. He is therefore faced with the problem of what his next step will be. It is a sickening, discouraging moment as we sit here and watch this country becoming consumed by racial hatred and animosity.

It is a time when little dictators are born—a situation in which the tactics of Hitler and Mussolini come to the fore. With people emotionally upset and distracted, it is a perfect moment for the rabid to spread unrest and to lead the assault against democratic institutions and policies.

I have been powerless to do anything. The President's advisers have not asked me my thinking on these matters, and I am too well-schooled in protocol to advance any uninvited ideas.

In my desperation I called Tom Stephens, former Appointment Secretary to the President and presently assisting Governor Adams in some areas, to ask him to sit down and discuss the entire situation with me. Tom has more political savvy than almost anyone else in the White House, and he is a man of action.

I told him that I felt that the time had come when the President must take a more effective stand on this situation and perhaps speak out to the country about it. He can no longer use platitudes and give lip service to democratic ideals; he must take some positive action that will put the Governor of Arkansas and other persons of his ilk back in their place. It is just not enough to make a speech to the country; there also must be some program of action.

Tom said he had already talked to Sherman Adams and Jerry Persons this morning about the same thing, but he had no hope that anything would be done about it. He suggested that the President call Governor Faubus' bluff by asking him if it were true that the only reason he had troops in the streets of Little Rock was the inability of local police officials to control the situation. If this is true, then the President could use his emergency fund to give the Governor the money he might need to employ additional civilians as police officers. We, of course, realize that this is not the true reason for the troops being there, but at least it would call the Governor's bluff and show that the President is serious in his efforts to remove the troops from the streets of Little Rock.

The other problem I discussed with Tom was the possible composition of the civil rights commission that the President must appoint to carry out one of the provisions of the civil rights law. There have been rumors at the White House that a Negro will not be a member of the six-man commission. This seems incredible to me, but it could well be that this is the thinking of some of the advisers. I do know that scores of Negro names have come to the White House from ambitious persons seeking nomination to the commission, and a lot of these names actually scare me. One of the difficulties of a Negro's becoming a member is the fact he will have to be approved by the Senate and that any professional social worker or member of the NAACP, etc., will have a hard time being confirmed. What will be needed will be a name that stands above the crowd and that has not been identified with active participation in any of the civil rights efforts.

I talked to Max Rabb about this before I talked with Stephens, and Max told me in confidence that the only name that had been considered so far was that of Dr. Frederick Patterson, former president of Tuskegee Institute. He felt that Patterson would be acceptable to the South and that his experience there would be valuable to the commission.

I pointed out that I felt that since Dr. Patterson had left Tuskegee and had become the head of the Phelps-Stokes Fund he had grown in stature and had indicated his real ability. Unless someone else who would have no difficulty being confirmed by the Senate could be found, I would certainly have no objection to Dr. Patterson being named to the commission.

The only thing that annoys me about this whole matter is the fact that things like this that vitally involve the Negro race are decided by men who have had little or no experience or contact with Negroes, and who must base their decisions almost entirely upon their own meager knowledge—or often upon the suggestions given them by social or political friends who may be equally uninformed.

I have repeatedly stated that I would not, under any circumstances, be the President's full-time adviser on minority problems, but I should think that when it comes to a question of choosing the right person for the right post, my intimate knowledge of the Negro community would be of some value. It is not a question of knowing all the answers—or even being unbiased in some opinions—but at least I would strive to protect the interests of the President and would recommend persons who are stalwart and responsible representatives of Negro ambitions and desires.

I don't know where this will all end or what the final outcome will be, but I wish my own state of mind was less disturbed right now. Catherine and I are to be married in just a week. I have a deep need for someone to share the burdens and problems that I have had to carry alone for so long.

OCTOBER 7, 1957

I RETURNED to the office this morning after our three-week honeymoon. I was anxious to get back to my desk. There have been some grave happenings in these past few weeks, and I knew that many matters needed my personal attention.

I had hardly put foot in the White House before Sherman Adams called me to come to see him at once. Our meeting was delayed temporarily because Senator H. Alexander Smith of New Jersey was with him, and several people were waiting in his outer office, hoping to get a few minutes with him.

Under the civil rights law, the President must appoint an investigating commission which will make recommendations to the Congress on the plague spots it uncovers. Up to now, the President has not appointed a member of this commission, and it is obvious that he has been combing names that have been submitted to him.

Sherman Adams wanted to talk to me about several that had been given to him for consideration. He asked me—in strictest confidence and in the form of hypothetical questions—what my reaction would be if Adlai Stevenson was made a member of the commission; or a man like Justice Stanley Reed of the Supreme Court. Obviously, on such a commission, all political faiths and all shades of opinion—southern as well as northern—should be represented. I thought Mr. Adams' suggestions were good ones. Stevenson would contribute real ability and stature, and it would be a political coup if the President named the man who had opposed him in a campaign; it would show a desire to handle the subject on an objective and nonpartisan basis.

Sherman Adams doubted that Stevenson would accept, but hoped he would. He also asked me what I thought of Ernest Wilkins. I told him that I felt that Secretary of Labor Wilkins was well qualified, that the Senate would confirm him without difficulty, and that he was esteemed by both Negro and white citizens. He is an able man and could bring objective thinking to this delicate problem. Then Adams asked: "If Wilkins turns this down, whom do you suggest?"

This was a difficult question to answer. While there are scores of highly educated, widely respected Negroes in this country, the character of this commission demands an exceptional Negro member. It is obvious that we cannot appoint any outstanding professional "race-saver" or anyone who has been prominent in the civil rights fight. This would make the Southerners see red from the very beginning and would cause a fight on the Senate floor when it came to confirmation. Everyone has agreed that Ralph Bunche would be an excellent choice, but he could not serve, because he's connected with the United Nations—an international body. Jackie Robinson has developed significantly in the past year, but the current feeling is that he is so adamant in his convictions that it might be difficult to effect any kind of compromise between him and the other members. Dr. Patterson has been ruled out on the grounds that he is a member of the "Old School," and because his former connections with Tuskegee would handicap him in trying to convince Negroes that he held a modern viewpoint on integration, etc. Other Negroes were rejected for various reasons. Mr. Adams has given me the next few hours in which to try to think of someone who can meet the qualifications he outlined. It is a difficult task, and I am hoping that Ernest Wilkins will not turn down the request.

October 9, 1957

WE HAD the usual pre-press staff conference this morning, and one of the things that came up was a story in the evening papers about Ghana's Finance Minister, H. A. Gbedemah, who had been evicted from a Howard Johnson restaurant in Dover, Delaware, the night before, because "colored people are not allowed to eat in here."

Gbedemah, in this country on official business, stopped at the restaurant for breakfast and was crudely insulted by a waitress and requested to leave by the manager. It has created a first-class international incident.

With Mr. Gbedemah was his private secretary William Sutherland, a young American from New Jersey, and a lifetime friend of mine, who had gone to live in Ghana many years ago. Perhaps this kind of treatment in a Delaware restaurant was not new to him as an American Negro, but it certainly shocked his boss.

On top of the Little Rock situation, this is the kind of thing that makes our country look bad abroad and gives the world the idea that we are first-class hypocrites when we prate about our wonderful democracy.

The President was incensed, and without any prompting from his aides, invited Mr. Gbedemah to have breakfast with him at the White House the next morning. This gesture on the part of the President is an eloquent rebuttal to the Delaware treatment.

Later in the day Jim Hagerty called me. There was a story on the ticker that Mr. Gbedemah would be leaving the country the next day. Jim was disturbed, because he wanted to know whether or not there had been a slip-up in signals and the breakfast invitation had been ignored.

Here was an incredible state of circumstances. The Vice-President and I had been entertained in Mr. Gbedemah's home during our trip to Ghana last March. Jim asked me to take the responsibility of phoning him at his suite in the Waldorf in New York to find out whether the acceptance for the White House breakfast the next day was firm. I could not get Gbedemah in New York, but called the embassy in Washington, and the second secretary assured me that the invitation had been accepted and that the minister would be there.

October 10, 1957

MR. GBEDEMAH arrived on time for his breakfast date with the President this morning and remained with him for over an hour and a half. Bill Sutherland spent this time with me, and we went over to the front steps of the big house in time to see Gbedemah saying good-bye to the President and being photographed with him and the Vice-President. The newspaper corps was out in force, as well as all the photographers, who had a Roman holiday with this distinguished visitor. He was very photogenic in his flowing African garb, and his handling of the press questioning was deft and intelligent. He seemed highly pleased with his visit to the President, and I gathered that it had erased his resentment.

Sometimes great good can result from an evil situation. Governor Faubus may have used bad judgment in calling out the National Guard in Little Rock, and setting off a mob violence that had to be quelled by Federal troops sent in by the President, but the resulting publicity did more to make Americans conscious of this plague spot in race relations than anything else could have done. Similarly, this Gbedemah incident has pointed up the state of the Negro's position in another area of this country. On the whole, it is difficult for any thinking American to be complacent about the fact that color can deny any human being the right to use a place of public accommodation.

I am off today to keep speaking engagements in Minnesota.

October 17, 1957

LAST week my wife and I received an invitation from the President and Mrs. Eisenhower to an evening reception planned for Queen Elizabeth and Prince Philip of England for tonight.

This was quite a day in our house. Catherine is just back from Chicago, where she's been closing her former home and arranging to have her furniture shipped East, and she was in a very natural state of excitement about our invitation to the royal reception.

Tonight was my own first time at an evening affair of this kind. A single person just can't function effectively at such parties; wives are a vital part of the social scheme in Washington. All evening I found myself glowing with appreciation for my marital status!

The guests assembled in the ground floor reception room to await the summons upstairs. It was a very elegant gathering, but I have never been more proud of anyone than I was of Catherine; she was particularly beautiful in every way.

We were both aware that we were in some kind of spotlight, being the only Negroes present, and most of the guests knew that Catherine was a recent bride—always a source of interest to other women. We walked into the reception room with a heavy sense of responsibility. I was thankful that I knew many of the guests, and the really big men of the staff were quick to bring their wives around for introductions and to offer congratulations. There was the usual small group which didn't know quite what to do, but I was more amused than annoyed over their behavior.

All couples finally in the line, we walked up the beautiful marble steps from the ground floor to the first-floor foyer where the Marine Corps Band was playing, and we moved through the Red Room into the Blue Room. The President, the Queen, Mrs. Eisenhower, and Prince Philip were standing on a slightly raised platform, receiving the guests. Each man preceded his wife and gave his name to the military aide who in turn gave it to the President, who passed it on to the Queen. The President spotted me, even before the military aide could get my name, and in typical Eisenhower fashion, said: "Hello there! This is the first time I've seen you since your marriage. Congratulations!" The Queen was smiling at this, and when Catherine shook hands with the President, he wished her happiness and told the Queen that she was a new bride. Catherine was so busy looking at Philip (as were most of the women) that she didn't even notice what the Queen was wearing! Mrs. Eisenhower received her in a manner that affected Catherine deeply, saying, "Oh yes, this is the bride. You are radiant tonight! I want to welcome you, my dear, and wish you every possible happiness."

After shaking hands with Philip, we both sort of stumbled the rest of the way to the East Room, where the musicale was to be held.

After the President and the Queen had received all the guests, the Queen came into the East Room on the arm of the President, and Mrs. Eisenhower on the arm of the Prince, and they sat in the front of a small platform. Fred Waring's Pennsylvanians and his choir gave a forty-minute program that was a combination of American folk songs, patriotic airs, and songs about holidays that have been developed in this country over many years. It concluded with the "Battle Hymn of the Republic," one of the President's favorites. Then we all stood up, and the President said: "Good night, friends," and left with the royal guests.

We went into the State Dining Room to a buffet champagne supper. This was an opportunity to exchange greetings with staff members and other friends, and it was a pleasant hour.

The Vice-President and Mrs. Nixon were particularly glad to greet Catherine, and told her that they were very fond of her husband. The Vice-President quipped: "Keep your eye on him and make him stay in line." She got a big kick out of this. He also said: "We couldn't get to your wedding, but we hope to see you real soon."

The good nights were friendly, and many people came up to say how happy they were to meet my wife and that they looked forward to seeing us socially. I was pleased that so many of the male members of the staff remarked on what a stunning woman Catherine is and how fortunate I am to have her. This I believe too.

October 20, 1957

> Once to every man and nation
> Comes the moment to decide . . .[1]

THESE lines from Lowell have been ringing in my ears for days. What they are saying is that the time has come for me to sit down and decide once and for all what I am going to do about remaining in this job.

Of late I dread going to the office. The letters and phone calls are from irate friends and citizens who are fed up with the President's moderate stand on civil rights and allied problems. They accuse him of refusing to assume the moral leadership of the country at this time, and with resolution and affirmative speech, take a stand in favor of every American having the right to walk this land in dignity and peace, unfettered by any restricting bonds.

I feel ridiculous standing on platforms all over the country, trying to defend the Administration's record on civil rights. While it is true that the Administration has made more significant appointments than any other in recent history and that gestures have been made—such as sending troops into Little Rock to maintain law and order so that Negro children can go to school—there is no strong, clarion, commanding voice from the White House, righteously indignant over the plight of the 18,000,000 Negroes in the United States, who are fighting for their God-given rights of human dignity and self-determination.

At this critical time in human history American Negroes have

1 *The Present Crisis*, James Russell Lowell, 1844.

only one way of estimating friend or foe—either you are for us or you are against us. If you are for us, then you will stand with us in the four corners of the land and cry out against the sins of oppression.

Well, specifically, what is my problem? Didn't I expect abuse and slander in a political setup? Yes. Didn't I expect disagreement and bitter opposition to some Administration policies? Yes. Did I expect that the President was going to champion Negro rights at every turn? No. Did I expect to be popular with Negroes because of my position in the White House? No. What then?

First of all, any Negro who is worth his salt must look at any vital question from two sides—first as a Negro, and then as an American. This double responsibility is a heavy cross upon the mind of any black who must make a decision in a dual society.

Then, no matter how high you ride on a job like mine or how acceptable you are to your colleagues or how triumphant you are in your accomplishments, you must always keep in the back of your mind the fact that after this pomp and ceremony is all over you must return to a Negro community to live out your days. If in the eyes of this exacting, demanding, righteous group one has not—while having the opportunity—planted his flag high on the mountaintop of uncompromised citizenship, he is an exile and a leper. The problem? How to be loyal to two opposing responsibilities.

As I have done for years, I will spend the weekend in the beauty of the Berkshires, and there in quiet and peace make a final and binding decision on my future with the Administration.

October 21, 1957

EARLY Monday morning the White House called me, announcing that Sherman Adams wanted to talk to me. In his typical fashion—without saying hello, or any other preliminary—

he asked me: "Fred, how much of your time do you give to your job?" I was trying to think what he was driving at, and said that my job consumed a great deal of time. He said: "Well, maybe you won't be able to do what I have in mind, but I wish you would talk to Arthur Larson about it. We're thinking about making you an assistant to Larson in his new post." Having no idea what Arthur Larson was going to do, I tried to beg off, but the Governor would have none of it and told me to talk to him after I had talked to Larson.

This is very disquieting. I have established a routine in my office, things are going well, and I have no desire to change positions or situations.

I went over to the United States Information Agency to see Larson in the afternoon. He had just resigned his position as director of USIA, and the President had appointed him a special assistant on the White House staff. The newspapers had indicated that Larson would probably be engaged in international fields—perhaps in psychological warfare—but no one knew for sure exactly what his new assignment would be. He confided to me that he was to become the principal speech writer for the President, establishing a White House speech-writing section manned by himself and two assistants. The idea was to develop an agency that could collect material for speeches and then write them in such a fashion that the President would appear able and scholarly whenever he had a pronouncement to make.

The old hodgepodge method of developing presidential speeches was out. Under that system, the President had first accepted invitations to speak and it would later be decided what area he would cover. For example, if the speech was to be about agriculture, the Secretary of Agriculture would send rough notes over to the White House for possible use in the speech. If it was to be about civil rights, the Attorney General's office would offer suggestions, etc. Various staff members versed in these subjects would try their hands at developing certain segments of the speech. There was always a mad rush to make the deadline, and each speech had to pass through a half dozen hands before it was ready to go to the President for his approval.

Larson's idea is to have on hand up-to-date material and rough drafts on all vital areas on which the President might wish to speak. For example, a speech developed on civil rights would be ready when the proper occasion arose. In other words, except in national or international crises, the subject matter of the speech would determine when the President spoke.

Larson told me that they had scoured the country, but had not come up with anyone they felt was suited for the job. He said that he had collected all my speeches over a period of two years, read them, and had the feeling that I was just the man he needed to assist him. I told him that *I* felt he needed a professional speech writer. He said no, that what the job called for was a person who had a spiritual feeling about the President and the Administration—someone who was truly saturated with this atmosphere and who knew the President as a man and was dedicated to him. I was the one for the job.

All this was flattering, but I had no desire to accept. My position in the White House has been unique. To Negro Americans, I am a symbol of achievement. The Negro press watches every move I make, and would be the first to question my move from Administrative Officer in the President's office to a job as assistant to a presidential special assistant. Even though the White House calls this a promotion, it would be difficult to explain to the Negro public.

There are other factors. Every Negro delegation of any consequence that comes to Washington wants to come to the White House to see me. I welcome these opportunities to get to know such groups better and to have them get to know me. It has been possible to meet them in my offices because of the spaciousness of the rooms in the Executive Office Building, but the new Larson setup will have a very small cubbyhole in the East Wing of the White House in which it would not be possible to entertain large or even small groups.

On my own, I have been putting out a lot of "brush fires" around the country during the past two years, as well as making scores of speeches. The new job would be a confining one.

I argued all of this out with Larson and Staff Secretary Goodpaster, but neither of them would budge, and they have indicated that it has been decided at the highest possible level that

I will take the job. This would seem to put an end to all discussion. I move into this new post with great trepidation, and can only hope that I will be pleasantly surprised by the outcome.

October 29, 1957

DR. WILLIAM J. BARNES of Great Barrington, Massachusetts, is one of the really great practicing Christians I know. With the exception of my father, no man has made the impact on my life that he has. All my adult life he has been my friend, father confessor and benefactor. His beautiful estate in the Berkshires has been my refuge and sanctuary during the difficult years since the war. I have always gone there when vital questions plagued my soul, and it was there this week that he helped me to come to grips with my problem.

After a sojourn at "Point of View," the Barnes' place, I can understand Thoreau and other great nature lovers. There in the woods, with an ax in my hands, I literally carved out a course of action and chopped down all the little obstacles in my head that were barring the way to peace of mind and firm decision.

I resolved to stay on at the White House. This opportunity of service to both a President and a race has never before come to a Negro American. It may be a long time in coming again. To put personal difficulties above even a little good that might flow from this relationship is cowardice. But the real clincher in the decision is this—it was a struggle to get there and the opposition was severe. It is quite possible that if I resign, no similar appointment will be made. The Administration is not obligated by personal pledge to any other Negro. Then, too, my very presence on the staff does do some good. While I am certain that many things are not done despite my presence, it does prevent some anti-Negro acts from being attempted. Also, as long as I am there there will always be a pipeline to the President and the top members of Government.

As to my present and future standing with members of my own race, it is out of my hands. I can only hope that they will recognize my efforts to chart a sensible, sane course in a position with little choice.

I could never be disloyal to Dwight Eisenhower. I realize that he is straining every nerve to serve, to the best of his ability, the interest and the welfare of all the people of the United States. In his decisions he has to estimate what is best for all the people, and while he should show concern and deep interest in the ignoble plight of 10 percent of the population, his ultimate decisions must be based on what he determines is best for the welfare of the whole.

This point of view does not dismiss the President's derelictions as regards the Negro, but it does seem to me to be a mature and nonemotional view of a difficult human problem.

For a minority member in this kind of a spot anywhere, there is always the haunting specter that to quit gives delight and comfort to your enemies and oppressors. It indicates that you could not take it. It makes them line up more solidly against any newcomer, and the opposition becomes more active and determined.

I will continue to press for what I believe to be right, and I will not compromise with conscience or principle on my brothers' basic aspirations for human dignity and human rights. I would prefer to be fired for aggressiveness and forthrightness, rather than resign because our petitioning had fallen on deaf ears.

NOVEMBER 9, 1957

THIS has really been a hectic week. Things have been happening from all angles, and I've had little opportunity to catch my breath. First of all, there was a shift of my physical office from the Executive Office Building to the East Wing of the White House. Even though this appears to be a temporary move, I am sorry to have to give up my spacious accommodations for this small new suite. To the unwitting, I suppose there is more prestige in being in the White House than in the EOB, but for many practical reasons—including peace and quiet and being a short distance away from the accelerated tempo in the White House—the EOB is a much more desirable place.

As soon as word got around that I was to move, there was a universal scramble to take over my former offices. I can understand this, because offices in the EOB building are larger than any others in Washington. They were designed for the State Department and Army and Navy bigwigs back in the days of pomp and ceremony, and have man-sized fireplaces, tiled bathrooms, ceiling-to-floor window casements, etc.

I've had no opportunity to get started on my new assignment. It is a frightening one! Mr. Larson has not talked to me at any length about what is expected, but he has already handed me a portfolio containing departmental and Cabinet officers' reports on their functions, and this material will be culled, sieved, and developed for the President's State of the Union address.

Heretofore it has taken scores of persons to develop the State of the Union Message. It is a tedious, confining, alarming task. The major problem is not what to put in, but what can be left out judiciously. At this critical period in American history, it is doubly difficult to write a presidential speech that can be delivered to Congress within an hour. I hope Mr. Larson is not expecting me to develop the speech, but rather to give an assist on making suggestions on what it should contain.

Another startling thing happened this week. Bernard Shanley resigned his position as Appointment Secretary to the President. Shanley has been absent from his post for weeks, assisting in the gubernatorial race in New Jersey. The party suffered an ignominious defeat in this election when our candidate Malcolm Forbes was soundly trounced by the incumbent Governor Robert Meyner. Meyner has been an able and popular governor, and it was apparent to me all along that Forbes could not defeat him. Forbes is an aggressive, effective and youthful state senator, and is probably as handicapped by his wealth as by his intense desire to be governor. He worked very hard for the nomination and for his election, and resorted to spectacular campaigning. Shanley spent considerable time in New Jersey, assisting in this campaign, and reports indicated that some of his speeches had not set too well with top party officials or with the rank and file of the party.

It has been known for some time that he was interested in securing the nomination for U. S. Senator from New Jersey for himself, and the daily papers have indicated that he will contest for Senator Alexander Smith's seat in next year's April primaries. Shanley's announcement has set off a real Donnybrook among Republican politicians in New Jersey. Senator Smith is in his late seventies, and it is not known whether he will run again. There are many ambitious young candidates in New Jersey who want the nomination, and this situation promises a knock-down, drag-out primary fight in the Republican party next spring.

Yesterday fifteen prominent Negro newspaper publishers came to the White House for a meeting with Sherman Adams. They are holding one of their quarterly sessions in Washington, and sought this opportunity to present to the Governor, for the attention of the President, matters pertaining to the unrest among Negroes in this country due to the Little Rock situation and the wave of violence now sweeping the South.

I did not know that this meeting had been scheduled, and it was only by pure accident that I found out about it. However, after the meeting got underway in the old Cabinet Room, Sherman Adams had Max Rabb phone and invite me to attend and to sit next to him.

The newsmen made an able and objective presentation, and Mr. Adams skillfully fielded the hot ones thrown his way. The newsmen felt that the President had skirted all around the problem and had not stated effectively that he was for integration. They felt that his press statements to the effect that no matter how he felt about it, this was the law of the land and he intended to enforce it, indicated a negative attitude and gave the impression that he was not for integration, but was merely carrying out his legal responsibilities. They requested that the President make a speech on the necessity for respecting Constitutional recommendations, Supreme Court decisions, etc., and that he leave no doubt about the fact that America must accept the inevitability of integration.

Sherman Adams tried to point out the fact that Eisenhower is the President of all the country and could not make speeches designed to influence or castigate any segment of the American public. However, he told the publishers that he would like them to write the kind of speech that they thought the President should deliver, and send it to him. This of course does not mean that the President will deliver such a speech, but merely that Adams and the rest of us are interested in what these men would like the President to say.

The Governor asked me to make any remarks I cared to, but I merely said that I was glad that these men, who were molders of Negro opinion, had this opportunity to meet and talk face to face with the President's assistant. One of the first questions always asked me is: "What about this man Adams?" For the first time, the publishers were able to see him in action, and he was his usual terse, crisp, unsmiling self. He never dodges any issue and hits squarely from the shoulder; he neither appeases nor promises. I am certain that the publishers left the White House with the impression that Adams is tough but unquestionably fair.

November 26, 1957

THIS is an anxious day as we await the latest bulletin on the President's health. He suffered a chill on his return from meeting the King of Morocco at the airport yesterday, and his doctors ordered him to bed immediately. He had to miss a state dinner for the King, and the Vice-President acted as host in his stead, escorting Mrs. Eisenhower to dinner.

Any illness of the world's number one statesman throws foreign relations into a tailspin. The stock market always reacts to a president's illness, and there is a general feeling of anxiety and dismay throughout the nation.

4 P.M.

The latest bulletin on the President's health has just confirmed our worst fears; he apparently suffered a slight stroke. There seems to be some confusion on the exact diagnosis, but the bulletins indicate that he has suffered a speech impairment, although this has improved since last night.

DECEMBER 3, 1957

I HAD lunch to day with Major General Synder and Gabe Hauge, and the topic of conversation, very naturally, was the President's health.

Both the country and the world are still reeling under the impact of the slight stroke that the President had last week, and despite all signs of rapid recovery, there is a degree of apprehension among staff members. We alone know the tremendous burdens and problems the President carries and how discouraging it must be to him, despite physical frailties, to be subject to so much abuse and speculation—not only from the press but from his own party—over whether he should resign. And now everyone seems to be a medical doctor and able to diagnose the President's problems and troubles from afar. It is a very confusing situation.

Dr. Snyder indicated that the President is getting along very well and that perhaps his greatest battle will be overcoming the depressing fear that any subsequent ailments, no matter how slight, could be attributed to the results of his stroke. It is difficult for a patient to remain cheerful under such circumstances, no matter how obvious his rate of recovery. There is always the dread of a recurrence.

Snyder and Hauge apparently were sticking close to the scene, and before lunch was over, they were handed proposed preliminary press bulletins to edit.

The afternoon papers indicate that the NATO trip is off and

that Hagerty is speeding back from Paris, where he has been setting up preliminary plans for the NATO conference next month.

All officials are trying to maintain an outward calm, but all of us are deeply affected by this latest illness. We feel certain that if the President determines he is not physically able to carry on in a satisfactory manner, he will resign. His complete honesty and dedication to his country will make him think long and hard about his duty. While the bulletins indicate that rest is the primary need at the moment, we all hope and pray that this will solve the situation. We can only stand by and mark time and wait.

December 4, 1957

THIS latest illness has been the subject of much editorial comment and feature writing. With Hagerty away, Associate Press Secretary Anne Wheaton handled the original reports. It is unfortunate that she should have been subjected to such a prominent incident so early in her tenure at the White House. This kind of situation is enough to try the soul of a veteran. Not only that, but it was obvious that she could only give the press what she had received from the doctors and that she was in no position to elaborate on or give technical details of what was happening. As a result, she got unshirted hell from the press, and it was fortunate that Hagerty flew back from Paris immediately and took charge. With a few deft strokes, he was able to repair some of the damage, but now the newspapers have taken another tack and are accusing him of smoothing things over and giving oily reports about a situation that is more severe than has been indicated. At any rate, I was glad to get, firsthand, General Snyder's reasoning behind this whole situation.

He said he felt that the President would be able to go to the NATO meeting. He thought this would be good therapy, because the President wanted to go very badly, feeling that his presence was necessary to save this organization. General Snyder said that they would make every effort to cut down on the number of dinners and luncheons the President would have to go to, and would conserve his strength as much as possible.

As of this writing, the NATO meeting is still more than ten days away, and as yet there has been no positive statement that the President will go to Paris. However, from what General Snyder has said, the chances would seem good, if he has no setback between now and the time he should take off.

December 6, 1957

LIONEL HAMPTON, the celebrated bandleader, came to the White House today to see Max Rabb and me before taking off on another world tour. Hampton has been a good friend of the Administration and has been distressed by not receiving the kind of recognition that other people in the entertainment field have—Louis Armstrong, for example.

Hampton is now embarked on a trip that will take him to Africa, Israel, and other places in the Far East. Wherever he goes he serves as an unofficial ambassador of this country; young people are continually asking him for his impressions of the United States and how it feels to be a Negro citizen there.

I regret that neither the State Department nor the White House has seen fit to give Hampton the kind of blessing that would let him travel as an official ambassador of goodwill for this country. He feels this very keenly too. Armstrong has played to the hilt the idea that he is serving as such, and all of us have been terribly disappointed in the past few months because of Louis's distasteful abuse of the President in the Little Rock case. I can see that there is great hostility between Hampton and Armstrong. Hampton felt that something would have to be done to counteract the damage that Armstrong seems to have caused.

Because the President was at Gettysburg, I was able to take Hampton through to see the President's office and the Cabinet Room, and to meet some of the staff. He was in high spirits.

December 22, 1957

THE Vice-President and Mrs. Nixon had a reception at their home last evening in honor of newly appointed Attorney General William P. Rogers and his wife. Catherine and I were invited, and we had a delightful evening. I had been asked to the Vice-President's home before, but had never been able to accept, because of the press of duties.

He lives in a magnificent house in an exclusive section of Washington, and I can remember when he bought it, just before leaving on his trip to Africa last March. On the plane going over, Mrs. Nixon told me about the purchase and was very excited about her new home. She had a right to be—it is a gorgeous place.

There were all the notables present at the reception that one would expect to find at the Vice-President's home. It was a bright and gay party, and the guests were free to roam about the entire house.

There were some raised eyebrows when we entered, but Mrs. Nixon is such a gracious person that she immediately puts her guests at ease. On our way up to the second floor to leave our wraps I ran into a very excited and not too sober female guest who rushed up to me and demanded: "Where did you put my coat? I need it right away." She was a little unhappy about my slowness in grasping what she was saying, but became quite sober when I told her that I was not an attendant but a newly arrived guest and had no idea where her coat might be.

As I've said, I no longer get angry over incidents like this— they're too frequent in my official line. Actually I thought this one was funny and found myself chuckling over it through the evening. It's just plain difficult for some people to realize that a Negro can appear in mixed gatherings in any other role than that of a servant.

The most interesting group at this affair gathered in the spacious recreation room in the basement. There was a well-stocked bar and plenty of space for relaxation around the huge fireplace or among the group singing at the piano.

I was pleased to see Ann Whitman, the President's personal secretary, there. This was Catherine's first opportunity to talk to her at length, and they liked each other immediately.

We stayed for about an hour and then left after thanking the Nixons for what we had genuinely found a very refreshing evening.

December 23, 1957

OUR social life has really been stepped up. Today we went to Gerry Morgan's home in Gaithersburg, Maryland. Gerry is one of the men in the White House whom I genuinely like and trust. He has a real country-gentleman's estate with rolling acres, swimming pool, stables and such. We enjoyed the trip out to it—the day was one of glorious sunshine, and the road to Gaithersburg runs through one of the most beautiful sections of Maryland.

I still don't know why Gerry invited us at this particular time; the luncheon did not turn out to be a staff affair at all. Gabe Hauge and his family were there, along with Wilton Person and his wife, and the Brundages, but all the other guests apparently were friends who lived on adjoining estates. One of the couples arriving just as we did seemed shocked at seeing us. I'd be willing to bet they thought we'd wandered into the wrong place by mistake.

The Morgans were perfect hosts and went out of their way to make us welcome. This takes courage under these circumstances, and I thoroughly admire people who simply do what they feel is just and sincere. They didn't have to invite us; it was obvious that they had done it because they wanted to. We had a delightful time.

December 31, 1957

My first assignment in my new job was to assist in writing the President's State of the Union Message for 1958 which is to be delivered within the next week. Other than assembling some material, I have not been given a chance to take part in its development in any way. This has been humiliating. There was great fanfare when I was given this assignment, and both staff members and friends think I am working on it. The former ask me about the status of the speech daily, and it's embarrassing when I have to reply that I don't know.

Arthur Larson doesn't seem to be staff minded. He keeps everything to himself and never takes his people into his confidence. Apparently the State of the Union Message is to be his personal version and he doesn't want an assist from anyone. If it falls short of the mark, it will be difficult for me to defend myself as not having had any part in it. By the same token, I certainly can't afford to take any bows if it succeeds.

I do not want to begin a new year as a mere wart on the White House staff. My other efforts have been of real substance and consequence, and for my own peace of mind I must have a real job to do. I hope that the new year will give me one.

JANUARY 7, 1958

I AM no better informed about the State of the Union Message than I have been in the past few weeks. It will be delivered two days from now at the opening of Congress. There are all sorts of rumors as to what the President will say. I can only guess that he will spend most of his time trying to reassure the nation and our allies that we are in a fairly healthy state as far as armaments are concerned and able to defend ourselves against any sudden atomic attack.

At no time since I have been in the White House have I been so discouraged about my status. This last assignment promised to be one of my most challenging. It has turned out to be—at least in my own mind—both disturbing and humiliating.

For the past two weeks Fred Fox, who writes presidential greetings to organizations and individuals celebrating fiftieth anniversaries or birthdays past seventy-five, has been on vacation, and I have been doing his work. With his return, that has come to an end, and I now have no idea how or if my ability will be utilized.

Sherman Adams called me to his office the other day to talk to me about an official matter, and in the course of the conversation asked me how I was getting along. I told him that the job had failed to produce the challenge that he intimated in the beginning and that apparently Mr. Larson was a "lone wolf" operator and did not confide in his colleagues. The Governor said he understood that was the way Mr. Larson worked, and that he felt I should "have it out with him."

This is cold comfort. No matter how I feel about the matter, Larson at present is bogged down with the responsibility of getting out the speech, and this is no time to approach him with my problems. However, as soon as the President's message has been delivered, I intend to get an official clarification on my status and what it is to be in the future.

I went into the White House mess this morning for coffee and ran into Fred Seaton.[1] He greeted me with: "When are you going to quit this crazy rat race over here and come over to Interior to help me?"

It is true that Seaton has been after me for some time to be one of his assistants, but I felt that this kind of change would be difficult to explain to the public. People look upon an assignment on the presidential staff as the highest privilege that can come to anyone in Government, and when one leaves the President's staff to join that of a Cabinet member, it has all the earmarks of a demotion.

However, I appreciate Secretary Seaton's invitation, and will think about it. I like him very much as an individual, and he was one of the original members of the Eisenhower campaign train team. We have always gotten along together very well and think alike on many vital issues.

January 22, 1958

SHERMAN ADAMS is the main topic of conversation in Washington today. Two days ago, in a speech in Minneapolis, he made a sharp political attack on the Democratic party's defense record precisely at the moment when President Eisenhower was in Chicago appealing to everybody to keep politics out of the defense debate.

[1] Secretary of the Interior.

The Democrats are up in arms and there is a great deal of sound and fury.

One of their accusations is that Sherman Adams shoots from ambush, since "he cannot be questioned by the Congress or the press, as the President or the Cabinet can." And they resent his revival of the old fighting implications that the Democrats were responsible for Pearl Harbor; for "the scientific catastrophe of losing our atomic secrets"; for the Communist invasion of Korea; for the tragic loss of China; and for limiting the area of the Korean War.

I have no explanation, but it certainly shows the tremendous power Sherman Adams has in the Administration. Newsmen state that he is without doubt the most powerful White House adviser since the late Harry Hopkins in the Roosevelt Administration.

January 23, 1958

JOSEPH V. BAKER of Philadelphia, Republican party stalwart of many years and prominent public relations man, was in Washington for a meeting yesterday and invited me to his hotel for dinner and a talk. For many years, Baker has been handling race relations for such outfits as the Railroad Association of America, United States Steel, and the Radio Corporation of America. He has the ear and confidence of some of the most powerful men and some of the largest contributors in the Republican party. Whatever he says is worth listening to.

He indicated that Republicans all over the nation were alarmed about the way the party had disintegrated. The feeling is that the President has lost his grip because he cannot be a candidate for re-election. A great many people feel that the President has no sense of politics at all and constantly weakens the party because he will not use his power to chastise those who step off the reservation.

Baker also said that many old-time Republicans are very interested in Nixon. They feel that he is an extremely practical politician and can give the party a sense of direction and leadership.

Then Baker said that the Attorney General's recent statement that he did not propose to offer any civil rights legislation in the present Congress and that there should be a cooling-off period on the whole problem of civil rights had infuriated most Negroes in the country. They felt that I had sold them down the river, because—despite my protestations that I am not the President's adviser on minority problems—I could not escape the moral responsibility of failing to go to bat for my race in situations like this; that the President has made many blunders in race relations and that it was incredible that a Negro could be on his staff and permit him to stumble this badly.

Baker felt that the Republicans had done me an injustice by not giving wide publicity to my actual role in the White House. He added that at the moment—in the eyes of many Negroes—I was a traitor and would have to work very hard to overcome this disadvantage before leaving the White House.

This shocked me, of course. I have known that the Negro press has been somewhat unfriendly to me, but this has been understandable because, as a member of a Negro publishers' association stated, "You don't give us any tips."

My sole effort in this job has been to try to convince the President and other high officials around here that if an American Negro with proper background, character, and training is given an opportunity, he will be able to measure up as well as any other American under the same circumstances. My job is to serve the President in the capacity to which he has appointed me. It is neither feasible nor wise for me to advise him on anything outside the scope of my responsibilities, unless he requests it. It should be perfectly apparent to Sherman Adams, the President, and any other members of the Administration, that if for no other reason that the fact that I am a Negro, I have the ability to advise them on matters that affect the Negro race. The fact that they seek and obtain this advice and information from others, while it may be of concern, is not in my power to alter. However, I suppose there is little I can do about this situation until I am actually out of the White House, unless someone of real stature can appreciate this conflict and will make it known to the Negro public.

MARCH 10, 1958

I HAVEN'T been able to record anything in several weeks, primarily because of an extended trip to California. I left for San Francisco on February 4 and returned to Washington on February 24. It was a stimulating trip. I took my wife with me, and we went by train so that we could enjoy the beauties of the western section of this country. The idea behind the trip was for me to make several California speeches which would give impetus to Republican activity.

I was not interested in promoting any particular candidate, but I did hope to make the people aware of the Administration's program in various phases of national life. I was particularly interested in the sentiment in the San Francisco-Oakland area. Oakland is the home town of Senator Knowland, who is resigning his Senate seat next year in order to seek the governorship of California. There has been a great deal of speculation as to why he would step down from the Senate, where he is Minority Leader, to risk running in the primary for the Republican nomination for Governor of California. Rumor has it that he feels the governorship would be an easier springboard to Republican nomination for the Presidency in 1960. It is said that he feels he would have greater opportunity to develop his machine if he were on the scene, rather than trying to work from Washington.

I was therefore surprised to find sentiment among minorities running steadily against Senator Knowland. He is particularly unpopular among Negroes, and will probably lose the labor vote because of his advocacy of the "Right to Work" bill. Many in the laboring field feel this is a union-busting device and does not mean what the title indicates.

Negro leaders were particularly surprised when the Oakland paper owned by Senator Knowland's family gave me front-page prominence. They indicated that the family attitude toward Negroes is more condescending than earnest.

This is more or less the attitude I found among white Republican leaders in their relationship with Negro leaders or voters. There is sort of a paternalistic attitude, and Negro politicians do as they are told. In most instances, Negro leadership has been selected for them, and it has been selected on the basis of the person's ineffectiveness rather than ability. This method was used over fifty years ago, when Negroes were without the intellectual capacity to paddle their own canoes, but today this method is an insult and only leads to indignation and loss of votes.

My own position is a case in point. It was difficult for the heads of the Republican party in California to accept the fact that I was a presidential assistant and should be accorded the same respect and courtesies that would be extended to anyone from the President's staff. They were prepared to accept me as "a Negro assistant" who was merely sent to chitchat with Negroes and give them a feeling of achievement. I refused to accept this role, and because of this, made many Republican officials uncomfortable.

At my first conference at the Saint Francis Hotel in San Francisco, a public relations man from the Republican State Central Committee was sent to my room fifteen minutes before a press conference to tell me what to say. I dismissed him as courteously as I could, but intimated that this was a distinct insult to a member of the President's staff whose daily responsibilities made contact with the press a routine matter.

However, despite these problems, my wife and I enjoyed the little time we could spend together in San Francisco. Without doubt, it is one of the most appealing cities in the world. It has a more continental air than any other American city, and I believe that if I had adequate income I could live there happily the rest of my life.

We found more of the same racial situation down in Los Angeles, that big, sprawling country town with a Negro population of more than 300,000. While there is a colony of extremely wealthy Negroes there, the great bulk is leaderless and without a respected spokesman. Here again the Republican party is missing a great bet. These Negroes, given adequate opportunity for participation in party circles, and their leadership given opportunity for expression, could become a great bulwark of strength to the party. An example of the irony of this situation is the fact that James Roosevelt, eldest son of the former President, is a congressional candidate in a district where he does not live and where more than a majority of the residents are Negroes. The Republicans have selected a brilliant Negro candidate, Crispus Wright, to oppose Roosevelt in the next election, but Wright is having a difficult time trying to obtain funds and tacit support from the white leadership of the party.

I tried to do what I could to put new life in the movement and to challenge the people to greater efforts. It was a difficult period to appear on Republican platforms. We have to admit that we are in some kind of recession, and there is ominous unemployment all about us. In every question-and-answer period after a speech I was attacked, rather than questioned, on the fact that the Republicans had sat by and let this country drop off into another recession. Republicans who have enjoyed the Eisenhower prosperity for years were the most bitter in their denunciation of him. This sort of thing made these public appearances difficult and unhappy, and I returned from this trip a very tired man.

I have been back at my desk two weeks now and I have still had no word on what my future White House status is to be. The speech-writing business has dwindled to practically nothing, and I have no idea what Mr. Larson is doing. We were sitting together in the dining room the other day, and he confided to me that things had not worked out as he had dreamed. To me this seemed a masterpiece of understatement.

I have requested that General Goodpaster talk to me about my status, but as yet I have had no word from him.

During my absence there have been three rumors in the

Negro press that I was being groomed for an ambassadorship, probably in Ghana. There is no support for this supposition, except that I have been seen in the State Department once or twice during the past few months. It is true that occasionally I have expressed a desire to represent my government abroad in a non-Negro country. I think that this would be an excellent move for combating Russian propaganda about the falseness of our democracy. I did go to the State Department to be interviewed by Christian Herter, Undersecretary of State. He wanted to meet me, talk with me, and apparently size me up for any possible future State Department assignment.

One significant thing that happened during my absence was the resignation of Harold Stassen from his post as Presidential Adviser for Disarmament. Stassen has been a very colorful figure in the Administration and a rugged individualist. He weathered many storms when he took a position completely opposite to that of the Administration's viewpoint. Apparently he ran into difficulty over his latest opposition to Mr. Dulles on the matter of disarmament and the feasibility of a summit meeting, etc. We will hardly see his likes again, and certainly not the kind of staff he had around him—one which was blindly loyal and would do anything to help him have his way.

March 19, 1958

I HAVE finally had a long talk with General Goodpaster. I told him that my present position with Arthur Larson was untenable, that I had been taken from a perfectly good spot where I had apparently functioned satisfactorily, and placed in a position where I had neither title, function nor self-respect. He said that he could not think of anything to assign me to at the moment, but would give it a great deal of thought. "And," he added, "since you know the way the White House operates, why don't you look around and see if there is anything you might want to do?" He dismissed me on this note.

I do not know what has caused the sudden downhill drop of my stock. There is no obvious explanation. Perhaps some of the background ogres of prejudice have been busy.

I have discovered certain peculiarities in the White House top staff. There is little sentiment at anyone's downfall. There may be outward expressions of sympathy, but each man is primarily concerned with his own survival, and there's always the possibility that another's misfortune will ease the pressure on *him*. Not unlike the rest of the world!

I hope it won't be long before I know what the score is.

March 20, 1958

EARLIER this week I sent Sherman Adams a memo requesting a conference with him at the close of business on Saturday. I had made up my mind that the time had come for me to go to the mat with him on my future status on the White House staff. He phoned this morning to ask what he could do for me. It is difficult to discuss a personal problem of this scope over a telephone, and I had hoped that I could see him in person. However, I told him that in view of the fact that nothing had developed in my case, I would like his permission to return to my former position as Administrative Officer for Special Projects. The Governor said he had decided that I was needed out in the field, to make more speeches. I replied that I had been doing this, but to continue it I needed some kind of defined White House status and a valid title. He suggested that I take the matter up with Andy Goodpaster and said that after that the three of us would sit down together and discuss the whole situation.

I immediately called Goodpaster and requested another audience. He told me to come right over. Again I went over the situation with him and said that my position was now a subject of discussion among even the messengers and White House employees. It would be just a question of time before the matter became public property and we would be forced to answer queries from the press.

He agreed that something should be done immediately. He reiterated his conviction that, if at all possible, I should not return to my old assignment, as it would indicate a defeat. The speechmaking assignment was supposed to have been an advance, and going back would be difficult to explain. He was still hoping that something could be arranged for me within the White House, rather than my returning to the Executive Office Building. However, I was still uncertain as to what the new assignment could be.

I made it very clear to him that I was not interested in "made work." I had not volunteered to come to the White House, but had been invited; the present situation was not of my own doing, but had been brought about by someone else. I did not want him or anyone to feel that they had created something for me because I was "the President's boy." I was quite willing to pit my abilities and qualifications against anyone on the staff, and I wanted a responsible job of some consequence, based on ability and merit. Short of this, I was not interested. He said he would dig into the matter and let me know very shortly.

Later in the afternoon, Howard Pyle came in to ask me to substitute for him on a speaking engagement at Georgetown University. He asked me what I was doing and whether I was happy doing it. I felt I had nothing to lose by telling him the truth, since my situation was no longer a secret in the White House.

Howard Pyle was one of those who, at the very beginning, had fought against any change in my position because he felt that it would not work out. He was familiar with Mr. Larson's reputation as a "lone wolf" worker, and understood what had happened to me.

He spent some time trying to assuage my feelings, saying that there were many others on the staff who did not know what their status was from day to day. He appreciated that my abilities were not being utilized, but this was not a unique situation. He told me to be of good cheer.

At any rate, I feel relieved that the matter has been brought to a point where a decision will have to be made. When it is, then it will be up to me to choose. At least this will be better than the indecision and uncertainty of the past four months.

APRIL 1, 1958

THE last ten days have been eventful ones here in the White House. There have been several changes in job designations—including my own—which have surprised a great many people.

For example, Tom Stephens has returned as Appointment Secretary to the President. This is the second or third time Tom has been in or out of this position, and this latest return is somewhat of a surprise to me. Bob Gray has been acting as Appointment Secretary ever since Bernard Shanley resigned the position in October 1957, to go back to New Jersey to lay the groundwork and campaign for the Republican nomination for Senator from that state. From all appearances, Gray did a fine job, but there have been continuous rumors that the President missed a familiar face in this important and personal spot and needed more strength in this area as regards political sagacity and the ability to say no to important persons without hurting their feelings.

I feel certain that this is a blow to Gray, because this is a position anyone would like to have, not only because of its outside prestige, but because of its importance in White House circles. The Appointment Secretary, in a large measure, determines whom the President will see, and of course sees the President more during the day than any other member of the staff. It is always difficult to have had a taste of greatness and then have it snatched from you through no personal fault.

In my own case, I finally got a call from General Goodpaster, informing me that he and Sherman Adams had finally decided that it would be best for me to return to my former position in the President's Executive Office. I regretted this. I had hoped that there would be developments in some other area, but since these things had not jelled, it was thought advisable for me to return to my old post. While this in some manner relieves my mind and frees me from the boredom of my recent do-nothing spot, I regret that it displaces a friend—Douglas Price—who did a marvelous job as Acting Administrative Officer. To the uninitiated, my return to the old job could be interpreted as a defeat or even as a demotion, but at this time I cannot concern myself with what others may think about this White House game of musical-chairs.

A day or so ago I had a very interesting few minutes with the President. Claude Barnett, Director of the Associated Negro Press, came to the White House to present the President with a gift tray, made by one of the finest silversmiths in Tripoli. During our visit in Libya last year, the silversmith, Fazi Naas, told Claude that he wished to make the largest and most beautiful tray of his career as a gift for the President. He was very excited about the President's reputation for being concerned about the underprivileged throughout the world, and wanted his tray to be a symbol of appreciation from all the downtrodden people in Africa. The tray was a beautiful work of brass and had taken Naas approximately nine months to complete. It had been flown to this country on a plane carrying some of our military, and had been sent to me at the White House for safekeeping and eventual presentation to the President.

I was given the job of trying to arrange for the presentation, since this was a little unusual and the kind of thing that the White House likes to avoid. There can be all kinds of complications involved. First of all, the gift was a personal one from a citizen of another country. Normally, such presentations would be made through State Department channels, and the ambassador of the country making the presentation would be invited to attend. However, the State Department called me, indicating that it wanted to keep this informal and very simple. We agreed that only Barnett and I would be present on this occasion.

We found the President cheerful, alert, and his usual charming self. It was the first time that Barnett had met him, and he was amazed at his sincerity and simplicity. Following the presentation, newsmen and photographers dashed in to get the story, and the President was affable and willing to pose with Barnett and me with the huge tray placed in front of us. The morning papers carried the story and picture.

At this writing, I have returned to my old offices in the Executive Office Building and am happy to be back in these spacious quarters. It was nice to have offices in the White House, but they had seemed small and cramped.

I'm also glad to be back with my former secretary, "Junior" (Mary O'Madigan), and have brought Peggy King with me as a new addition to the staff. Once more we have a very effective team, and—while the job may get rougher—we're expecting busy, rewarding times together in our familiar surroundings.

April 7, 1958

I'VE told a few friends of my desire to find a suitable position for myself when my tour of duty is over here in Washington. Tom Stephens has encouraged me in this and has tried to utilize his friendship with some of the prominent businessmen in the country to help me pick up leads. Tom is obviously experiencing the same difficulty that I had; many leading American businessmen are aghast when it is suggested that a Negro be given a position of consequence or influence in their organizations. A number of them still think of the Negro in terms of "a boy," and their attitudes have not changed very much since the Civil War. Despite my status here at the White House, it is incredible to many of these men that my job consists of anything more than being a glorified messenger boy or a political sop to attract Negro voters to the party.

This morning Tom made an appointment for me with one of the most prominent lawyers in Washington, who is a personal friend of the President and has among his clients Coca-Cola and other great corporations of the country. Tom had sent this man a note about me, asking his assistance in helping me pick up some leads. The lawyer, whom we shall call "Mr. Jones," had me come in to see him today at 8:45 A.M. He told me that he had played golf with Sherman Adams the day before and that the Governor had spoken very highly of me.

From his opening sentences, however, I was aware that this gentleman had no conception of my desires, abilities or present position. He asked me what my salary was, and when I told him, he was shocked! He had no idea that Negroes made more than fifty dollars a week, and he asked me point-blank if I believed that such a fabulous salary would continue after I left the White House. He then proceeded to give me a lecture on the detriment of the Supreme Court decision on civil rights. He felt that it was a sad mistake, that it had merely increased race conflict in this country and caused men of his generation to become more embittered; as a result, they are teaching their children that integration must never happen.

It was difficult for him to believe that I had worked for CBS in my former capacity there, and it was also difficult for him to accept my education. He had originally wanted to help, but he was thinking in terms of my having some kind of a job that "a nice colored boy would have." He wanted to know if I would be interested in selling automobiles. He said that Coca-Cola hired three "Negro boys" here in Washington to do some public-relations work for them, and that their principal job was to keep Negro dealers happy. "However," he said, "these three boys combined don't make the salary you make now."

By this time I thought I had better end the interview by telling him that I appreciated his seeing me and felt that he had given me enough of his time. He said he would keep trying to think of helpful ideas and would see me again.

I left his office thoroughly shaken and discouraged. I had

been hoping continually, despite many bitter past experiences, that strides were being made in this country—particularly in industry and business—so that a person could be accepted on the basis of his ability alone. Apparently this is not true. Mr. Jones had indicated to me that it would be a long time before bias would vanish in America; that one would have to work and be accepted as a Negro and not as an American who had something to offer his employer.

This is a discouraging moment. But—as I have had to do all my life—I must rise above it and try to prove that the Mr. Joneses have a misconception of America in 1958.

April 10, 1958

CLARENCE RANDALL, formerly Chairman of the Board of Inland Steel, and for the past few years Special Assistant to the President for Foreign Economic Developments, is one of the most competent and interesting men I have ever met. He is one of several businessmen who, though retired, have come into the Government, at the insistence of the President, to utilize their talents and experience in making its program more effective and efficient.

Randall has done an exceptional job, and because of the great respect industry has for him, has been able to bring in other able retired executives who have caught his fire and zeal and are making a significant contribution to their Government.

He has just returned from a several weeks' visit to Africa, and this morning at staff meeting spent a half hour giving us his impressions. It was a brilliant performance! His report was of particular interest and value to me, since he has covered some of the same territory I had on my trip with the Vice-President last year. I was happy when he said that our visit had made a tremendous impression on the Dark Continent and that everyone had high praise for what we had done.

Randall came back to this country with a shocked reaction to the treatment Africans receive from the various nations still holding spheres of influence on that continent. He was incensed by the attitude of the whites in South Africa, and shares the opinion that a change is inevitable and that it will probably be brought about through great bloodshed. He also feels that the governing whites there realize that their methods are bound to fail and that they are at the end of their tether, but perhaps pure fright prevents them from making any change or even admitting to themselves that their seventeenth-century methods can only lead to disaster and death.

He reiterated my conviction that Ghana is a jewel in the crown of Africa; that the British have done a great and enlightening job on the Gold Coast by not only bringing the Africans along economically, but also developing them socially in the matter of education, health and welfare. They are much more ready to govern themselves than almost any other section of the continent. He feels that Prime Minister Nkrumah, who spent ten years in America getting an education, is essentially pro-American, despite the fact that he must have suffered many insults and abuses during his stay in this country. The Prime Minister realizes that he carries the hopes of all Africans that Ghana will succeed, thereby proving that it is possible for Africans to govern themselves with intelligence and ability.

Liberia, of course, is the most "American" country in Africa. This is because it was founded under the auspices of our Government and its first citizens were former American slaves or their offspring. However, Mr. Randall discovered, the same as I had, that there is a great deal of anti-American feeling in Liberia and that this is true even among its top officials. America has not done the kind of job of promoting this country that the British did in the Gold Coast, or even that the French have done in their area. We have given only token assistance to Liberia, and its people are resentful and unhappy.

Mr. Randall said that he hesitated to give us the following information, but felt that he was morally bound to do so. He revealed that one of the sources of this anti-American attitude is the undemocratic and almost uncivilized attitude of the great

American companies that practically dominate Liberia and its economy.

Apparently these companies have made no effort to give the Liberians even the barest considerations of decent living. The wages are insufferably low, the education is negligible; and no effort is being made to train Africans in technical or supervisory positions. There is absolutely no mixing socially, and company officials have made no effort to remedy this. This makes it appear that these companies are in Liberia purely to exploit the country and not to make any contribution in the field of human welfare.

It is interesting to note that, even in the past few weeks, the Liberian legislature passed a law making discrimination in business or in other endeavors a crime. This is an effort to secure for the Liberians some kind of equality in the commercial and business world.

I remember a news story a few weeks ago where a white official of one of these companies was fired because he had married an African girl. I feel sure that this kind of situation agitated the condition and made passage of the Antidiscrimination Bill easy.

I have been aware of this anti-American attitude for a long time, and some of my Liberian friends in this country have even come to my office in the White House to plead with me to try to do what I could to urge the Administration to show a more friendly attitude toward this nation.

I am quite sure Mr. Randall has returned to this country aware of the fact that the rapid economic development of this vast continent is inevitable and that if this anti-American attitude persists, we will be completely shut out of an almost virgin world whose minerals and other necessities inherent in our civilization are available in undisclosed quantity and bulk.

The development of great dams and power sources throughout that continent will make the acquisition of these raw products easy, and Africans will welcome those nations that have shown an inclination to help them develop their area to the maximum.

During my visit there I was able to see the way Russia is coveting the resources—both human and natural—of Africa, and that is why we can no longer afford to send incompetents and misfits to represent us there. We must send only fully trained and equipped people who will reflect the best in American life and attitudes.

I feel that Clarence Randall's report will serve both his own country and the future of Africa well.

April 16, 1958

MY WIFE is a very wise woman! She is intelligent, well-traveled, well-educated, and instinctively does the right thing at the right time.

Since she came to Washington, she has been very careful about accepting social invitations, not wanting to create the impression that she was overly eager to share in functions given by the wives of White House personnel or official Washington. She has been very selective in this matter.

Yesterday she went to a luncheon given for the White House wives by Mrs. Amos Peaslee at historic Gunston Hall on the Potomac. Mrs. Peaslee is one of Washington's distinguished hostesses and a regent of Gunston Hall. Her husband is Deputy Special Assistant to the President.

When the invitation first came, I had some uncertainty about Catherine's acceptance. Gunston Hall is in Virginia, and that state still has oppressive laws about socializing between the races. It actually can be a penal offense for Negroes and whites to socialize in Virginia. With this in mind, and without Catherine's knowledge, I called Mrs. Sherman Adams to ask her if she felt Catherine would have any difficulty. I told Mrs. Adams that I was used to rebuffs and insults and had grown quite hardened to them, but that Catherine had led a very sheltered life, and, since her father had been a man of means, had been brought up in an atmosphere of culture, friendliness and good breeding. While I never doubted her ability to handle any situation, I did not want her to be hurt by discourteous people.

Mrs. Adams immediately offered to have Catherine go with her. Mrs. Adams is the "Third Lady" of the nation, and few women would risk her displeasure by being rude to anyone in her party.

Catherine went and had a very interesting time. Her experience, however, duplicates mine. The wives who are socially secure were kind and friendly. The socially insecure—because of personal backgrounds or their husbands' average positions—were unfriendly and nervous.

An interesting thing happened when some of the women, fascinated by the historic surroundings of Gunston Hall, began talking about their own ancestries, trying to establish themselves as having roots deep in American history and culture. Catherine innocently asked how far Gunston Hall was from Gordonsville, Virginia. Someone asked her why Gordonsville would be of interest. She said it was the birthplace of her father, that she had been born a Gordon, and that the town was named after her family. (Her father's people were the bankers and merchants of that historic area.)

Amazement ran through the group. It was immediately apparent that this girl had some of the bluest blood of Virginia in her veins, and despite her copper-colored skin, had as much right as anyone to claim herself as an FFV. The information put a decided chill on the ladies at her table.

These experiences, even if you have a sense of humor, take a great deal out of you. There is never an opportunity to relax completely; one is always on display. If you're completely relaxed, it looks like presumption, and to be too reserved looks like snobbishness! The happy medium is the only solution.

I am very proud of Catherine. She is making a wonderful contribution to democracy here in official Washington. But it may take her several days to recover from her "ordeal," and each such experience makes her more reluctant to accept other invitations. However, we both realize that she must continue to accept, because—here again—she must try to pave the way for an understanding of what tolerance really means.

April 25, 1958

LAST night I was sitting at home looking at television when the 11 P.M. news came on and I heard the startling announcement that Max Rabb had just tendered his resignation as Secretary to the Cabinet. I knew that with Max's resignation the question of who would handle this delicate problem of civil rights and Negro affairs would be one of the most pressing matters to confront both the President and Sherman Adams.

I have been with Mr. Adams today, along with Max Rabb. In his typically terse manner, the Governor told me that the President had agreed that from this point on I would handle all correspondence and all problems coming into the White House dealing with civil rights and Negro affairs. *That was all!*

There is a tremendous irony about this whole situation. After the President was nominated in 1952, and there were discussions on who would accompany him to the White House, I refused point-blank to come to Washington to be his adviser on Negro affairs. I held out for many months and said I would only come to Washington to assist him if I could be given the same recognition, responsibilities and privileges of any other staff member. There was something abhorrent to me in being a professional "race-saver." However, at this writing, with the exception of our unsettled relations with the Russians, there is no problem that gives this Administration more concern or more anxious moments than civil rights. Max Rabb indicated to the President and to Sherman Adams that it would be discrimination in reverse if they did not turn this responsibility over to the one staff member who had the ability, knowledge and tact to handle it.

It is with deep emotion and mixed feelings that I leave tonight for a speaking engagement in Tallahassee, Florida. The very thing that I have fought so long to avoid is now an important part of my daily life. The test will come when other crises such as Little Rock arise to plague this country, and I must rid myself of all personal emotions and make a cold-blooded analysis of the situation in order to give the best possible advice to the President. It will not be easy. I can foresee my former colleagues in the NAACP and the Urban League berating me for being "soft," "unrealistic," and even "traitorous," but I have resolved that one of the prime requirements of first-class citizenship is to put race and color in their true perspective and to try to estimate all problems and situations from the standpoint of an American.

MAY 13, 1958

AFTER great effort on the part of the Negro Publishers Association, the President finally consented to address a summit meeting of Negro leaders, called here in Washington yesterday by the Publishers Association. Some 400 prominent Negroes in all avenues of life came, at their own expense, to discuss problems involving their continuing fight for first-class citizenship. The President agreed to address an afternoon meeting.

In his typically honest manner, the President told them that while laws should not be ignored in bestowing citizenship rights upon Americans, it had to be acknowledged that prejudice because of race and color is deeply rooted in the hearts of men and can only be changed by education and by constant work on the part of enlightened citizens. He then chose what might be considered an unfortunate term. He asked Negroes to be "patient" and to use forbearance in their efforts to gain citizenship privileges.

From the expression on the faces of the audience, I knew the President had struck a sensitive nerve. I could imagine the reverberations.

They weren't long in coming. In the evening meeting, Roy Wilkins devoted a great part of his address to a denunciation of the President's conservative attitude on civil rights. It was a difficult thing for me to take, sitting there in the audience, but I realized that the privilege of free speech enables anyone to express his disagreement in vigorous terms. I am more and more conscious of the great personal problem of having to resolve the conflict of being two personalities at once—a Negro and an American. Add to that my love and devotion to the President—despite his conservative views on civil rights—and one can see that there will be a never-ending conflict as long as I hold this job.

May 14, 1958

THIS has been another eventful day in the White House. At an early morning staff meeting, we discussed the possible domestic and international issues that might come before the President at today's press conference.

The problem that occupied most of our attention was the situation in Caracas, Venezuela, where hundreds of fury-spouting demonstrators attacked Vice-President Nixon's car with rocks and heavy sticks upon his arrival from Bogotá, Colombia. About ten minutes later another mob, described as being in "a lynching mood," had tried to assault Army and Navy attachés of the United States Embassy at the National Pantheon. The Americans were there to attend the laying of a wreath by Mr. Nixon. The ceremony never took place, and two companies of helmeted infantry with bared bayonets were necessary to escort the attachés to safety. Three windows in the Vice-President's limousine were smashed by large rocks, and Mr. Nixon was covered with shattered glass. The Venezuelan Foreign Minister, riding next to the Vice-President, was struck in the eye by a piece of glass.

President Eisenhower had already ordered four companies of Marines and paratroopers to the Caribbean bases to back White House demands that Venezuela guarantee the safety of our Vice-President. A statement by the Department of Defense said that the combat-ready troops were being moved "as a precautionary measure" to be used "if assistance is requested," in case of further violence.

In addition to this, during the night French troops had seized government control of Algeria, and were demanding the return of General Charles De Gaulle as Premier of France. In Paris, a Right-Wing mob marched on the French National Assembly, but was stopped by armed forces just short of its goal. The march began as news of the riots in Algeria reached Paris.

From Beirut, Lebanon, dispatches indicated that the Foreign Minister accused the United Arab Republic of having instituted and aided the rebellion.

I could not help but remember a thought that I had tried to pass on to the Vice-President's office four or five weeks before his trip to South America. I was aware of the fact that he would be visiting a section of the world where the countries are made up of many mixtures of blood. I remembered the success of our African trip, when the Administration had had the foresight not only to send me along with the Vice-President as a representative of the Government, but also to see that the trip was covered by Negro newsmen. I had hoped that this would be standard operating procedure in the future for all government-sponsored trips by Administration officials.

With this in mind, I had called the Vice-President's office, suggesting that a Negro—not myself—be taken on the trip. This would be good public relations and visual evidence of the effort of the United States to indicate its complete belief in not only a democratic form of government, but democratic representation in any of its missions at home and abroad. The Vice-President was out when I called, and I talked with one of his young assistants. After I had made the suggestion, the young man replied, in a very smart-alecky manner, "What the dickens would he take a Negro with him for? These are white countries he is visiting. If anything, he ought to take an Indian. Ha, ha." I begged his pardon and asked him to forgive my interference.

I am not saying that the mere presence of a Negro, or several Negroes, would have prevented this outburst in South America, but I do believe that it might not have been so violent. If the trip had been well-publicized and it had been known that a Negro would be an official member of the party, the mob might have looked a little more kindly upon the Vice-President's visit.

Whether we accept it or not, white men are very unpopular in a great many areas in the world where there are colored people or where the people are considered "nonwhite." Despite the great amount of mutual aid we are sending abroad, it has been obvious to me in some of my visits that a great part of the aid does not trickle down to benefit the downtrodden. They are often totally unaware of our hopes of brotherhood, goodwill and cooperation, and they only know that the very elementary benefits of Democracy are not available to them.

To these people, white men symbolize arrogance, success and superiority, and it does not take too much to incite them into rioting or strife. We blame most of these incidents on the Communists, but I don't believe this is the whole story. There are a great many other elements involved. However, the Communists are able to benefit from dormant possibilities. So much for the foreign side of the picture!

On the domestic side, is the burning question of civil rights. This has all been pointed up this week by the two-day meeting called in the capital by the Negro Publishers Association.

I have reported that the President spoke at this meeting Monday and made what I thought was a creditable speech. However, his statement, particularly his call for "patience" on the part of Negroes in demanding their Constitutional rights, drew strong criticism from the conference body after the speech and heavy fire from the officials of the NAACP and the other leaders attending the meeting. On Tuesday, James P. Mitchell, Secretary of Labor, told the meeting that the civil rights act passed last summer was weak, watered-down, and in his opinion ineffectual. He set off a dispute by suggesting that civil rights leaders have been responsible for amendments to the bill. Clarence Mitchell, Washington representative of the NAACP, shouted from the floor, "That's not true!" Later he unsuccessfully tried to get the floor, to reply to Secretary Mitchell.

This was an unfortunate occurrence, and it left a bad taste in the mouths of Administration leaders. It was the only black spot on the record of the conference, and it was rather tragic that a

responsible citizen such as Clarence Mitchell should have embarrassed both the Secretary of Labor and the conferees. The
chairman of the meeting apologized to the Secretary for this
intemperate outburst, and thanked him for his remarks. This
brought thunderous applause from the audience.

All these elements have been a part of a wild and exciting
thirty-six hours, and today's press conference was jammed by
reporters representing almost every news service in the world.
The President handled himself very well. I, of course, was particularly interested in his answer to the powder-loaded question
on civil rights.

He was asked whether or not any efforts were being made by
the Federal Government to lay the groundwork in Virginia so
that the state would comply with the Federal Court decision
that the secondary schools in its principal cities must be integrated in September. Both the governor of the state and the
Attorney General have indicated that they would not comply
with the Court's decree. The newsmen wanted to know what the
President would do in this case. He replied that he never gave
answers to suppositions or to possible future situations, that he
would have to look at the facts at the time. He said, however,
that any decree issued by a duly constituted Federal court must
be respected by all citizens and officials, regardless of their personal views. He said that as President of the United States, it is
inherent in his oath that he carry out all decrees of duly constituted Federal courts and all the provisions of the Federal Constitution. This he would do.

I felt this was an eloquent answer, not only to the press, but
to all the critics who had scorned him twenty-four hours ago
because he had counseled patience and forbearance in our struggle for citizenship rights.

May 23, 1958

YESTERDAY some of Max Rabb's many friends in Washington held a farewell luncheon for him at the Press Club. It was well attended by many of the leaders in government, industry and civic affairs. Vice-President Nixon, Sherman Adams, Senators Saltonstall of Massachusetts, Case of New Jersey, and Javits of New York were on the dais and had warm words of praise for Max's efforts during his term of office. His friends presented him with an oil painting of himself by Dr. Oppenheim, and a plaque expressing warm sentiments. It was a very nice affair.

Thus comes to a close the official career of a colorful individual. He will be missed in the White House. Although I did not always agree with his actions in handling minority group affairs, he was pioneering in a difficult and complex field. Max Rabb has a high code of ethics, and is certainly an honest man of great integrity. There were many times, however, when his soul was sorely tried by pressures within and without. I must honestly confess that he was perhaps the only one on the White House staff who showed deep personal concern about the plight of the Negro and other minorities in the country.

JUNE 11, 1958

THERE has been little time to make any notes on daily events in the past two weeks. My new responsibilities keep me so busy, in addition to the speeches I am making across the country at this graduation season, that there is no time left for personal life of any kind. This constant running about the country, trying to inspire youth and to give a lift to the flagging spirits of Negroes in the South and elsewhere, is putting me in the doghouse at home. My wife is concerned about my health as well as the fact that we have little time together to enjoy our very pleasant home and gardens.[1]

A long, dusty ride to Fayetteville, North Carolina, to speak to the graduating class at the State Teachers' College there was a rewarding experience. Most of these youngsters are from farm communities and farm parents, and I felt a duty to try to inspire and challenge them. If only one or two persons out of a group such as this are moved to perform beyond their normal capacity, it is worthwhile.

There has been much excitement in the field of civil rights in the past ten days. A Negro college professor by the name of Clennon King, of Mississippi, attempted to enroll in the University of Mississippi to work on his Ph.D. He was escorted from the university by the state police and committed to a psychiatric

[1] At that time we were fortunate enough to be living in northeast Washington, near the Maryland line, and our garden was formerly a part of the beautifully tended Franciscan monastery grounds that adjoined our place.

hospital on the grounds that he must be insane because of his presumption in attempting to enroll. The reactions in the country have been swift and gratifying, and the President's mail has been heavy with letters and telegrams from white and Negro citizens imploring him to take some action to protect the civil rights of Clennon King.

The weekend was rather explosive, with another disturbing incident in Terrell County, Georgia. In the little country town of Dawson, a plantation section of the state, newspaper stories revealed that several colored people had been killed without just provocation in the past few weeks and that the conditions are worse than those in Nazi-occupied countries during World War II. In an interview, the chief of police said that terror was necessary in order to keep Negroes in their place, and that killing a few of them once in awhile was always good medicine for the rest of them.

Just before the newspaper exposé, I received a letter from John W. Dobbs of Atlanta, Grand Master of the Negro Masons in Georgia, who asked me to request the President to take some action to stop the horrible brutality going on in Terrell County. It was a bizarre story of Negroes having their eyes beaten out and their skulls crushed for no apparent reason. It seems that this was an accepted sport for the local police. He attached copies of letters from Negro ministers in the area who gave pitiful reports of the need for Federal intervention in order to save the lives of the people there. They told the story of one lad who was severely beaten and later died merely because he had begged the police officers not to pistol-whip his father. The ministers went on to say that it was even dangerous for their people to go to church at night, because the police would prey upon the communicants. They said that if the FBI or someone could not send help at once, it would be necessary for them to get out their shotguns and resolve to die trying to protect their own families.

Though I was up to my neck in official responsibilities, I went over to the Attorney General's [2] office this morning to consult with the Assistant Attorney General in charge of Civil Rights.

2 William P. Rogers.

His coolness and nonchalance about the whole matter disturbed me no end. I realized, of course, that in the spaciousness of his air-conditioned office it would be difficult for him to visualize the situation of the poor devils who had asked me to try to get them some help. The FBI had been sending in reports, but apparently the Federal Government had no intention of interfering. I realized that in many cases the Federal Government cannot enter unless it can be proved that some Federal statute has been violated, but in this particular case it is prima-facie evidence that the civil rights of Negroes are being ignored and that they are suffering wanton brutality at the hands of conscienceless police officers. Certainly their rights and privileges as citizens are being denied without due process of law.

I requested the Assistant Attorney General to do all in his power to see to it that some kinds of pressure were brought to bear to stop this brutality. I then called Mr. Dobbs to tell him what I had done, expressing the hope that some action would result from my visit to the Attorney General's office. I will never forget his choked voice, thanking me for moving so swiftly and telling me what harrowing days these were in Terrell County.

Another event of this week found me in the middle, trying to help make decisions. Dr. Martin Luther King had again petitioned the President for a meeting of Negro leaders to discuss the many problems facing colored people today in the area of civil rights. Reverend King had been asked to come to the White House to discuss his request with Rocco Siciliano [3] and me. A member of the Attorney General's office was also present at the conference. Reverend King pointed out that this was a strategic time, with the schools closed for the summer, for the President to meet with Negro leaders and talk about the future of integrated schools in the country, as provided for in the Supreme Court decision in 1954. He felt that the signs that Virginia would oppose the Court order to integrate schools in Arlington, and similar indications in other places, could lead to serious rioting and perhaps bloodshed in the fall. To effect plans

3 The President's Special Assistant for Personnel Management.

to meet this situation, he thought the President ought to have a free, honest and factual discussion with leading Negroes.

Siciliano and I were in agreement that such a meeting should be held, but who would the Negro leaders be? And how would they be determined? This is always a sore point. Every knowledgeable Negro believes himself to be a leader in some area, and any Negro of national prominence might feel that he should be a candidate in any meeting where the future of his people was discussed. I realized that Roy Wilkins ought to be present, being Executive Secretary of the NAACP, but I also knew that he was in the White House doghouse because of his forceful attack upon the President during a speech he had made before the summit conference of Negro leaders in Washington in early May. However, Dr. King pointed out that it would be unthinkable for him to come to the White House without Wilkins and that it would be difficult to explain to the Negro people why Wilkins was not included in such a conference. We all agreed that A. Philip Randolph should be at the conference, because he is a respected citizen in whom most Americans have complete faith.

Rocco Siciliano and I conferred with Reverend King in a preliminary conference two weeks ago. It was finally agreed that A. Philip Randolph, Vice-President of AFL-CIO, and head of the Sleeping Car Porters Brotherhood; Roy Wilkins, Executive Secretary of the NAACP; Lester B. Granger, Executive Secretary of the Urban League; and Dr. King himself, should form the delegation.

The name of Adam Clayton Powell also came up. The President had promised to see Mr. Powell sometime this year, but his recent indictment for income tax problems by a Federal Grand Jury posed a delicate situation. If he came to the White House, critics would say he was there to make some kind of deal about his case. If he were not invited, his friends would say that despite his support of the Administration—which caused him to lose his party's support—the Administration was kicking him when he was down. What to do about Congressman Powell will take further consideration.

June 19, 1958

THE President has consented to see four national Negro leaders, and last-minute preparations are being made for this meeting. It will be historic—the President's first face-to-face encounter with Negro leaders since he took office.

At present we face a very great problem: the involved selection of the persons to attend. I suppose almost any literate Negro with a few friends believes himself a "leader." Certainly any heads of large churches or groups consider themselves important. Perhaps they are right, but great care must be taken in selecting people to represent 18,000,000 people, in this kind of a conference.

Our troubles had begun when the New York *Amsterdam News* scooped all other papers in the country with a front-page story on the meeting. They quoted an "unimpeachable source." As soon as the news spread through the country, we began to receive requests from countless people who wanted to be a part of the delegation. I have an unlisted telephone, but somehow people discovered the number and phoned me at home night and day, pressuring me to add this or that name to the delegation.

To add to the confusion, Representative Powell informed the press that the meeting was the result of his suggestions to the White House, and that the persons named in the delegation were those he had urged the President to see. This gave the impression that Powell was responsible for the decision and that he had named the representatives. This put the White House in a spot—the President's daily program is seldom published that far in advance. Hagerty generally issues an announcement twenty-four hours before such an event is to take place. In this instance, however, it was necessary to rush a story into print to counteract Congressman Powell's.

Powell then sent a telegram to the White House, demanding that a Negro woman be added to the delegation. He was interested in a specific candidate who was president of the National

Council of Negro Women. In addition to his telegrams, many telephone calls were made, and this was the beginning of a barrage from prominent Negroes in all sections of the country. In order to make myself unavailable, I left town.

When this is all over, I will have to defend myself against the accusation that I discriminated against Negro womanhood!

June 20, 1958

THIS is the close of one of the most dramatic and tragic weeks in the Eisenhower Administration. For months the House Subcommittee on Legislative Oversight has been conducting an inquiry into the operations of Federal agencies and whether officials of these agencies have been subjected to political pressures to influence their decisions.

On June 10, committee investigators introduced records to show that Bernard Goldfine, a New England industrialist, had paid hotel bills of around $2,000 for Sherman Adams in Boston, over a period of more than two years. Mr. Goldfine has had cases before the Federal Trade Commission and the Securities and Exchange Commission.

This information dropped on Washington like a bombshell and spread across the world like a prairie fire. The situation was incredible. To the politically wise, and especially the Democrats, the Governor—for all his toughness and experience—had apparently made a colossal political blunder.

On June 12, Mr. Adams sent a letter to Representative Oren Harris of Arkansas, Chairman of the Subcommittee. The Governor said, in part:

> Since this Committee has chosen to make public the extent of the entertaining of myself and my family, on the part of an old friend, Mr. Goldfine, and has insinuated that because of this entertaining or this friendship, Mr. Goldfine has received, on

my intercession, favored treatment from the federal agencies, I feel that I should set the record straight. I categorically deny such insinuations. They are unwarranted and unfair.

He went on to explain that he and Mrs. Adams had known the Goldfines for more than fifteen years, and that each had been entertained in the other's home. It was a close personal relationship. Mr. Goldfine had told the Governor that whenever he had the chance to come to Boston, he hoped that he would stay in Mr. Goldfine's suite at the Sheraton Plaza, where he maintained an apartment. Whenever Mr. Adams had been in Boston, he accepted this offer.

He admitted that he had called the Federal Trade Commission once or twice to secure what he felt was routine information for Mr. Goldfine. He felt that this information was the kind that any citizen could get from any Federal agency merely for the asking. He had done the same thing in relation to the Securities and Exchange Commission. When Mr. Adams received the information, he did nothing further in the SEC case; relative to the FTC, he merely passed the answers on to Mr. Goldfine.

Among the other charges the subcommittee was studying were: that Goldfine gave the Governor a $2,400 Oriental rug and other expensive furnishings for his home, a $700 vicuña coat and other presents.

On June 17, Sherman Adams requested an opportunity to testify before the subcommittee, and his request was granted. He was subjected to pitiless questioning for two and a half hours. He testified that he may have acted a little imprudently in making phone call inquiries to the FTC and the SEC for his friend, but insisted that this was mere routine and the same services he and the White House staff performed in connection with many such requests.

"I have no excuses to offer. I did not come here to make apologies to you or to the committee," Adams told Chairman Oren Harris. "I do not wish to testify that I am a fledgling in this business of politics." But then he added, "If I had the decision now before me to make, I believe I would have acted a little more prudently."

He said that there had been no strings attached to the exchange of friendship he had from Goldfine. His home in Washington does have a $2,400 Oriental rug, as has been rumored, but it is only on loan from Goldfine to remedy the "shabbiness" Goldfine found in the rug they had had previously. He also admitted that his friend had adorned his home with two other small rugs.

Goldfine did give him a vicuña coat and had it tailored for him—but the actual skins cost Goldfine's mill $69—nowhere near the rumored price of $700. Mr. Adams said that his friend was proud of his mills and their products, and also had garments made up for Mrs. Adams and himself, just as he had done for each of the governors of states and territories in 1955.

Sherman Adams insisted that Bernard Goldfine had not benefited in any way in his relations with any branch of the Federal Government because he was a friend of Adams, and by the same token, Adams did not secure any favors or benefits for Goldfine.

This was a remarkable performance of courage and forbearance, but it did not stem the tide. Instead, from every corner of the nation and particularly from the Congress, came bitter denunciations of Mr. Adams and demands that he resign or be fired by the President immediately. Perhaps the most disheartening aspect of the whole event was the fact that so many Republican Congressmen and Senators joined with the angry pack snapping at Mr. Adams' heels. Senator Edward Thye of Minnesota, Senator William Knowland of California, Senator Charles Potter of Michigan, Senator Barry Goldwater of Arizona—all Republicans and all up for re-election—demanded the Governor's scalp.

The pressures upon the President to fire the Governor have been tremendous. Everyone waited to see what the President would say about the matter at his Wednesday press conference.

I squeezed into the conference behind the President's Secret Service bodyguards, because I realized that this was an important occasion. The room was crowded to the eaves. The President began by reading a statement, so that there would be no misunderstanding or misquotations from his pronouncement. He said, in part:

Anyone who knows Sherman Adams has never had any doubt of his personal integrity and honesty; no one has believed that he could be bought. But there is a feeling or belief that he was not sufficiently alert in making certain that the gifts of which he was the recipient could be so misinterpreted as to be considered as attempts to influence his official actions. To that extent he has been, as he stated yesterday, "imprudent."

The utmost prudence must necessarily be observed by everyone attached to the White House, because of the possible effect of any slightest inquiry, suggestion or observation emanating from this office and reaching any other part of the Government. Carelessness must be avoided.

My own conclusions on the entire episode are as follows: (1) I believe that the presentation made by Governor Adams to the Congressional Committee yesterday truthfully represents the pertinent facts; (2) I personally like Governor Adams; (3) I admire his abilities; (4) I respect him because of his personal and official integrity; (5) I need him.

Admitting the lack of that careful prudence in this incident that Governor Adams yesterday referred to, I believe with my whole heart that he is an invaluable public servant, doing a difficult job efficiently, honestly and tirelessly.

Ladies and gentlemen, so far as I am concerned, this is all that I can, all that I shall, say.

This honest assertion by the President has merely added more fuel to the flames. Today the cry is even greater than it has been at any time during the week—Adams must go!

This is a shocking series of events for all of us who met Sherman Adams at the same time the President did—back in 1952—and have been a part of the team ever since. It is a tragic thing to sit here and watch Adams grow thinner and sadder day by day. One wants to go up and tell him to have heart and to hold on, but it is difficult to do this to a man who for so long has had the reputation and demeanor of an iceberg.

That day, after he returned from testifying on the Hill, he came into the dining room with his wife and his friend Gerry Morgan. Despite the fact that he had given an admirable performance before the committee, he appeared blanched, tired and sad. I came back to my office that afternoon and wrote him a little note, telling him of the homely philosophy of my grandfather, who had fought his way out of slavery to become a free man and a foremost citizen. The essence of his philosophy had been that no matter how tough things get, "one must keep on keeping on." I also telephoned Mrs. Adams to tell her that my wife and I were with them in spirit and prayer.

The next day the Governor sent me a very cordial note of thanks for my personal support and faith in him. It is one I treasure.

June 23, 1958

THE Negro leaders have had a pleasant meeting with the President, and A. Philip Randolph did a masterful job. The problem of greatest concern to the conferees was the matter of the district federal judge in Arkansas who had given the Little Rock board of education a stay of two and a half years before starting to integrate the school system there. If the stay was permitted to stand, it would mean that the eight Negro children who had already been admitted to Little Rock Central High School last year would not be permitted to return, but would be sent to enroll in Negro high schools.

This is certainly a slap in the face as far as the Supreme Court decision is concerned, and there was strong feeling at the meeting that the Federal District Court's decision had been made from the standpoint of personal bias rather than from that of law.

The President listened with deep attention, and this in itself was reassuring to the delegation. Attorney General Rogers was there, and tried to answer some of the questions. The meeting was supposed to last thirty minutes, but because of its intense interest to the President, it stretched to almost an hour. The press came in to take photographs, and after this the delegation was ushered to an anteroom where it met the reporters. The delegation did a sensational job of parrying loaded questions. It was a creditable performance, and I feel that both the President and the group benefited by the meeting.

JULY 9, 1958

ONE of the enigmas of my relationship with the White House has been the answer as to why I was not given the position promised me at the beginning of the President's term in 1953, and why I had to wait almost two years before a place was found for me on the White House staff. I had resolved that sometime before I left the White House I would simply ask Sherman Adams. From time to time, Max Rabb had hinted at various reasons, but he was never very specific. I believe that my conference with Governor Adams today has brought me nearer to knowing the answer than I have ever been.

Earlier this week I had sent Sherman Adams a memo telling him that I felt I deserved a raise. For the past two years I have had to entertain visiting dignitaries from nonwhite countries, at the request of the State Department or others. In addition to this, as I have grown in stature in the Administration and my presence on the staff has become better publicized, the members of Negro groups meeting in Washington, or here for any other reasons, call and ask to see me in my office or at home. I always try to see as many of these people as I possibly can. I feel that in answering their questions or letting them talk to me I help them understand the philosophy of the Administration and particularly that of the President.

I am being asked to speak to many more groups throughout the country, and more often than not the fee available is not sufficient to cover my actual expenses. Before I was married I used my own funds to cover these deficits, but that is no longer possible. So it was with some alarm that I realized that my savings account was terribly small and that a part of each salary check was earmarked to pay for obligatory entertaining.

Sherman Adams has asked Andy Goodpaster to explore the contents of my memo, so he and I had two meetings, and I went over all these details with him.

Mr. Adams has a reputation for not being happy about paying high salaries or for increasing those already in existence. The conviction that one should always be able to live within his means is a part of his New England tradition. It did not surprise me that so much time was spent in making an analysis of my situation with strict concern as to whether my request for a higher salary was warranted.

This afternoon Mr. Adams called me and Andy Goodpaster into his office to give me a firm but gentle lecture on my financial condition. He felt that no man should be in a position where the demands were greater than he could afford, and it took considerable determination on my part to explain that these social demands were not at my request or desire, but were a part of my official duties and the requirements of my position.

I had explained to Andy Goodpaster that I had exhausted my life's savings trying to protect my home and my mother's health before I came to Washington and that this had been my situation when the White House disappointed me in employment after I had been advised to resign at CBS and told that I would be reporting for work in Washington within a month. For more than a year after this I had had to try to make enough money to live on and support my family, had never been able to recover from this financially, and a large part of my present problems stems directly from this.

I could tell that this matter had preyed upon Sherman Adams' mind and that he felt he still owed me some kind of explanation. He was his usual clear, frank, honest self. He very distinctly remembered the promise that had been given me. It had not materialized at that time because no one had had any clear-cut idea of his own job and certainly none as to what I could do that would not result in unfavorable comment. He said he recalled discussing me with the top aides and telling them that I was coming to Washington and to the White House, and their asking him, "But what will he do?"

Adams said that there had been no answer to that and that the decision had been that something would have to be worked out so that my job would be more than just a sinecure. He said he hoped I understood.

I understood very clearly. But, again, I have never been able to understand why someone in the Administration—particularly on the White House staff—didn't have the courage and the courtesy to call or write me and tell me honestly what had happened. All of these people knew me and what I stood for, and they should have known that they could be frank with me. I can only imagine that the general embarrassment was so great that no one wanted the distasteful assignment of "belling the cat."

Well, finally I have been able to get a partial answer to a question that has worried me more than any I have ever had to deal with.

I don't know what the outcome will be on my legitimate request for a raise, but at least today's conference has been helpful in supplying a part of my long-sought answer to a difficult personal riddle.

This is the first conference I have had with Sherman Adams since he has been involved in the hideous Goldfine matter. He looked better than he has looked in several weeks, and he was thinking clearly and talking with assurance and conviction.

At the end of our conference he stood up and gave me a particularly firm handclasp, and we looked each other as straightly in the eye as we have always done.

(P.S. I got the raise.)

July 17, 1958

IT has been reported here that J. Ernest Wilkins, Assistant Secretary of Labor, has resigned but that his resignation will not be announced for awhile yet. The real story behind this is not available, although I understand that there have been personal differences between him and Secretary of Labor James Mitchell. Because of my official position here, I have been aware of the impending resignation and have even seen the proposed letters to be exchanged between the White House and Mr. Wilkins. I was shocked today to discover that his successor has already been chosen and that he is white.

Present plans call for a friendly exchange of letters between Mr. Wilkins and the President, and Mr. Wilkins will come to the White House for a farewell with him. Then the exchange of correspondence between them will be given to the press.

There will be a horrendous explosion in the Negro press when it is discovered that this sub-Cabinet position is lost to Negroes. Mr. Wilkins, or rather, the job he held, was a symbol of positive achievement to Negroes. It is the first time in history that any Negro has been a member of the President's Cabinet, and it was a definite step forward on the American scene. With this highest appointive position lost, there will be much disillusionment and dismay about the Eisenhower Administration.

It is difficult for me to understand this kind of bungling. It may be a personal thing on the part of Secretary James Mitchell, who received rough treatment at the hands of Clarence Mitchell, NAACP executive, during the newsmen's conference here early in May. At that time Clarence accused Mitchell of telling an untruth when the Secretary observed that we could have had a stronger civil rights bill if the liberals had held fast during the critical period of debate in the Congress. Mr. Mitchell may have decided that he has had enough of the whole thing, and perhaps this is his method of indicating displeasure. On the other hand, he has always been a liberal and a friend of the Negro, and I cannot believe that he would let emotion and personal feeling enter into a decision of this kind.

It distresses me that there is no Negro Republican politician with stature enough to fight this thing. Val Washington is a close friend of Ernest Wilkins and probably had a hand in securing his appointment, but whether he has been able to do anything or reach anyone in an effort to secure this job for another Negro is not known. If there is a weakness in this Administration as far as Negroes are concerned, I feel it is because there is no strong political group which can do battle with any degree of effectiveness in a crisis such as this. There is no outstanding individual who can throw his weight around—no one like the late Oscar dePriest of Chicago, who could stand up and bellow any place in the country and get results from the leadership of the party.

July 30, 1958

I WENT to see the Vice-President on personal business today. It had to do with my decision on whether I should make a career out of government or go ahead with my present plans to leave here at the end of this Administration and go back into business. As much as I like working in the White House, a possible change of administration would naturally mean the resignation of all of the present presidential staff. This would seem to be a good time to be thinking seriously about what one should do and the best time to do it. The President is beginning to receive a great many resignations from members of his personal staff, and there have been several important changes in the Administration in the past two or three years. This means that men are going back to private business while they are still on top.

I asked the Vice-President whether he thought my pioneering job in Government had borne fruit and whether he felt that there would be a place for one of my talents in any future administration. I told him I had come to him as a personal friend and not because he was Vice-President, and I wanted his honest opinion and advice.

He urged me to continue to plan making a career out of government. He said that I was not only a rare "Negro," but a rare human being with qualities that were valuable to the Government. He felt that I must continually break through into new areas, achieve goals and help blaze a trail that would make it easier to integrate other Negroes into top Government echelons. He said that one of my greatest assets was the fact that I did not resent being a Negro; that I did not use my color as an excuse for any misfortune I might encounter.

He gave keen observations on his whole attitude toward the position of Negroes in the Federal Government. He was critical of naming a Negro to any position that had to deal with race relations or "minority matters." He said that his attitude and view on this were different from many men in public life and even different from that of the present Administration. For example, he felt that despite the fact that Val Washington was doing a good job, it was a mistake to have a Negro in that spot; that he would not only be emotionally involved in any problem concerning the race, but that it is rather pathetic to see a Negro laboring on something that consistently points up race or color.

He was critical of the position that Max Rabb had held in the White House as a minority adviser to the President. He felt that this merely made it possible for prejudiced persons to feel that Max's job consisted of looking out for the welfare of Jews or Negroes and trying to make it possible for them to reach places of influence in Government. He felt that if anyone had to be placed in these spots, it should be someone who was not a member of a minority, and if they had to deal with matters of race, it should not be a Negro. He was in favor of qualified Negroes being designated as ambassadors, but felt that they should not be sent to all-Negro countries.

I agreed with the Vice-President's views wholeheartedly and was pleased that he should be thinking in such a progressive vein. He said that not only now, but if he ever achieved any other position in Government, he would utilize it to permit Negroes greater opportunities to serve their country in positions of prestige and influence.

July 31, 1958

KWAME NKRUMAH, the Prime Minister of Ghana, has been in Washington and is now enjoying a pleasant visit in Chicago. His three-day stay here was interesting. Upon his arrival at the airport, he was given a 19-gun salute and met by the Vice-President, the Diplomatic Corps and Government officials. I was in the receiving line when he got off his plane. That noon the President gave an official White House luncheon for him, and I was one of the guests. The guest list was studded with persons prominent in Government and in the industrial world and was a very enjoyable affair.

A rather queer thing happened during the Prime Minister's visit. There were several official affairs, such as the Vice-President's formal dinner, the formal dinner given by the Secretary of State, the formal dinner given by the Ambassador to the United States from Ghana, and Nkrumah's dinner for the Vice-President. I was not invited to any of these affairs, and it caused some eyebrow raising and direct questions from the press and other interested persons. There have been many feasible explanations offered as to why I was not in attendance. One is that persons invited to White House luncheons are seldom included in the guest lists for dinners given by the Secretary of State or the Vice-President. This was by no means a full explanation. Many have attended two or more of these affairs.

This is the first indication to me that there has been some undercover work in this matter of the suggestion of guests for these functions. I rather think I know who is behind this, but it is too early to give any definite opinion. Some persons here in Washington who have a degree of influence and who like to masquerade before the public as persons with tremendous inside power, as far as the Administration is concerned, will never forgive me for quietly arranging the meeting between Negro leaders and the President last month. These persons were not consulted, and have a feeling that their bailiwick was invaded.

I have no intense feeling about this, except that in the matter of the visit of the Prime Minister of Ghana, it was rather expected that I would be present at official affairs. I had represented the President, along with the Vice-President, at the birth of the new nation of Ghana in March of 1957. There has been and will continue to be considerable speculation as to why I was omitted from the guest lists.

AUGUST 22, 1958

AFTER much indecision and debate, the President today consented to see the leaders of the Negro Elks who are holding their national conference here in Washington. The original request was for him to review their parade, but this was turned down as not feasible. Many staff members were against the President's seeing the leaders, but Republican National Chairman Meade Alcorn, Speaker Joe Martin and others urged the White House to reconsider. The leadership of the Elks is Republican, and they supported the President heavily in 1952 and 1956. After some complications, we finally got them into the White House, and I presented them to the President at 11 A.M. this morning.

It was an outstanding group that trooped in to extend greetings to the President and to praise him for his sympathetic and humanitarian leadership. He was deeply impressed, and instead of shooing them out of the office as had been indicated before the meeting, he made a couple of informal speeches which warmed the hearts of the visitors. He then had pictures taken with them and gave each one of them a small souvenir from his desk—to the men, pocket-sized knives with his initials engraved on the blades, and pens inscribed with his name to the women.

The most significant part of the day for me was the five minutes before the Elks met the President, when I went into his office to brief him on their activities and what he might say to them. He asked me to sit down, and indicated that he was in a mood to talk to me about matters other than just the Elks. I told him that this was one of the largest Negro fraternal organizations in the country, that their activities were educational and charitable, and that their scholarships were available to white as well as Negro. He seemed pleased by this, and it gave him a cue for a short speech he wanted to make to them about their activities.

Then, without warning, he said to me, "Tell me, what is the feeling in the country on this fellow Powell?" I was startled for a minute and obviously showed it. He said, "You know—the Congressman in Harlem who won the overwhelming victory against Tammany Hall. What do the people think about his indictment for tax evasion?" I said, "Sir, the common feeling in Harlem is that Adam Powell is being given a 'ride' not only because he bolted and supported you, but because he is such an outspoken individual, not only in Congress, but on every public platform in the country when it comes to speaking out in behalf of civil rights and first-class citizenship for Negroes."

The President seemed interested in this information.

This is the end of one of the busiest weeks in my memory. Catherine and I left Washington last weekend, headed for the wilds of Michigan, with a short two-day stay in Chicago. We had hardly arrived there when telephone calls from the White House suggested my immediate return to cope with very pressing problems. The second day after our arrival in Chicago, Sherman Adams called to ask my assistance in dealing with a request made by Mrs. Daisy Bates of Little Rock, Arkansas, for the President to see her and the nine Negro children who had attended Central High School last year. At the present time these nine youngsters have achieved some kind of fame for enduring strife and abuse and even bodily assaults at the high school last year. It was because of them that the President had to order the Army into Little Rock.

Mrs. Bates' request could not have been more ill-timed. At the moment, the country is seething with unrest prior to next month's new school term. Virginia, Arkansas and other southern states have already determined that they will close their schools or risk bloodshed rather than see Negroes in attendance.

Mr. Adams asked me for a straight opinion as to whether I thought Mrs. Bates' request was a wise one at this time. I have tried to free myself from all emotional feeling on racial matters and to deal objectively with them whenever I am asked for advice by the White House. It is a difficult thing to do, but my usefulness here would be at an end if I did not make an honest attempt at it.

I told him that in view of the current unrest throughout the country, I did not feel that it would be wise for the President to see these youngsters and Mrs. Bates. It could be misunderstood. Anti-integrationists would use this for propaganda purposes, implying that the President was giving these children his complete blessing. He would not be dealing with this school situation as an impartial judge or on the basis of what is best for the entire country; he would be dealing with it on the basis that he was thoroughly sympathetic with the aspirations and ambitions of these nine Negro children. In this case it is not a question of whether the President's seeing them is the right or usual procedure; it is a case of how the meeting could be used to destroy the President's future usefulness in connection with this highly emotional national problem.

I also suggested that this meeting could subject these students to more abuse than ever before, and certainly the President did not want to be an innocent party to this kind of affair. Segregationists have already accused the NAACP of dictating the President's position and attitude on integration, and there have been articles in southern newspapers indicating that I, as a former staff member of the NAACP, was calling the shots on racial matters in the White House. All this added up to the fact that we could not keep this visit within normal channels; it could balloon into a *cause célèbre* which would do more harm than good. The Governor said: "You are absolutely correct. That was also my thinking on the meeting."

He then asked me, if I thought it wise, to call Mrs. Bates and in an honest and forthright manner tell her why it would not be feasible for the President to see these youngsters. I dreaded making this call. Mrs. Bates was friendly enough, but obviously distressed and disappointed. She felt it was the human and patriotic thing to do and that it would destroy a great deal of adverse criticism abroad, where Communist propaganda and other propaganda had given substance to the theory that the Government and the Administration were not solidly behind civil rights and democratic policies.

I tried to point out to her that the President had demonstrated his sincerity by sending troops into Little Rock last year and that his many pronouncements since then have shown that he would uphold and defend the Constitutional laws of the country. I told her that he was terribly alone in many of his actions, and to subject him to further abuse and criticism from the hostile South would be thoughtless and unkind. Furthermore, I told her that I could not make the President or anyone else see these youngsters, but that I would report her feelings and call her again on Thursday when I had reached Washington and had talked to other officials in the White House.

I flew back to Washington and immediately went to work on this. One fortunate thing had happened during my absence. At the President's press conference on Wednesday he had issued another clear-cut statement on his responsibility as far as carrying out the oath of his office is concerned. He had made it clear that whenever the laws of the land were challenged by anarchy, he would do all within his power to restore law and order, even if it meant the use of troops. This is part of his statement:

> The very basis of our individual rights and freedoms rests upon the certainty that the President and the executive branch of Government will support and insure the carrying out of the decisions of the Federal Courts.
>
> Every American must understand that if an individual, community or state is going successfully and continuously to defy the courts, then there is anarchy.
>
> I continue to insist that the common sense of the individual and his feeling of civic responsibility must eventually come into play if we are to solve this problem.

Perhaps the punch line was the statement: "My feelings are exactly as they were a year ago." An interpretation of this means that, if necessary, troops will be sent wherever they are required, to implement the law.

I called Roy Wilkins to tell him our attitude and to ask his help in making Mrs. Bates understand that the President's decision was not a matter of discrimination but one of sound judgment. When I asked Roy to request her not to insist further upon the meeting, he acted as an intermediary for me in explaining the attitude of the White House.

I talked to Mrs. Bates in the afternoon, and she was very cooperative. She had been greatly impressed by the President's statement the day before, and she was in a better position to realize the pressures that were on him because of that statement. She could understand that it would merely add to his burdens if the children were formally presented to him at the White House. I told her that we would see to it that the young people were put on one of our specially conducted tours and that they would see every part of the White House that was open to the public. I also told her that if she would contact my office, my secretaries would be happy to help in any way they could. This program seemed acceptable to her.

Mr. Adams was very pleased with this solution, and he told me it was a good job.

It's probably difficult for outsiders to understand our concern over what seems to be a routine request, but those of us who are close to the scene know that the country is just about ready to split in half over this matter of school integration. The rumblings are severe; even staff members are in violent disagreement as to the wisdom of the President's statement at his Wednesday press conference. In any organization of this type there are bound to be all shades of opinions and feelings, and some of the southern members of the staff feel that the President has gone too far in proclaiming his insistence upon using all the strength at his command to carry out the provisions of the Supreme Court decision. Some feel that he should have canceled the press meeting so that he would not have been forced into making a statement which would completely antagonize the segregationists.

There is a tense feeling within the White House at this time, and this merely points up the attitudes throughout the country.

Right now, any projects or meetings involving Negroes are not looked upon very kindly in some areas of the White House. These are difficult hours for me as I try to carry out my responsibilities to the President and not appear completely disloyal to my race in the eyes of my friends.

The average intelligent Negro feels that it is now or never, and no matter how painful this period may be to the country, righteousness always comes out of conflict and strife. It can never just happen! Negroes feel that to back down or agree to compromise will merely postpone for another 300 years their visions of complete citizenship. Only a Negro can understand this attitude. For those who have always enjoyed first-class citizenship, it is difficult to appreciate the black American's burning desire for complete recognition.

SEPTEMBER 11, 1958

I ATTENDED another historic event today when I went up to the Supreme Court to hear the final argument on the Little Rock case.

It took quite some doing for me to get into the courtroom, which holds only 150 people. Gerald Morgan, the President's Special Counsel, had called Solicitor General Rankin's office to try to get me a seat. He was told to have me in the marshal's office at 11:40 and Rankin would try to get me into one of the alcoves off the courtroom.

I arrived at the marshal's office to find thousands of people lined up outside, trying to get in. They were flashing identification cards, claiming to be friends of high officials—using every kind of influence or threat to get a seat. But the Supreme Court aides were adamant and admitted only those with proper credentials. They did not have my name on their list, so I had to stand around and wait for the Solicitor General.

In the office were many prominent Negroes who asked me to help them get in, but I explained how helpless I was and that I was not even certain I'd get in myself.

When the Solicitor General did arrive, everyone began pleading with him. I tried to identify myself to him across the uproar, and he suddenly thrust his large briefcase into my hands and said: "You are now my messenger."

I was a little taken aback at this, but then realized that it was his strategy to get me past inquiring officials. The only bad thing about it was that several prominent Negroes heard him refer to me as his messenger, and their eyebrows went up. However, I got into the courtroom and had a front-row seat.

The attorney for the Little Rock school board pleaded, as he had two weeks ago in his first argument, that Little Rock must be allowed a "reasonable delay" in its plan to desegregate the school. Otherwise, he said, the school board would be helpless in the face of opposition from the public and the government of Arkansas.

At the start of the session, Chief Justice Earl Warren announced that the question before the court was: "Does violent local opposition to school integration justify postponement of a desegregation plan?" District Court Justice Harry Lemley had granted Little Rock a postponement of two and a half years. The Court of Appeals for the Eighth Circuit reversed him.

Today's session brought out a few issues that had not been thoroughly argued two weeks ago, or were positions changed, but the drama of the jammed courtroom and interest in the justices' questions remained high. Both Thurgood Marshall, representing the NAACP, and Solicitor General Rankin spoke of the provisional constitutional rights of Negro children to non-segregated schools. They said that those rights were "present and personal." They said that in allowing implementation of its 1954 decision the Supreme Court had put the burden on defendant school boards to show some constructive reason for any delay. Unless there is such a reason, they said, the constitutional rights must be granted forthwith.

Mr. Rankin went on to say that the United States had been created by the separate states, precisely to resolve the bitter controversies that arose between them. He said that the United States must be supreme, and he derided the school-board argument that two sovereignties were at war.

Before going up to the Supreme Court, I had gone to an interesting meeting in Gerry Morgan's office—along with Assistant Attorney General Wilson White, in charge of the civil rights division of the Justice Department; Gordon Tiffany, Executive Director of the Commission on Civil Rights; Bryce Harlow,

Presidential Assistant; and Rocco Siciliano—to discuss what the President's role ought to be in this raging controversy. I had requested this meeting after receiving a letter from Roy Wilkins, who portrayed the bitterness among Negroes in this country because of the recent arrest of Martin Luther King by Montgomery, Alabama, policemen, his subhuman treatment, and the general feeling on the part of Negroes that they were being ignored by the leaders of their Government and would have to "go it alone."

Bryce Harlow reported that he had recently returned from a trip through certain sections of the South and the Southwest, and said that the feeling in those areas was that the President was not showing leadership or initiative in this crisis and that the country was slowly drifting toward chaos and confusion over the bitter school controversy. He felt, as I did, that there are certain forces for good in this country that, given leadership, direction, and encouragement, would be a great boon toward any effort to mold sentiment in favor of carrying out the Supreme Court's original decision.

We feel that no matter what the President's personal views may be, this is a clear mandate for him to take the initiative to put his views before the country, request the citizenry to put their personal feelings behind them, and try to make this facet of our democracy work. We felt that the President must—at the earliest possible moment after the Supreme Court handed down its decision on this present case—go to the country on television and radio to stress the moral necessity of Americans' obeying the Supreme Court's decision.

I was pleased at the apparent unanimity of opinion. It takes a certain amount of courage for staff members to tell the President that their feeling is that he must take this or that action. We all realize that this is a distasteful situation. Most of us would like to avoid it, but all of us were aware of a strong sense of responsibility to both the President and the country, and it was our considered judgment that a committee must wait on the President and request him to speak out.

We talked to the Attorney General on the telephone and told him our feelings. His advice was that we should have some kind

252] BLACK MAN IN THE WHITE HOUSE

of prepared script to put into the President's hands for a possible speech. This made sense, and Judge W. Wilson White of the Department of Justice and I were appointed to try to put together some kind of a rough draft.

The President will speak to the nation tonight on the dangers we face in regard to the situation in the Quemoy Islands, where the Red Chinese are threatening invasion and our Seventh Fleet seems to be the only thing between their success and the Chinese Nationalists who occupy the island of Formosa. It will be difficult to try to get to the President during this short period while he is here from his summer place in Newport, Rhode Island, and to try to convince him that he has another chore that he must perform right away. I do hope we will have the opportunity to do this. If not, we will all be severely disappointed.

In our meeting today it was brought out that right across the bridge in Alexandria, Virginia, may be the beginning point of another Civil War. The schools open there Monday. If the Supreme Court sustains its original decision that Negroes must be admitted to secondary schools without delay, the Governor of Virginia has promised to close those public schools that Negroes have tried to enter. If this happens, there will develop a bitterness that will be difficult to defeat or stamp out. Pupils will be angry—particularly those in high school senior classes who are looking forward to college and will not be able to be certified for it because of missing precious school time. Parents will be angry because children will be under their feet with nothing to do. Besides that, there will be a wholesale denial of educational opportunities for all young people.

There is only one bright spot in this dark picture. Many of these parents, who are opposed to the closing of the schools for any reason, may have the courage to speak out if there is some evidence of leadership and direction on the national scene, and if help is available to them. I believe that when intelligent citizens are faced with the stark prospect of having their schools closed because of the admission of some Negroes to classes, they will be unwilling to go along with this edict without fighting back. But until this hope is crystallized and until leadership is furnished, there will be confusion, bitterness and perhaps bloodshed.

This is the stark picture that faces us today as we await the Supreme Court's latest decision.

September 23, 1958

SHERMAN ADAMS announced, in a dramatic national radio-television speech last night, that he has resigned as the Assistant to the President.

"I have done no wrong," he said.

Thus comes to an end the career of a most able and dedicated public servant.

I seldom agree with David Lawrence, columnist of the New York *Herald Tribune,* but today Mr. Lawrence brilliantly and succinctly expressed my views on what happened to Sherman Adams. He wrote:

> An innocent man went to the gallows of American politics tonight—convicted, not by a jury of his peers, but by the political hangmen of the hour. His head was not bowed in shame, for his conscience was clear. He yielded only to the law of expediency, which enforces its criminal verdict to satisfy the passions of the mob, even in politics.

Mr. Adams' address to the nation was a masterly, solemn, dignified performance, and at the close of his eight-minute talk his voice appeared to break and he seemed on the verge of tears. As Catherine and I watched the performance we were extremely touched. Sherman Adams meant more to me, perhaps, than any other member of the White House staff, with the exception of the President.

Since I first met him on the campaign train in 1952 he has taken a distinct interest in my career and welfare and he has never hesitated to help me wherever and whenever he could.

There was a camaraderie between us that is hard to define. It was he who brought me into the White House after two years' delay while a "climate" was being fashioned for my entry. His door was always open to me, and his remarkable wife Rachel has been my wife's friend and protector. No matter where we met her or under what circumstances, she always made certain that we felt welcome and relaxed.

It will be impossible to fill his place. Perhaps it is true that no human being is indispensable, but Sherman Adams comes pretty near to filling this role in this present situation. Perhaps the President is the only living man who knows what Adams has shouldered and what he has done in helping to carry the burdens of the President's office. Only those of us who worked with him knew of his selflessness, dedication, fierce loyalty to his country, and incomparable integrity.

OCTOBER 21, 1958

FOR the past few weeks I have been active in making speeches across the country in an effort to help Republican candidates. I spent about ten days in California, concentrating in Los Angeles and San Francisco, to bolster the sagging spirits of Senator Knowland's cohorts.

At this writing it all looks like a lost cause, despite the fact that the President is out there now, making hard-hitting speeches. It seems incredible that California, as far as Republicans are concerned, can have gone so far downhill since the 1956 election. There is intraparty strife, and the major candidates—Senator William Knowland, who is running for Governor, and Governor Goodwin Knight, who is a candidate for Knowland's Senate seat—are at odds personally, and this feud and their stubbornness threaten to carry the party down to a humiliating defeat in November.

This was a difficult assignment for me. I fought it up to the last minute, but the Knowland forces had asked for me and had requested the National Committee to pressure the White House into getting me.

I had visited California in February and reported the belief in various areas there that Senator Knowland would give up his Senate seat to run for the governorship. Governor Knight has been an extremely popular individual, and has had heavy support from Labor. He is anxious to be re-elected to the governorship, and his friends indicate that he feels he was double-crossed when Senator Knowland decided to run for governor, which more or less forced Knight to run for the Senate seat, in which he was not particularly interested.

Labor has poured a great deal of money and talent into California to help defeat Knowland, who is actively supporting his right-to-work proposition. This bullheaded attitude of the Senator's—despite all indications that this proposition will lose him the election and will defeat the party—is a bitter thing to Republican leaders within and without the state. It is difficult to understand why he is putting personal ambitions or feelings above the fate of the party.

There was little I could say in favor of Mr. Knowland's candidacy. Negroes by and large are opposed to him, because they feel that the Oakland *Tribune,* owned by his family, has not supported ideals and propositions close to Negroes in their struggle for recognition. They think that he has small sympathy for their efforts. However, the present Attorney General, Pat Brown, is very popular with Negroes, and apparently has been much closer to their thoughts and aspirations than Knowland.

I spent most of my time meeting with small groups of Negro leaders, listening to their gripes, and trying to counsel with them on future methods of dealing with our problems. It would have been fatal for me to have gone out there and demanded or insisted that Negroes support Mr. Knowland completely and that they ignore their personal feelings in the interests of an over-all success. Negroes today are voting for men and measures that are in sympathy with their determination to become first-class citizens in this generation. I would have been accused of high treason if I ignored their attitudes and bullheadedly pleaded for support of a political party whose candidates were lukewarm toward these hopes.

Sherman Adams is preparing to leave, and there is a barren atmosphere in his old office, and a deep melancholia among those of us who were close to him, both officially and personally. I congratulated Wilton Persons upon his appointment to the old Adams post, and received a very friendly reply from him. I believe that Persons will do a good job, because he is completely dedicated to the President. I am certain, however, that from this point on it will be difficult to get through to the President any observations, suggestions, or counsel on the matter of racial problems and particularly in the present delicate field of civil rights and desegregation.

I am already beginning to miss Sherman Adams. He solidly supported me in my activities, my thinking and my efforts to make both the President and the Administration look good in the eyes of Negro Americans. But the present atmosphere among staff members indicates that I will be in for heavy sledding in the future. Already, there have arisen little incidents that indicate jealousy and petty feelings over the role I am playing in White House affairs.

There have been obvious leaks from my office about personal matters, and these could only have come from some staff member working with persons not completely happy about my position here. It is very trying to have to be on the alert twenty-four hours a day to avoid any kind of inadvertency that could be magnified to destructive proportions.

People who recognize my bond with Sherman Adams now realize that I am more or less alone as far as having a strong friend at court is concerned. I must face the fact that all may not be well in the days to come.

October 24, 1958

THE fast tempo of the past few weeks goes on as S.O.S. calls continue to come into the Republican National Committee for me to speak for candidates who seem to be in trouble. I have never even met half of these people, but by some magic they seem to know about me when they find themselves in difficulty with Negro voters. More often than not, these candidates have a terrible record in the field of civil rights or in supporting the Administration's legislation, and this always makes it difficult for me to accept their invitations with a feeling of complete honesty. Considerable pressures have been brought to bear in high places in the White House to get me to reconsider engagements that I have turned down, and I am always faced with the fact that as a team player, I have no alternative but to go out into the field and help the beleaguered candidate.

The President returned to Washington yesterday from the first of a series of campaign speeches he will make in various sections of the country. The staff went out to meet him, and we were all pleased when he came down the ramp looking well and in a jovial mood.

I went to the airport in a staff car with several other members of the President's official family. Among them were: Bob Merriam, Dr. Saulnier, Wayne Warrington, and Jack Anderson.[1] Homer Gruenther,[2] who normally supervises these activities, was running around outside the west entrance of the White House, dispatching cars and their occupants. Homer is a lovable personality and reminds one of a big, playful Saint Bernard dog. Noticing his hectic activity, Jack Anderson said that the best description of Homer was one given recently by General Persons, who said: "Homer reminds me of a nigger rat running into an ambush of white mice." Sitting in the rear seat, I did not quite catch what he had said, so I asked him to repeat it. He turned around, and facing me squarely, repeated the remark. I was aghast and noticed Merriam flush while the others gave embarrassed chuckles. Jack laughed hilariously, obviously enjoying not only the story but the look of amazement on my face.

My first impulse was to get out of the car, but I remembered that I am supposed to be impervious to these things.

When I returned to the White House, the first phone call I had was from Bob Merriam, telling me he was terribly sorry the situation had occurred and that he had been embarrassed

---

1 Merriam, Deputy Assistant to the President, for Interdepartmental Affairs; Saulnier, Chairman of the President's Council of Economic Advisers; Warrington, Special Assistant in the White House; Anderson, Administrative Assistant to the President.
2 Assistant to the Deputy Assistant.

beyond description. He wanted to apologize for his unthinking companions and hoped I would not let this situation make any difference in my relationship or attitude toward the staff. I assured him that my quick hurt had healed and that I would try to overlook the matter, which I was sure had come at an unthinking moment and was not vicious in intent.

But this is one more indication that things will not be the same with Sherman Adams gone. The staff has developed toward me a kind of respect that, whether genuine or not, has been decent and impassive. But in the past few weeks there have been increasing signs that more liberties will be taken with me now. I'm not going to go out of my way to look for incidents, and will not begin to wear my feelings on my sleeve, but I am determined that in the future I will speak out boldly and unequivocably in situations where persons are so crude as to forget that I am a human being before I am a Negro.

NOVEMBER 21, 1958

THE campaign has left me no time for journal writing. The defeat in the November 4 elections across the country was devastating. Since the party had to lose, I am glad it was a crushing kind of defeat. This should indicate, even to the most obtuse, that something must be done organically from top to bottom if Republicans are to survive as a party.

Every place I spoke during the election, the atmosphere was heavy with defeat; in every place there was an indication that the leadership was archaic, misinformed, and still holding onto blueprints of the dead past. In most cases where Republicans were defeated, the opposition candidate was young and vigorous and had an exciting program. Most of our men were running on a platform and a record that were not too impressive, and those who tried to hang on to the President's coattails and run on the national platform had, in many instances, been individuals who had opposed his program at every turn and had been effective in blocking its introduction.

The situation in California was pathetic. I spent more than ten days there, and tried to be honest in my approach. I told the leadership that I did not see how it could possibly win with the program it had outlined for the electorate. There was bitter intraparty strife. The pro-Knight forces felt that Senator Knowland had double-crossed Governor Knight and that Senator Knowland wanted to become governor for selfish reasons which would permit him to control the state delegation in the 1960 presidential election. There was no cooperation between the candidates, and the entire campaign had a hollow ring.

I went to California because it was a duty and not because I had any heart for it. Negroes by and large were not interested in Mr. Knowland's candidacy or in the Republican party generally. His "Right-to-Work" issue was the one that defeated him.

In my native state of New Jersey, Congressman Robert Kean was running against a personable, youthful and dynamic Democrat by the name of Harrison Williams. Whenever these two men appeared on the same platform or over television, the contrast was obvious and devastating. Mr. Kean came from a distinguished family and had an honorable record of many years of service in the Congress, but he is a deliberate man and no match for the scintillating Williams.

All over the country it appeared to me that people were not voting against the Republicans so much as they were voting for a hope that new faces and a new party would give leadership in these perilous times, and that new individuals would attack the difficult measures of the day with more determination and vigor. It was also obvious that the people were afraid of war and recession and the ultraconservative policy of the present Administration. It is an era of dynamism, and this was evident in the fact that many youthful men were swept into office on the wave of the Democratic landslide.

It is interesting to note that Negroes had a large hand in this Democratic victory. Despite the record of the Republicans in the field of civil rights, it is apparent that Negroes are interested in economics first and foremost, and through union activities they are being taught to believe that the Democratic party offers them greater hope for job opportunities and for participation in party politics at a local level.

A few days after the election, I drew up a memo for the top leadership of the Republican party. I pointed out that in the key cities in the country where Negroes held the balance of power, the Republicans had made little or no effort to interest them, to give them an opportunity to participate in party councils, or to become an integral part of its day-by-day efforts.

In most of the areas where I had been, the Republican leadership was aloof, still looked upon Negroes as a lower class, and talked down to them rather than giving them any chance of equality. This conduct and attitude is fatal in this area of struggle for equality in every facet of American life, and despite the southern wing of the Democratic party and its bitter feelings, the northen wing is doing a very effective job in making it possible for Negroes to share in party councils and in appointing them to jobs of influence and prestige in northern states and cities. Unless the Republican party can come up with a new format in a very short time, it is doomed to defeat and failure in 1960.

Several very interesting things happened to me in the past three weeks. The presidential mail has been heavy on the question of Little Rock and on desegregation of schools in the southern states. These letters have been bitter in their denunciations of the President and his action in sending troops to Little Rock and his determination to uphold the law of the land. It has been difficult for me to phrase thoughtful and objective replies to the writers of these derogatory letters.

As a result of this complex situation, my name has become anathema to a great many southerners. Few of them are aware that I am a Negro, and I believe that if they realized this when they received letters from me in behalf of the President, it could almost lead to another Civil War! At any rate, many of them do not like the replies they receive to their letters to the President, and they immediately sit down and write another letter to me, giving me the same kind of unshirted hell that they gave him.

A few weeks ago, an irate white man from North Carolina came to my office looking for me; luckily I had just left the office on official business. He muttered something about returning to see me and indicated that he was deeply angry about the kind of letter he had received over my signature. The members of my staff were afraid that I might come back to the office while this man was there. If he had met me, I'm sure there would have been fireworks. My color would certainly have enraged him further.

About two weeks ago the President invited Catherine and me, along with some other staff members, to join him and Mrs.

Eisenhower in the East Room Sunday night to hear the Mormon Choir from Salt Lake City. It was a deeply moving experience, and despite my feeling about the Mormons, I have to admit that they have one of the finest musical groups I have ever heard.

Salt Lake City is a difficult city for Negro residents. It has deep-seated, relentless discrimination, and, since the city is run, controlled and practically owned by Mormons, it is only natural that I have developed strong feelings about them.

Two weeks ago 1,000 Negro and white youths descended upon Washington to march from the center of the city to the Lincoln Memorial to listen to speeches pointing up the tragic situation in Little Rock and generally emphasizing the country's undemocratic resistance to integrated schools. A delegation of marchers, led by Harry Belafonte, came to the northwest gate of the White House with a petition which they wished to deliver to the President. They were denied admission, but only because their request for an audience with the President had not been granted. The march through Washington was led by Jackie Robinson, Harry Belafonte, A. Philip Randolph, and many other Negro dignitaries. The Negro community was partially divided on the usefulness of such a march.

Ten days before, the Attorney General had called me to ask if I knew the purpose of the march and why the participants felt that it would be effective. He felt that it was just an opportunity for a demonstration that could only offer an occasion for radicals to get out of hand. Prior to that, I had been familiarized with a Government report that indicated that in many cities the committees for the march had been infiltrated by Communists, who planned to use this event as an opportunity to berate the President and his Administration. For this reason, his advisers were against his seeing this group or any other on this matter.

Jackie Robinson was in town for the Afro-American Cooking Show, and when he called my office I suggested that he come by, as I had something to tell him. I took him into my confidence and told him of my knowledge of the Government report on the composition of the march. I told him that I felt he had nothing to gain by leading such a demonstration, and as a matter of fact it might be disastrous for his future if he became involved in any situations where the Communists were able to capitalize upon his mistakes. I told him that I felt that the march would prove nothing.

The Supreme Court had handed down a decision that made it clear to the whole world that Negroes should and would attend integrated schools. The matter was still in the hands of the Court, and that is where it should remain. Also, the President, in his press conferences and in his meeting with Negro delegations, had indicated that he would support and defend any Supreme Court decision because such actions were inherent in his oath of office. There was, therefore, nothing more that anyone needed to tell the President about the situation in the country; he unquestionably is well-informed on matters of this kind. In my estimation, all the march could do would be to frighten and alienate further those who might be on our side; it would also give the radicals another opportunity to point out that Negroes were merely troublemakers and interested in perpetuating a feud.

I do not know what Jackie did when he left my office, but I do know that within the next thirty-six hours the Negro press began calling to ask: "What did you tell Jackie Robinson in your office at the White House?" This put me in a very embarrassing situation—I had used confidential material to try to help a friend. It also gave me a black eye as far as Negro leadership was concerned, because it looked as though I was against their effort to enlighten the country on the matter of school integration.

This was a valuable lesson for me. I resolved that never again while in this position would I attempt to help individuals reconsider a position that they had taken. When people are emotionally involved in matters such as this, objective thinking and reasoning go out the window. I don't know what the repercussions from this controversy may be, but I only tried to do a duty that I felt I owed to the President as well as to my race.

We're still receiving rabid letters from irate people across the country, damning the President because he did not receive the group. It is my responsibility to answer these letters, trying to point out that the President knew all the facts involved and that it was not necessary—from any standpoint—for him to see another group telling him the things he had heard so often from so many people.

DECEMBER 3, 1958

THIS whole question of race and color—not only in the United States, but around the world—seems to engulf me. Everywhere I go, everyone I see appears to be heavily burdened with problems in this field. It is a real chore for my wife and me to attend social gatherings these days; so many participants seem to delight in launching bitter attacks upon the Administration for its alleged "softness" in not implementing the Supreme Court's decision, or rather for the Administration's lack of leadership in preparing the country to accept the inevitability of desegregation.

At times it is difficult for me to hold my temper and to ride with the punches. Negroes look upon me as a symbol of disloyalty and a kind of benevolent traitor. People so often believe that while my philosophy is like theirs, I hold on to my job because of its prestige and salary. If they could only know the tides that swell within my breast twenty-four hours a day as I try to carry out the responsibilities of this office and remain loyal to the President and to my racial identity, they might be a little more charitable. There are valid arguments on both sides, but it is difficult to meet upon common ground, because of the emotionalism involved. It is a question as to how long I can remain in this uncomfortable position.

Dr. Francis Hammond, brilliant young Negro Public Information Officer for the United States in Morocco, came in to see me today. He is preparing to return to his post there. Francis is a sensible, unemotional man who was formerly Professor of Philosophy at Seton Hall College in New Jersey. He has done well in his field and is not the kind of person to hold resentment without adequate reason. He has done an exceptional job in Rabat, and has come in for considerable news comment because of the nine children in his family—the oldest of whom is eighteen —which he has packed up and moved all over the world with the ease of a daily commuter. He has made many friends among the high officials in Morocco, and his oldest daughter is a confidante of and companion to the young princess of the ruling family.

These achievements have puzzled and angered many of the American officials in Morocco, and Francis has had some difficult times. Every effort was made to prevent him from returning to his post. He was stymied by red tape, and as a last resort, had to spend two weeks in a hospital while doctors looked for non-existent ailments. He knew all along what the score was, and in desperation called his Senator from New Jersey, who demanded that he be released and returned to his post immediately. This got action from the State Department, and Hammond is on his way back.

We talked at length about the "American attitude" on the matter of color and race both here and abroad. It is inconceivable to us that certain elements in the State Department are adamant against having Negroes in positions of responsibility in many legations. He said that what I had seen in Africa and Asia a year ago is even truer today—that the Africans are on the direct road to "Nasserism" because of American duplicity and because the American white man, with his double standard, has made himself *persona non grata* in that area of the world.

If we make a loan to one of these countries, we insist that the money be spent as we want and on the projects we select, and that we maintain leadership and direction in specific instances. There are so many strings attached to our benevolence that these people would rather take their chances with any other "friend."

Here are natural spots for America to station some of its qualified young Negro men and women. These are areas where race and color can lead to confidence and mutual trust; where Negro Americans could render a great service to their own country and to the entire free world. And yet, little if any effort is being made by our country to enlist qualified Negro personnel or to afford opportunities for them in this section of the world.

We discussed the composition of the new secretariat of the new Division of African Affairs in the State Department. Perhaps the man who heads the division and his deputy are pleasant social individuals, but to my mind they are not qualified for effective leadership in their areas. It seems to be no secret that the man who heads the department was suggested as Ambassador to Morocco some time ago, but when feelers were put out by the United States Government in Rabat, he was rejected by the Moroccan Government. Nowhere in this new secretariat on African Affairs is there a Negro deputy, adviser, or anyone in a position of competence and responsibility. This annoys the African nations and is humiliating to American Negroes. Just common sense would seem to dictate that somewhere in this hierarchy black people should be in evidence, if only to impress or pacify the Africans who have to do business with our State Department.

Hammond is returning to his post with great misgivings. The Moroccan Government is reviewing the matter of American bases in that country, and it would be a tragic thing for us if they decided that they wanted Americans out of it. Hammond is certain that he will be more hamstrung than ever and that his effectiveness will decrease as Stateside officials try to get even with him for returning to a post in which they did not want him to remain.

On the home front, bombings and racial strife continue. The school situation in Little Rock, Virginia, and other areas is at a stalemate. No leadership seems to be emerging, and if the tensions and bitterness increase, one wonders what the end will be. There are cries on all sides for the Administration to call a conference of Negro and white leaders under the auspices of the White House to see if some sane understanding can't be obtained. The Administration continues deaf to these pleas. It still does not see what good could come out of a rehash of sectional prejudices and bias.

There is one ray of hope in the Department of Health, Education and Welfare, where Secretary Flemming has come out with a positive statement about the tragedy of the closing of the schools and the disastrous effect it is having on the lives and future of American children. Perhaps Health, Education and Welfare might well call a meeting of the educational heads of the country, and under its direction and leadership, attempt to offer some solution. To my way of thinking, the question of whether such a conference would succeed is far less important than the fact that it would indicate that the Administration is trying to offer sound leadership and direction in this critical period.

December 12, 1958

SINCE Governor Adams' departure, the White House machine has stalled almost completely. There is an atmosphere of indecision and fear which seems to be affecting the attitude and the morale of the entire staff.

I went to Bob Gray's office this afternoon to talk to him about official matters, and we got into a discussion of the present state of White House affairs. I was amazed at how thoroughly we agreed on this. Bob said that he was completely dedicated to Sherman Adams and had intense admiration for him, but felt that he had made a serious mistake in leaving his former duties in the hands of the present occupants.

It is difficult to describe or estimate the position that Adams held and the myriad things he did. He played an active part in nearly every decision made in the White House in the last six years, and he took the brunt of almost every fight and skirmish, no matter with whom it might be. He never shirked a duty or put off making a difficult decision. When hell broke loose because of some White House decision, Adams—without debate or self-pity—would take the responsibility for the decision.

In all fairness, it is easy to understand how any new person would find it difficult to step into his shoes. His responsibilities have been divided among several persons, and this is one of the factors that make it difficult to get a quick, clear-cut decision on anything. There is vacillation, indecision and lack of leadership. No one wants to accept the responsibility for making tough decisions, and consequently, matters are piling up that should have been decided many days ago.

Gray made a further observation—that no matter how busy Adams might be, a memo sent to him during the day would have an answer and a decision before the close of business. Also, if you stepped into his office and he was not busy at the moment, you were free to discuss anything pertinent. Today it takes a long time to get paperwork moved, and this is being felt down in the lower echelons.

I can testify to this personally. I asked for a title that would enable me to sign presidential mail. This memo has been kicked around from desk to desk, there has been complete silence on it, and I am still being embarrassed by having to sign such correspondence without an adequate title. Although this seems an important matter to me and one that could be decided without much ado, there is still no decision forthcoming.

I do not know whether the President has felt Adams' departure as much as some members of the staff, but if what has happened to us is any indication, he must feel it keenly.

December 15, 1958

JAMES HAGERTY never ceases to amaze me. He is a strange person who can be very friendly or very cold—very vocal or very silent. He can also be completely objective or extremely narrow.

When he comes into the staff mess, it is his custom to choose the table occupied by the highest-ranking White House officials. Lesser individuals generally pick any other table in preference to the one where Hagerty is hobnobbing with the top brass. This is because one can't be sure whether Jim will be suffering from his ulcers and not happy to see small fry, or engaged in confidential conversation.

However, I have occupied a table with Jim several times and have always found it interesting. He can be very free in talking about pending problems or matters that have been decided, but the intimate details of which are not available to the average person.

The Republican leadership has been at the White House today, conferring with the President on the legislative program for 1959. There may also have been a discussion on the State of the Union Message. Apparently there has been strong disagreement between some sections of the group over what the new program should be and what the Message should include.

I sat with Hagerty at lunch, and he was adamant on what he felt the President's speech should contain and what he considered the major issues before the nation today.

Jim thinks that both nationally and internationally the pressing question of the moment is that of school integration. He feels that no matter how we hide our heads in the sand, this situation will not go away or be solved until there is active, vigorous leadership on the part of the White House, supported by the liberal members of the party in Congress. He, too, feels that it is a shocking sight to see the schools closed and thousands of youngsters being denied a normal education, merely because adults refuse to yield their personal prejudices to the law of the land.

He finds it shocking that governors and other elected officials thumb their noses at the Constitution and generally discredit and attempt to humiliate the President of the United States. He feels that there are thousands of people in this country awaiting leadership and a display of moral courage on the part of the Administration, and he believes that the time has come when the President must strike out vigorously and assume the leadership of the forces for moral good. I was amazed to hear this recitation, and yet this is consistent with the kind of thing Hagerty has done through the years since I have known him. He instinctively seems to be on the side of the downtrodden, and he is always in favor of bucking the whole world if one honestly believes in the measures he champions.

If most members of the staff had Hagerty's courage and willingness to speak out when the chips were down, this Administration would have a far more impressive record for courage and leadership. Howard Pyle and Anne Wheaton were at the same table, and they agreed with Jim.

I thought this was a good time to ask their advice on what I should do about the complaints that come to me from African diplomats to this country when the State Department is unsympathetic with their problems. I said that in the past months several ambassadors had indicated that while the State Department is coldly precise and correct in its relations with them, there is absolutely no sympathy or human interest expressed in their problems. I felt that it was a tragedy that no Negro served on the staff of the Secretary for African Affairs; this in itself indicated to the Africans an indifference and a bias that could not be concealed.

Hagerty again was very sympathetic and helpful. He suggested that I write Secretary Dulles, but I pointed out that such a letter would never reach the Secretary's desk; it would be routed to the Bureau of African Affairs for evaluation. The reply would be obvious, for one could not expect an office to investigate itself. Whereupon Hagerty suggested that I send the letter to him and he would see that it got into the hands of the Secretary and received attention. This I will do forthwith!

JANUARY 10, 1959

MY NOTES have been interrupted by the Christmas holiday, which Catherine and I spent in Chicago. She still has a nostalgic feeling about that city and considers it home. It is where she was born and raised and has many friends and her only relatives—a sister and nephew.

While we were there I went down to Memphis, Tennessee, to speak at the Emancipation Proclamation celebration on New Year's Day. This is always a tremendous affair in Memphis, and it was an inspiring evening for me. Four thousand people pushed their way into the city auditorium that night. My speech was a hard-hitting outline of what Negroes still have to do to realize complete emancipation. It was the old theme of the necessity of accepting all the responsibilities as well as the privileges of first-class citizenship. I praised what had been accomplished in the ninety-five years since Lincoln's original proclamation, but pointed out that we still had a long dark road ahead.

The mayor and other city officials were there, and this gave me a good opportunity to comment on their attitudes, principles and policy during this critical period. The newspaper coverage was excellent, and the white dailies gave several columns to the speech.

We returned from Chicago on January 2, and I got back to my desk the following day. A friend had sent me the December issue of the publication of the White Citizens Council of Louisiana. The leading article was one attacking me, not only for being a member of the President's staff, but for daring to answer letters from white citizens writing to the President. The article, of course, was designed to incite the unreconstructed liberals and to point out to them that this was the President's method of humiliating southern white citizens, by having his "Negro Assistant" answer their letters.

In addition, articles in the Negro press painted me in a villainous role for answering a telegram to the President from the president of the Monroe, North Carolina, NAACP, in which he had asked the President to take official action in the case of two Negro boys, aged eight and ten, who had been sentenced to a juvenile correctional institution for kissing a ten-year-old white girl. In answering this telegram, I had pointed out that this was outside the jurisdiction of the President's office, since it was purely a local matter. The Justice Department had looked into the case and had discovered that violation of Federal statutes was not involved. North Carolina law permitted, in instances of this kind, the committing of children to institutional homes until the state social working agency had determined that they were ready to be returned to their own homes. No trial is held, and commitment to the home is not considered as punishment for a penal offense. Therefore, the only way the matter could be attacked is through the North Carolina courts, since it involves North Carolina law.

Certain members of the Negro press wrote as if I had been used as a presidential cat's-paw, to insult Negroes and to help the officials of North Carolina withhold their civil rights. It was a typical emotional, unobjective job, and I wrote strong letters of protest to the Negro press.

I went up to the Hill yesterday to hear the President's State of the Union address. It was not a forceful address, but it was a thoughtful one, and I was particularly pleased with the paragraph on civil rights. The President indicated that he would use whatever powers necessary to carry out the provisions of the Constitution. He indicated that officeholders had a particular duty to be in the forefront of those demanding the enforcement and carrying out of the provisions of the Constitution. Needless to say, these references were greeted with heavy silence on the Democratic side of the aisle.

There is every indication that the President is in for heavy going in these last two years. I only hope that he can withstand all of the physical and mental pressures they may hold.

January 27, 1959

TODAY, after almost five years in the White House, I finally received my commission signed by the President, and was officially sworn in to my job by Gerald Morgan in his office at ten thirty this morning. My wife and my secretaries were there, and three or four surprised staff members who dropped into Morgan's office, unaware of what was happening.

This marks the end of a long hard fight to receive proper recognition for my assignment here in the White House. At that, the swearing-in was not done in the usual style or manner. The President usually attends the swearing-in of any of his staff officers, but he was not present at mine. The White House is a little embarrassed about me. I should have been commissioned four years ago when I first came here, and to handle this in the usual manner now could open a Pandora's box of questions and difficult answers. If the President attended, the press would be there, and there would have to be some explanation as to why I was going back to the same job with the same title, and yet was being officially commissioned and sworn in. To prevent this, I agreed to a modest ceremony.

FEBRUARY 10, 1959

LAST week the Dominican Republic, through a public relations man, invited Catherine and me to go on an all-expense-paid junket to the Dominican Republic as guests of its government. Several Negro newspapermen and other prominent individuals have been rounded up and are being flown there for a week, ostensibly to view a horse show and other social events.

The invitation was extended to me by Val Washington at the request of the public relations man. I was shocked at the idea that any thinking American would fall victim to this kind of slick gesture on the part of Dominican officials. Trujillo is one of the most vicious dictators in this hemisphere, and his record of injustice is great. I would be risking my job and laying myself open to cries of "another Adams" if I had let myself be lured into this trap. This is the kind of "innocent" project that can develop into a serious situation for an unsuspecting man.

Another interesting thing has happened during the past two weeks. I had my first interview with Wilton Persons since he succeeded Sherman Adams as Assistant to the President. I requested the meeting, because I wanted to be reassured that the job I was trying to do met Persons' approval. It was rather disconcerting to me that he really had no idea of what I had been doing or what I was doing, and he asked me to brief him on my activities.

He was affable and friendly, and we chatted about the old

days on the campaign train. The General assured me that his door would always be open to me, and that I should directly refer to him any problems I thought needed his personal attention. However, he made a unique request. He asked me to discuss all civil rights and racial matters with Gerry Morgan rather than with him. He made this request on "emotional grounds." I could readily understand his feeling.

Persons is in a difficult spot. He was born and reared in Alabama, and comes from a very prominent family in that state. A brother of his was formerly a governor of Alabama. The General told me that the matter of civil rights and integration had almost divided his family and that they had agreed not to discuss them at all when they were together. A man with all the training, tradition and emotions of an aristocratic Southerner finds himself the number-one man on the team of a President whose Administration has done more than any other to advance the cause of the Negro in the field of civil rights. What a dilemma!

The White House staff personnel has been invited to a dance at Fort Meyer this Saturday. There has been a great deal of interest as to whether Catherine and I would attend; several staff members have asked me gingerly if we were going. I have let it be known that we are not. When pressed as to the reason, I have implied that I did not want to place the less socially secure members of the staff in the predicament of having to decide how to treat the Morrows in public.

Experiences in the past few months indicate that there are several such persons on the staff. Catherine has not even attended any of the White House wives' meetings since Mrs. Adams' departure—she has not been informed when these meetings were being held. Things have changed with the departure of the Adams family.

February 27, 1959

THIS morning's staff meeting was dramatic.

Wilton Persons, who presided, quoted at length from a recent article in the *U. S. News and World Report* which gave a very dismal picture of affairs in the White House since the departure of Sherman Adams. The article stated that staff members were at each other's throats; that they were choosing up sides; that paperwork was piling up because of the impossibility of getting decisions on important matters; and that there had been a general sloughing off of the kind and character of work formerly turned in by staff members. It further indicated that some individuals were even spending their time trying to jump aboard the Nixon or Rockefeller band wagons, and that they had grown severely critical of many Administration policies and moves. It gave the impression that Persons did not have the control over the staff that Adams had had and that he had not been effective in dealing with the many problems that came to his desk.

The article pictured the President as old, inept and worried in his job, and implied that he was becoming irascible and difficult to deal with. It even went so far as to indicate that staff jealousies had developed over who should see the President; that the conservative members of the staff were in the saddle at the present time, and that the President was not even listening to those with liberal views.

It is apparent that this article could only have been written with the help of someone on the staff or very close to it.

Persons handled the situation well. He said he had no fear for himself, but it did shake him to realize what such articles could do to the President. He deplored the fact that somewhere in the staff ranks there might be someone who was disloyal to the President.

He went on to say that if the staff had grievances, they should bring them out in the open. He and Jim Hagerty both warned us that few men have the ability to fence with qualified newsmen and that they generally come out of such bouts defeated. It was felt that whenever newsmen tried to interview individual members of the staff, this should be cleared with Hagerty, and his opinion sought. He often knows exactly the kind of story the newsman is after, and he can also warn of the pitfalls involved. However, the most important thing is that no staff member should set himself up as a spokesman for the White House or for the Administration, and he should bend over backward to see that he does not invade this delicate field which is the sole province of the President.

In all candor, I must admit that things are not running as smoothly as they did under Sherman Adams. He would stand for no interference with the primary business of getting the President's job done, and he held such tight reins on the staff that it had little time to engage in personal activities. Adams was a fair man but a tough one, and every staff member knew that to keep his job he must do a bang-up job every day. A dressing-down by Sherman Adams was something to be avoided. The situation that exists today could hardly have happened with him in command.

Wilton Persons is an easy-going individual but completely dedicated to the President. We have a great deal more leeway than we did under Adams, but he was familiar with everything that went on—from the smallest problems to international situations of major importance. He had a line on every member of the staff and knew what he was supposed to do and what he was doing. I think Persons relies more upon relaxed conferences and chance meetings with staff members.

APRIL 18, 1959

WELL, I have let them have it with both barrels!

Two weeks ago I spoke in Detroit, before the Wayne County Republican Club. Michigan has steadily been losing elections since 1950, and at long last the Republicans are concerned.

On the way from the airport to the meeting, one of the party officials asked me bluntly: "What do we have to do to make friends with the Negro and get his vote?" This made me extremely angry, but fortunately I restrained myself and tried to give a measured answer. The question, however, gave me added ammunition for my speech. The theme of my address was that the Negro is still on the fringe of party activity, and that until he is taken in, given a full-fledged part, and permitted to have a voice in party councils and aspire to office, it will be a long time before the party can count on his allegiance. It seemed incredible to me that in a city like Detroit—with its polyglot millions—party officials did not know the answer to this question.

The Negro never sees the top leaders; his desires and wants must be made known through some straw boss who takes it upon himself to offer stupid solutions. Governor Mennen Williams of Michigan, and the Democratic party generally, have gone out of their way to make friends of the Negro voters. Not only that, but the Governor has made some outstanding appointments of Negroes to positions of substance and stature. This is a record that the Republicans cannot match.

There were some slight repercussions to my speech, but nothing to match those that came after my address before the Republican Women's Convention held in Washington on April 14. Here again I used the Michigan situation for my theme, and— a little more sharply—tried to bring home the fact that Republicans could not expect Negroes to be extremely grateful for what Lincoln did, since in effect he had merely returned to them their God-given rights of freedom and personal dignity.

I had hardly finished my speech before hell broke loose. The audience had given me a standing ovation, but it was evident that the leadership on the platform was pretty sore about the whole matter. Officials soon started calling the White House to brand me as a traitor, an ingrate, and many other uncomplimentary names. It had not been intended that the press give any coverage to the speech, but, ironically enough, the Associated Press rushed in, grabbed the speech, put it on its wires, and it went around the world. Since then it has been bedlam.

The President has been in Augusta, but officials of the National Committee have certainly made known their displeasure to some of the White House deputies and assistants. I have been asked to interpret certain accusations in my speech in the hope that they did not mean what they said. They meant exactly what they said.

The representations from the Negro community have been tremendous. Telegrams, letters, and telephone calls have come from both Democrats as well as Republicans. The feeling is that this is the first time in the memory of man that a Negro jobholder with a position such as mine has dared stand up—while occupying that position—and tell off the party that gave him the job!

This was no smart-alecky stunt on my part. My conscience had been whipping me for many months as I watched the complete country-wide indifference of Republican leadership and of the national Administration to Negro participation in party life. In the beginning, the Administration did a good deal to appoint a few Negroes to prominent positions, but this stopped after a dozen or more had been named. Then, as these appointees resigned, were promoted, or died, there have been no Negro successors named in these or comparable positions. This means that Negroes actually have lost ground. By the same token, during the past four years, the Democrats have gained tremendously among Negro voters. It is safe to say today that approximately 75 percent of Negroes who vote, vote for Democratic candidates.

I do not know whether what I have done will do any good, because Republicans are reluctant to see the handwriting on the wall. But I feel that I have done my duty to my party and to the Administration, and—no matter what the consequences are for me—it is a tremendous relief.

MAY 7, 1959

ALONG with the rest of the staff members and the White House personnel, I was present today at what I believe to be the passing of a great era. We were assembled outside the North Portico of the White House when Sir Winston Churchill said good-bye to the President and Mrs. Eisenhower. He has been the President's personal guest for the past three days.

It was a tragically drooped and weary old man of eighty-four who came out of the White House door and stumbled into his car. He did not say a word, but merely waved and left. Many thoughts ran through my mind as I saw him go. One could not help but feel that this might well be the last time he would visit America, for despite his indomitable will and brilliant mind—which still functions—time has left its marks on his former bulky frame.

It is significant that he had been able to make this visit on the eve of the important Ministers Conference at Geneva, where the Western nations will meet with the Russians in an effort to arrive at some common agreement for a future summit conference of the executive office of each country involved.

Churchill is still a resolute symbol of courage and determination in the free world. Perhaps for the last time, his wisdom has been offered to an old friend, the President, as to how the free world must stand against Russia on every occasion.

JUNE 9, 1959

MANY reasons have kept me from any regular notes during the past few weeks, but the primary consideration has been the press of official business. I seem to have become involved in a myriad of operations at one time.

Meanwhile, the whole country has been saddened by the death of Secretary of State Dulles. His passing has had a tremendous impact, not only on the Administration and the country, but on the world. Even though his death had been expected for many weeks, it was still a sad shock.

I attended his funeral with the rest of the White House staff. The services were held at the National Cathedral and were impressive in their simplicity. There were neither ceremonies nor eulogies, but merely a few expressive hymns and inspirational readings from the Old and New Testaments. There was little of the pomp and ceremony which normally accompany such an occasion, but one could not help but be impressed by the distinguished world figures who had come to pay final homage to this great man who had been so active and dedicated.

June 10, 1959

THE President gave an outdoor supper party on his farm at Gettysburg last Saturday. He had held a similar affair in 1955 to which most of the staff members had been invited, and this party was to afford the same opportunity to those who had joined the staff since then. Not only executive members of the staff were invited, but also the household staff including maids, cooks, butlers, the White House police and the Secret Service men—all with their families.

It was a perfect afternoon to drive to Gettysburg, and the President's farm and home are really beautiful. I was happy to see that this place offers such rest, peace and satisfaction. It is my solemn hope that he will have many happy years to spend there after his retirement.

The President has nominated my brother, Dr. John H. Morrow, to be Ambassador to the Republic of Guinea in West Africa. Neither John nor I sought this appointment for him, and apparently the State Department decided on him solely because of his extraordinary ability as a French scholar, his knowledge of the area where he will work, and his personal friendship with many of the people from Guinea whom he met during his stay at the Sorbonne and on subsequent trips in France.

At this hour he is awaiting Senate confirmation, and as the President indicated in a little note to me a few days ago, he hopes "that the Senate will not give him too difficult a time."

The Washington *Post* raised the question of whether a scholar was the best person to send to such a difficult post—the Russians have made tremendous inroads there during the short span of Guinea's independence. The *Post* also dragged the racial question into the situation by suggesting that the naming of a Negro as a diplomat to a Negro country was presumptuous and condescending.

What the *Post* has forgotten or ignored is the fact that white men have lost face in Africa, and due to the previous policies of white countries, it is possible that Africans may be willing to deal more freely with a Negro representative than they might be with a white. The other factor is that ability should be the overriding consideration in any of these appointments, and color incidental. Interestingly enough, some of the southern newspapers have given John's nomination complete endorsement and seem very proud to point out that "one of our boys made it!"

JANUARY 7, 1960

I HAVE let the whole summer go by without making any entries here. I was very busy, and things were happening so fast that there was no time to record them. However, there are a few events of the last four months that I want to put down before my mind gets rusty on them.

My brother John's appointment as United States Ambassador to Guinea, West Africa, was confirmed by the Senate. We were delighted that his appointment was strictly on the basis of ability. This was a big step forward.

About a month ago I was summoned to Wilton Persons' office for a personal conference. This was unusual. I seldom come into contact with him and knew that this call must be of some consequence.

I long ago learned to respect this southern gentleman. I can appreciate all of the emotions he must experience when we have to meet socially or even on business. However, through the years he has learned to adapt himself admirably to whatever is happening, and we have a very cordial relationship. There are times when he seems quite self-conscious, but this is understandable.

When I sat down in his office, he began on the subject immediately, in characteristic fashion. He said that it was never his policy to prevent anyone on the staff from seeking new opportunities for advancement or other employment, but in this case he had been forced to interfere and wanted me to know about it.

The Nixon group had approached him a few weeks ago and had asked if he would be willing to release me so that I could go to work for the Vice-President, apparently on his preconvention campaign. Persons said that the Nixon forces were prepared to offer me a very responsible position, but that he had discouraged them. He said that I was one of the President's top staff men and if I left at this time, it would give the wrong impression to the public and the press and merely serve as an opportunity for writers and other guessers to have a field day speculating upon my decision.

He also felt that at this early stage of the game it would not be too smart for me to expose my hand as to what I would do in the coming election. He emphasized that to get too far out in front before a candidate is determined is to leave oneself wide open for attack and abuse. He felt that it would be smart for me to stay on the staff at least until a candidate had been decided upon, and then leave quietly if I wanted to.

Mr. Persons said he realized that he was usurping my prerogative to make decisions for myself, but that of course I was free to do whatever I wished. He was merely trying to give me fatherly advice and—very frankly—would not like to see the President's team broken up at this time.

The fact that the Nixon forces wanted me was news to me. Questions as to my attitude toward the Vice-President had come from various sources from time to time, but there had been no specific offer. This one seemed pretty definite, with the President's Chief Assistant being sounded out on the White House attitude toward it.

I assured him that I had no immediate intention of leaving the President's staff. I am dedicated to him and shall be eternally grateful for the exceptional opportunity he gave me.

My staying is going to mean a sacrifice, because this is the propitious time for current staff members to leave for other pursuits. Our worth will diminish as the term gets shorter, and many are already cashing in on their present affiliation with the President. I will stay on until the situation is clearer and I have been able to give the idea more thought and planning.

John came back to this country during the official state visit of President Sékou Touré in October. He had been in Guinea since July, but had already had a taste of the many complex problems that face a new country.

John, as a scholar, deals solely with the truth. When the facts have been arrived at, the solution seems to be simple. It is hard for him to understand why the State Department has so much difficulty in arriving at decisions once the facts are available. It is a difficult spot for an ambassador. His effectiveness in a country depends upon his honesty in dealing with officials of that country. If persons on the policymaking level back home at the State Department are hostile to the country where the ambassador is located, the ambassador is in trouble.

It has shocked me to discover how officials in the State Department let their petty jealousies, feelings, and attitudes interfere with carrying out their clear-cut duty. So many of them have deep feelings about race and color, and they communicate these feelings to others, despite the fact that this is injurious to the job they are supposed to do and to United States' reputation abroad. It seems difficult for many in the State Department— especially the Southerners—to be objective when dealing with black countries. This attitude communicates itself to Africans, who are very frank in their denunciation of the paternalistic attitude they experience from so many of our State Department's personnel.

On the surface, the Touré visit was a success, but there were great struggles behind the scenes. For example, Touré wanted to visit an important southern city. It was John's thought that Atlanta would be the place for him to see. While Atlanta has all the problems that plague every southern community, it also is the home of the great Atlanta University and several Negro colleges. Negro business thrives in Atlanta, and there are as many beautiful Negro homes there as one will find any place in the country. It was a unique testing spot for race relations, and John felt that this was the kind of situation that President Touré should see.

It is my understanding, however, that when the State Department went into action on the subject, the officials of Atlanta turned down the idea on the grounds that the reception for

Touré could not be a cordial one. In other words, the social aspects of the visit necessarily vetoed it. So the city of Durham, North Carolina, was chosen. Durham was a poor substitute; it is small in comparison with Atlanta and has few of that city's features or facilities.

Despite the fact that President Touré visited Duke and the University of North Carolina, only at a Negro institution— North Carolina College—was he given an honorary degree. This rankled with John as well as with some members of the Touré delegation. Going to the white universities was merely a token gesture, and it would have been politic of them to bestow an honorary degree upon this distinguished visitor.

January 15, 1960

THE Cameroons in West Africa came up for independence on January 1, 1960, and a few days later President William V. S. Tubman was to be sworn in again as President of Liberia. An American delegation was to be sent to both celebrations, and I had been named as one of those in the official delegation, which was to be headed by Ambassador Henry Cabot Lodge of the United Nations.

In preliminary discussions at the White House and also with the State Department, I was told that my wife could go along with the delegation, particularly in view of the fact that an Air Force plane would be used for transportation. In the event that commercial airlines had to be used, the wives would not accompany the delegates.

About six days before the trip was to begin, I had heard nothing from the State Department as to what would be required in the way of dress and when there would be briefings on the trip. I called the State Department for information, and was shocked when I learned that my wife could not accompany me on the trip because "all the spaces on the plane had been spoken for." The spokesman informed me that only the wives of certain members of the delegation had space on the plane. Ironically enough, these turned out to be the wives of the white men. None of the Negro delegates were to be permitted to take their wives.

I was so incensed that I told them to remove my name from the delegation, and I did not go.

NOVEMBER 10, 1960

IT DIDN'T have to be! The tragic defeat suffered by the Republicans two days ago was the result of incredible ineptness. Somewhere in the highest echelon of the party, decisions were made that foredoomed the Republican team. It is true that the Nixon-Kennedy debates were a sad mistake for Nixon managers to have made. Nixon was Vice-President, universally known, and had a legendary reputation for sound and logical debate. Kennedy was practically unknown and had everything to gain by this public debate. Nixon had nothing to gain—and a great deal to lose.

However, this wasn't the key blunder. That was the indefensible decision to ignore the Negro vote and go hell-bent-for-leather for the coy but predictable South.

Even without the benefit of polls or knowledgeable Negro advice, the dullest politician should have been able to figure that the Negroes held the balance of power in the pivotal and border states of the nation. These states were absolutes to any candidate who wanted to win. The Negroes, spurred on by the NAACP, organized labor, and liberal organizations, had registered in unprecedented numbers and were determined to play a vital part in this election. They stood in the wings, just waiting to be wooed and won by the candidate who understood their mood and concern over the matter of first-class citizenship. Despite the issue of religion, for the candidate who understood and listened, this was the easiest campaign of all.

As early as January 1959, the mood of the Negro was clear to me. I started early in the year petitioning the Republican high command to organize its activities locally and nationally to attract the Negro vote. I sent endless notes to Leonard Hall, chairman of the campaign committee, Senator Thurston Morton, and to staff members in Mr. Nixon's office, outlining what must be done if we were to hold what we had and try to gain more. Often the notes were ignored or the replies innocuous. It was maddening.

From time to time during the early part of 1960, a few interested staff members in the White House talked informally about the coming convention and election. Bob Merriam became the liaison person between the committee and the Administration. He helped work on the composition and strategy of the convention. It was largely through him that we got some slight Negro representation on the program. I was given a three-minute spot on the Salute-to-Eisenhower night, and Mrs. Jewel Rogers [1] of Chicago was selected to second the nomination of the vice-presidential candidate.

Vice-President Nixon's acceptance speech was a masterpiece, delivered with conviction and courage. He took charge in a manner that befitted a fighting candidate, and it gave heart to the flagging spirits of many apprehensive Republicans.

In retrospect, it is my opinion that Mr. Nixon reached the high point of the campaign and perhaps of his career with that speech. Never again did he attain such heights in conviction, sincerity, determination and boldness. His appearance, attitude, and self-determination reflected dynamic leadership. A deliriously happy convention audience saluted him. One of the unsolved mysteries of the 1960 campaign is what happened to that Nixon.

As far as the Negro was concerned, the campaign got off to a good start. Nixon personally invited me to the secret midnight caucus of the party greats to pick the vice-presidential candidate. It was the first time in history that a Negro had participated actively in such proceedings. Some of the participants seemed concerned when a Secret Service man escorted me into the

---

1 A leading Negro attorney who is very active in Republican circles.

heavily guarded room, but the Vice-President quickly assured them that I had been invited on the same basis as any of them.

It was a historic meeting. Some of the hopefuls—like James Mitchell, Secretary of Labor, and Fred Seaton, Secretary of the Interior—were present, but no holds were barred, and each man spoke his piece when called upon.

I was among the first to be asked by the Vice-President, who presided, who my choice was and why. I picked Henry Cabot Lodge, because "not even the NAACP can be against his superb liberal record."

The meeting went on far into the early morning—all the wheels had to speak ad infinitum. The final decision was Lodge. It was obvious that Nixon wanted him, and perhaps it would have been Lodge no matter what the majority vote.

It seemed to me that if Nixon had me in this vital spot, he intended to use me in the campaign, and this I wanted very much.

I had flown to the convention with the President in his new jet plane. I had gone up to his vacation retreat in Newport the day before, to be on hand for an early morning departure. I landed in Newport in the afternoon, and was invited to go for a sail on the presidential yacht. It was a delightful interlude and one of the most pleasant evenings I have spent with the top White House brass. Everyone was relaxed and friendly during the two-hour sail.

We flew into Chicago at noon the next day to a tumultuous welcome. We landed at O'Hare, helicoptered to a small field in midtown, then motored at a snail's pace past crowds of spectators who lined the streets all the way to the hotel.

The night of the "Salute to Eisenhower" was a trying one for me. I was originally allotted five minutes for my television speech. Then some officious character cut me to two minutes. At the afternoon rehearsal, I did not get a chance to "try out," and only through vigorous insistence got my speech put on a teleprompter.

When I arrived at the convention that night, I could not get in because I had not been given the correct pass, and the guards would not recognize my White House pass. By sheer luck, fifteen minutes before I was to go on, I ran into a Secret Service man who got me in. I was a nervous wreck.

The opening line of my speech was: "One hundred years ago today my grandfather was a slave. Tonight I stand before you a trusted assistant of the President of the United States."

The applause was deafening.

The President had arrived early enough to hear part of the program, and was seated off stage in the VIP lounge watching the proceedings on TV. He was furious when the station to which he was tuned cut me out for a commercial and some chit-chat by the commentators. He commented vigorously on this later.

These same commentators and this same network had cut out the Negro speakers at the Democratic Convention in Los Angeles a week before. It hardly seemed like an accident.

I returned home eagerly, enthusiastic about participating in the campaign and giving my best efforts for the party and Richard Nixon. However, the call was a long time in coming, and the part given me to play was insulting.

I took a two months' leave of absence from the White House without pay to work in the Nixon campaign. Since February, Leonard Hall had promised me a prominent and vital place in the campaign hierarchy, but it did not materialize. Nixon's young managers and staff had different ideas, and it became apparent to me at once that they had more zeal than knowledge. They never asked for or thought they needed advice on this delicate and vital campaign subject.

During the whole two months in the office I never had a secretary or anyone to answer my considerable campaign mail; I never had a dime to spend for anything other than personal expenses. No literature, no workers, no assistants.

I felt that this was a tragic moment. Negro leaders from all over the nation called me day and night for help, financial assistance and literature, and they could not believe me when I turned them down because we had none to give them.

Val Washington was in a similar boat. He had practically no money, and was trying to direct a nationwide campaign with a staff of about five people. His urgent pleas for help fell on deaf and unsympathetic ears.

The only national speaker of any importance we had on the road was Jackie Robinson. He made a great personal sacrifice to help Nixon, yet he, too, had a heavy heart from the ignorance with which the campaign was being conducted.

Late in the campaign I joined the Nixon entourage on the road. Unlike the Eisenhower campaigns of '52 and '56, I was never seen with the Vice-President. I rode in caravans in a rear car and was never called into parleys or strategy meetings.

In the closing days of the campaign, Reverend Martin Luther King, Negro idol and civil rights leader, was thrown in jail in Atlanta on a trivial charge. It was an international sensation. It was the moment for American leadership to speak.

I begged the Nixon managers, by memo and in person, to have the Vice-President make a statement deploring the situation under which King was jailed. They demurred. They thought it bad strategy.

The next day I joined the Nixon campaign train in Illinois. I urged his press secretary to have him take some action. I even drafted a telegram for the Vice-President to send to the mayor of Atlanta. The press secretary put the draft in his pocket to "think about it."

Twenty-four hours later, King was freed from jail. His freedom came after the intercession of the Democratic presidential candidate, John F. Kennedy. He had scored tremendously, not only by wiring the mayor of Atlanta, but by phoning King's wife to express his concern and ask if he could be of assistance. And his brother Robert had apparently talked to other Atlanta officials.

This act won the election. Kennedy's action electrified the entire Negro community and resulted in tens of thousands of Negro voters going over to the Democrats' banner.

Many factors contributed to Mr. Kennedy's election—which was close—but one incontrovertible fact is evident. He carried the crucial, essential Negro vote. He had keen, intelligent Negro advisers, and he obviously listened to them. In the Republican headquarters everybody was an expert on the Negro.

The results of this campaign should hold many valuable lessons for Republican leaders and politicians. The strategy of wooing the solid South and ignoring the available Negro vote was a costly blunder. The South is still too emotional over slavery and Reconstruction to come over to the Republicans in a wholesale manner. And white people must stop believing they "know the Negro." For a long while to come in this country, it would be well to ask knowledgeable Negroes for an objective assessment of the Negro attitude and mood on a given subject.

TODAY

THE preceding pages are excerpts from several books of notes I kept during my days at the White House. They were not kept with the idea of writing a book, but because of my sense of sitting in on history being made and—for the first time—being intimately witnessed by a Negro. Never before in the history of our Republic had an American black had the privilege of serving a President in an executive capacity.

Today my experiences on Dwight Eisenhower's staff become endearing gems of memories, perhaps of some value to sociologists and social scientists. For me, they will also form a valuable background with which to measure and analyze the efforts of other Presidents in coping with the same problems and heartbreaking tribulations that each must know.

Most of all, I have developed a sincere sympathy and understanding for any man elected to this impossible position. It would be helpful to the President and the American people if we could accept without question the fact that any man elected to the Presidency does his level best to serve his country to the satisfaction of his conscience. The cases of failure have been few in American history, and when Presidents have failed it has usually been in the field of human judgment.

It occurs to me that America has generally had the kind of President for which the tenor of the times called. This was certainly true in the case of Eisenhower. We needed a father image at that particular moment in world affairs, and he furnished this quality as few other citizens could have. We needed the security of the kind of thinking and leadership that a successful military mind could give. We needed his kind of patriotism and religious devotion to American idealism. And we needed a man of world stature who had won his honors on the international stage of achievement.

On the whole, those of us who had the privilege of serving under President Eisenhower in the White House not only admired him without reservation, but were devoted to him.

Whatever his defects, they were not those of indifference or lack of dedication. They were the faults that may have come out of past or present environment, out of the generation in which he was born, or out of the tastes supported by his own lifetime of experience.

For example, President Eisenhower's lukewarm stand on civil rights made me heartsick. I could trust this man never to do anything that would jeopardize the civil rights or the personal dignity of the American Negro, but it was obvious that he would never take any positive giant step to prove that he unequivocally stood for the right of every American to walk this land in dignity and peace, clothed with every privilege—as well as every responsibility—accorded a citizen of our Constitution.

His failure to clearly and forthrightly respond to the Negro's plea for a strong position on civil rights was the greatest cross I had to bear in my eight years in Washington.

It was incredible to responsible Negroes that I could—for high political office—forsake the principles and ideals that had become associated with my background of three generations of uncompromising service to my race in the field of human rights.

Their attitude was understandable. Negroes had bad memories of President Eisenhower. As a general, he had once testified against wholesale integration of Negroes in the Army. In speaking to a meeting of Negro publishers, while President, he had cautioned "patience" in their fight for integration. At Little Rock, he had used troops, but some thought only because Governor Faubus had insulted him and not from any strong conviction that a serious injustice had been inflicted upon a large segment of the American people. During his Presidency, he had generalized on the whole question of civil rights. At no time had he made any overt gesture that would encourage Negroes to believe that he sympathized with, or believed in, their crusade for complete and immediate citizenship.

In fact, during the Eisenhower Administration, the whole Republican party seemed to have been embarrassed by the civil rights question. Except for a few liberals in Congress and elsewhere, any discussion of this issue brought pained expressions and crafty evasions. It was a rough spot for a Negro official depended upon to point up, defend and secure positive action for his people.

Despite this atmosphere, some genuine good and progress did come out of the Eisenhower Administration as regards Negro advancement. I think one of its greatest accomplishments—and one for which little credit has been given or acknowledged—was the complete and effective desegregation of the District of Columbia. This was done overnight, without bloodshed or rioting, without strenuous opposition or counterattack—almost without notice.

President Eisenhower said he wanted Washington to be a "model city" in the matter of civil rights and democratic conduct. He was firm and resolute about this. In Washington today almost every area of life catering to the general public is open and available to Negro citizens.

However, the basic problems engendered through denial of civil rights to a segment of the citizenry still prevails to plague not only Washington but the entire nation.

President Kennedy denounced the Eisenhower Administration time and time again during the 1960 campaign for failure to eliminate discrimination in housing "by the stroke of a pen." Yet under the Kennedy aegis, the problem has worsened.

The Democrats gave Eisenhower a bad time when he sent troops into Little Rock during the school crisis of 1958. They felt he had acted imprudently and that civilian officials could have handled the problem more efficiently and with less rancor.

Yet now we see President Kennedy facing the same problems and making almost the same decisions President Eisenhower made. It drives home the thought that the man does not make the Presidency—the Presidency makes the man. No matter what great convictions and determination a candidate may have about burning issues when he is on the stump, their complexity and solution change when he becomes President.

He is thereafter afflicted by political considerations, sectional differences, expediency, what is best for the whole country, minority pressures, personal promises, and a host of other conflicting and intertwined problems.

President Kennedy did a whale of a job in wooing the Negro vote during the 1960 campaign; he made the Republicans look pitiful by comparison. He was a picture of conviction as he hammered at the point that this should and could be a land of equal opportunity for every man.

This sounded great coming from a candidate—especially a Democratic candidate whose strength and heartbeat resided in the South. It was incredible to hear, but impressive because of the apparent risk the candidate took in saying it.

But the old pros knew this promise could not be kept. It could not be kept by either a Democratic or a Republican president. The former would be hamstrung by the southern wing of his party; the latter would find the Right Wing of the party weaseling out on the issue when the chips were down.

Every President finds certain inevitable forces at work against him when he enters 1600 Pennsylvania Avenue. No matter what he promised in the exciting days of November, the stark reality of political life greets him the minute he crosses the threshold of the White House after the Inaugural Parade. He is never the same man again.

The basic problems that afflicted Negro citizens because of the lack of absolute freedom and complete citizenship in this country during 1952–1960 still bewilder and bedevil them today. There is a new Administration, there are new slogans, there is new lip service to human ideals, and there is a lot of petitioning at the bar. But little has changed, except the Negro's unrelenting and courageous determination to get freedom *now!*

The new Administration meets the problem a little differently than the last. Whenever the Negro community gets restive and digs up the campaign promises of 1960, the Kennedy Administration makes a sensational appointment of a Negro to a high office, and this takes the heat off for the time being. But the great masses of blacks today still stand in the four corners of the land and cry out against denial.

Someday, somehow, somewhere, Negro Americans will realize that without the tacit agreement, help and conviction of his party, no presidential candidate can deal out the great treasures that American Negroes have longed for and sought for over 300 years.

I am grateful to President Eisenhower for giving me the privilege and honor of aspiring beyond the former rigid boundaries of caste and class and permitting me to serve in a position formerly beyond the ken of an Afro-American. No other job, situation, period, honor or distinction I ever have will be quite like it.

Index